D1597795

WITHDRAWN

Byron in Geneva

Byron in Geneva

That Summer of 1816

DAVID ELLIS

LIVERPOOL UNIVERSITY PRESS

First published 2011 by
Liverpool University Press
4 Cambridge Street
Liverpool
L69 7ZU

British Library Cataloguing-in-Publication data
A British Library CIP record is available

ISBN 978-1-84631-643-2 cased

Typeset in Arno by
Koinonia, Manchester
Printed and bound in Great Britain by
Bell & Bain Ltd, Glasgow

Contents

Afterwords

Preface

The details of Byron's extraordinary life will always attract interest, yet there are already a sufficient number of biographical studies for this new one to require an explanation. The incentive for it came from reading what are still the most recent, large-scale cradle-to-grave lives of Byron, all of which have strong features. In *Byron: The Flawed Angel*, Phyllis Grosskurth makes excellent use of the numerous documents Lady Byron left behind – the so-called Lovelace papers now in the Bodleian library in Oxford – and as a result writes one of the best of the many accounts of his disastrous marriage and separation. But she dislikes her subject, or at least thoroughly disapproves of him. According to her, Byron 'frequently lied or insinuated something dire in order to heighten the drama of a situation'; he had 'a propensity all his life for assigning blame to other people'; and he tended to make friends 'with those towards whom he might have some slight reason for feeling superior'. 'An impoverished aristocrat who strutted about as though he were the Duke of Devonshire', Byron resented the waltz, she claims, 'not only because he could not participate in it, but because it detracted from the attention that might have been concentrated exclusively on him' (the list goes on).[1]

Benita Eisler, in *Byron: Child of Passion, Fool of Fame*, is not as overtly hostile as Grosskurth, and she pays more careful and intelligent attention to Byron's writing than most of his other biographers. But she accepts every discreditable rumour about him she can find, regardless of its source, and ignores the efforts Doris Langley Moore made in *The Late Lord Byron* to distinguish between those witnesses who could be trusted and those with an axe to grind. The result is that the Byron she presents is something of a moral monster, forcing himself on the 11-year-old daughter of his mistress, Lady Oxford, and repeatedly attempting the rape of his heavily pregnant wife.[2] When, three years after Eisler's book had appeared, Fiona MacCarthy published *Byron: Life and Legend*, it was not so much monstrous aspects of her subject's character which she wanted to highlight but his homosexuality. Recognising how much all biographers of Byron will always owe to the admirable work of Leslie A. Marchand in the 1950s, she claimed that he had been inhibited in what he could say by the conditions of his time, and that it was now possible to tell the whole truth about Byron's fundamentally homosexual nature. The unique selling point of her book was the claim that all his relationships with women were only substitutes for those which he would have preferred to enjoy with men or boys, had the laws against sodomy in England not been so severe. Thus she suggests that Byron's accounts of how hopelessly he had fallen in love with Mary Chaworth, when he was in his mid-teens, were in fact only attempts to distract attention from his 'real sexual proclivities', and that his accumulation of mistresses while he was living chiefly in London in 1808 was a result of his feeling that there was safety in numbers 'in a society proscribing relations with boys'. If he was moody and dissatisfied while attending dinners with compatriots in Smyrna in 1810, she goes on, it was because he was comparing the context they provided with 'imagined marble palaces of sodomy and sherbet', and she detects in his relations with women when he returned to England 'an element of cruelty engendered by the knowledge that he was being false to his own heart'.[3] This view of Byron, bolstered by many more similar interpretations of his behaviour than there is space to illustrate here, has been influential and, in ways for which MacCarthy cannot be held responsible, was particularly evident in a television documentary on his life fronted (the word seems apt) by Rupert Everett in 2009.

The point here is not of course that anyone could object to Byron being described as homosexual, or that such a description ought to be taken as a sign of hostility. Marchand accepted that Byron was bisexual and most commentators since have concurred. The idea that the heterosexual aspect of his nature was a front, improbable though it seems given the variety of his relations with women as well as the length and indeed depth of some of them, is also not in itself objectionable. But its consequence is that MacCarthy, who writes better than anyone about her subject's time in Greece, is driven to present a Byron totally lacking in either candour or self-knowledge, a man who combined in his dealings with others a 'high camp English manner' with what she calls at one point a 'lethal ... emotional duplicity'.[4]

Byron was certainly no angel, flawed or otherwise, yet it seemed to me, in reading these biographies, that he was receiving an unjustifiably bad press. No-one would want to attempt a rebuttal of all the charges made against him, and no-one could (since many of them are true); but by taking a cross-section of his life, and examining his behaviour and relations with others in more detail than a full-scale biography allows, I hope to take a step towards a more sympathetic and therefore, in my view, more accurate portrait. To provide an intelligible context for this portrait, it seemed necessary to sketch in his life before the point at which I begin to consider it, and to describe briefly what happened to him after he left Switzerland, so that the general reader has some sense of the whole shape of his life; but the main concentration is on a short period in order to convey the truest possible impression of what kind of person Byron was. Of course, that impression will alter according to which cross-section of his life is investigated. A different result from my own might well result from looking in detail at the period just before his time in Switzerland, when he was separating from his wife; or the one just after when he was settled in Venice and leading a life of frantic dissipation. Yet there are characteristics which are abiding and go through all the different phases of his life even if there are many others which appear or disappear as his character evolves.

The period I discuss was a crucial one for Byron as he tried to recover after the collapse of his marriage and become a different person. But its significance is as much literary as biographical. Of all the English Romantic poets, Byron was the one who had most influence abroad. The wild and stirring tales he told in his poems, incorporating in them as he often did elements of romantic love, constituted for many of his foreign readers the essence of what they thought of as Romanticism, as did also the willingness he always showed to talk about himself and his feelings in a manner wholly free of eighteenth-century notions of decorum. But in England itself what became known much later as 'the Romantic movement' was associated indelibly with Wordsworth and Coleridge and the publication in 1798 of *Lyrical Ballads*. The urge to describe the simple doings of simple people in simple language was a major feature of that work, with which Byron had not the slightest sympathy. His response to the attitude to 'Nature' which it evinced, and which became particularly evident in the poems Wordsworth went on to write, was more complicated. Baffled at first, it was in Switzerland in 1816 that, under the influence of Shelley, he tried to transform himself into a nature poet of the Wordsworthian variety. The failure of that attempt was also his failure to find solace for his acute unhappiness in landscape and, more particularly, in mountains, and was therefore one crucial step towards the decision he was to make later that he was not a Romantic poet after all, and that the Romantic movement as a whole, especially as it was represented by the Lake poets, was a mistake. This was towards the end of his life when he was increasingly turning to satire and comedy, producing in his final years those three masterpieces of English comic writing *Beppo*, *The Vision of Judgement* and, of course, *Don Juan*. It is in these works that the reader best discovers the same Byron who had always previously been apparent in his incomparable letters. This happy conjunction had not yet been reached in Switzerland, as *Manfred* indicates clearly enough; but it is one of the aims of this study to follow his steps towards it.[5]

Acknowledgements

I would like to thank the Leverhulme Trust for a travel grant which allowed me to visit Switzerland, Oxford and Edinburgh in order to carry out research into various aspects of Byron's life. John Worthen, Edward Greenwood and Grayson Ditchfield read drafts of this book and gave me good advice, and I am also grateful to Frank Cioffi, Michael Irwin, Alan Rawes and Christopher Thompson for several very useful suggestions. Angela Faunch and her colleagues at the Document Delivery Centre in the University of Kent at Canterbury have been as cooperative as they always are. In the Bodleian Library in Oxford, Dr Bruce Barker-Benfield was particularly helpful and I received kind assistance from librarians at the National Library of Scotland as well as those at both the university and city libraries of Lausanne.

I owe a particular debt of gratitude to Peter Cochran.

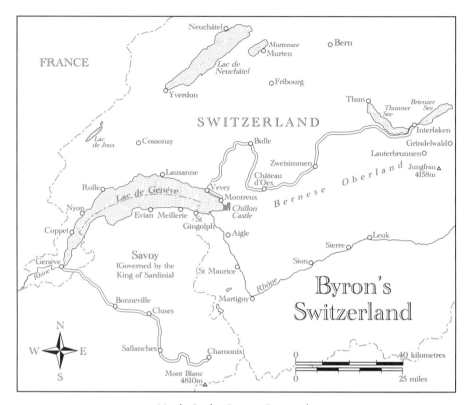

Map by Stephen Ramsay Cartography

Part One

1

Heading for Geneva

In the early morning of Friday 26 April 1816, after a Channel crossing which had lasted sixteen hours, Lord Byron landed in Ostend. He was heading for Switzerland, and more particularly for Geneva. For many of us now, Geneva is where the United Nations meet or where the very rich, who prefer not too much scrutiny into their financial affairs, keep their bank accounts. In 1816 its reputation was rather different. Although the town had only very recently become an official member of the Swiss confederation, it benefited from the warm feeling which had existed in Britain towards Switzerland in the late eighteenth century. Here was a conglomeration of small states, none of them very wealthy and all of them poorly resourced, which had fought for their independence and then heroically defended it against much more powerful neighbours. What made this feat seem especially impressive was that it had been achieved while those states (or cantons) continued to maintain a limited system of representative democracy. For the British, Switzerland was the only *other* country in Europe whose government was non-autocratic. This was why its invasion by the French revolutionary forces in 1798 had been such a shock to the liberal-minded. Looking back on that event, both Wordsworth and Coleridge identified it as the moment when their faith in the French Revolution finally collapsed. Byron was still then a boy, and he would never totally abjure revolutionary principles, but for him too Switzerland had high symbolic value.

However much they might admire Switzerland in general, the reason that many of Byron's compatriots had a special feeling for Geneva had little to do with politics. This was after all the town which had in the past established a sober, puritanical mode of living that served as both a model and an inspiration for many others. Thanks to John Calvin, it had become a Mecca of the Protestant

world, a beacon in a surrounding sea of idol-worshipping Catholics and a place
where respectable British tourists could take their wives and daughters without
misgiving. Visiting Geneva in 1817, Stendhal declared it was a town where one
met fewer cuckolds than anywhere else, although he then added that, were
he married, no amount of money would persuade him to live there.[1] This was
because its respectability could make it seem rather dull and self-satisfied. Some
visitors who had this impression preferred Lausanne, where they felt there was
'un calvinisme plus aimable'.[2] Madame de Staël, born in Paris but with strong
attachments in the region, expressed one aspect of the difference when she said
that whereas the people in Lausanne were always happy to welcome her, those
in Geneva would tell her how pleased she must be to find herself once again back
in their town.

Geneva had been able to export its Calvinist principles to several countries,
not the least of which was the Scotland where Byron had been brought up. His
mother was Scottish, fond of boasting that one of her ancestors was a daughter
of Scotland's James I; and she had taken him to Presbyterian Aberdeen when
he was two, in order to be near her relatives, and as far away as possible from
the creditors who in London were always pursuing her pathologically spend-
thrift husband. Byron stayed there until he was ten and the death of the great-
uncle from whom he inherited his English title. These were formative years and
it is often said that the 'Byronic hero', the central figure in many of his plays or
narrative poems, with his brooding sense of having previously committed some
obscure but mortal sin and thereby put himself beyond the reach of salvation,
owes a good deal to a Calvinist background (as Benita Eisler shrewdly notes,
being cursed is the 'mirror image of a sense of election'[3]). Certainly Byron was a
fatalist, able to point on the one hand to the death in battle of the young cousin
who would otherwise have succeeded his great-uncle as the arbitrary stroke of
fortune which had made him a rich peer of the realm; and, on the other, to the
considerable personal disadvantage of having been born with a deformed or
'clubbed' right foot. However much he made light of this disability, participating
as far as was possible in all the usual physical activities of boys and young men,
the idea of it haunted him and must occasionally have made him feel that he was
predestined to misfortune, marked with a sign of God's disfavour.

Seriously interested in biblical matters but no friend to religion as it was organised in Britain, Byron did not look upon his early religious training in Scotland
with any warmth or affection; and the respectability of a town (its greater or
lesser number of cuckolds) was never at the top of his list of desiderata when

he was considering where to live. As he set out for Geneva, therefore, he was less likely to have belonged to that majority of his compatriots who had Calvin in their minds than to the minority who remembered with respect and appreciation that this was the town of Jean-Jacques Rousseau. In the late eighteenth and early nineteenth centuries no other literary figure had a greater impact on European cultural and intellectual life than Rousseau. His political writing was widely credited with having paved the way to the French Revolution, although Byron hotly contested this interpretation, insisting that the 'cause is obvious – the government exacted too much, and the people could neither *give* nor *bear more*'.[4] Schools were founded on the basis of Rousseau's thoughts about the education of the young which he laid out in *Emile*, and his sentimental love-story, *Julie ou la Nouvelle Héloïse*, which somehow managed to combine passionate sexual feeling with respectability, was a European best-seller. In the *Confessions*, and other autobiographical texts, he developed modes of baring the soul which were prominent features of what came to be considered 'Romantic'. Calvin had been born in France and came to Geneva as a young man, but Rousseau had been born and raised there. He was the representative of much that was forward-looking and innovative in the late eighteenth century, or – to put it in a way which helps to explain his appeal to Byron – much that was also subversive and bound to upset the moral and political Establishment.

Calvin and Rousseau were names which the British associated with Geneva in 1816, but their chief reasons for going there were ones which still operate powerfully today. As a young Scottish doctor, tutor to the Duchess of Hamilton's children, had put it in 1779, the situation of the town was in many respects 'as happy as the heart of man could define'. There was, he explained, 'the long ridge of mountains called Mount Jura on the one side, the Glaciers of Savoy, and the snowy head of Mont Blanc on the other', and all of these served as 'boundaries to the most charmingly variegated landscape that ever delighted the eye'.[5] Increasingly alluring for visitors were those glaciers and Mont Blanc, and Geneva was the convenient location from which to visit them. A hundred years before Byron's arrival there, wanting to see the mountains would have seemed an eccentric enterprise and one which was hardly likely to improve the traveller's knowledge of human life. Even in 1753, when the sixteen-year-old Gibbon was packed off to Lausanne because at Oxford he had fallen into what his father regarded as bad company and temporarily converted to Catholicism, 'the fashion of climbing the mountains and reviewing the *Glaciers*, had not yet been introduced by foreign travellers, who seek the sublime beauties of nature'. But returning to that town thirty years later, now a famous author, Gibbon complained that it was precisely those mountains and glaciers which were opening Lausanne on all sides (as they did also of course Geneva) to 'the incursions of foreigners'.[6] The difference signals a radical change in sensibility of which he did not approve. One stimulus for it had been the letter which a character in Rousseau's *Julie* writes when he is on a trip to the Valais, that canton of Switzerland which lies south-east of Lake Geneva. Among other ecstatic statements in praise of a mountainous region, this includes the claim that 'it seems that by rising above the habitation of men one leaves behind all base and earthly sentiments, and in proportion as one approaches ethereal regions, the soul contracts something of their inalterable purity'.[7]

One went into the mountains in search of sublime feelings and because they offered an escape from society as well as the opportunity of experiencing the ineffable power of Nature. For those more orthodox in their Christian feeling than Rousseau, one went there also to reaffirm one's faith in God. This is the unequivocal message of Coleridge's 'Hymn before Sunrise, in the Vale of Chamouni', which was first published in *The Morning Post* in 1802. Coleridge begins this poem by picturing himself looking up at Mont Blanc as the light begins to break and then goes on to address the mountain directly. 'Who sank thy sunless pillars deep in Earth?', he enquires; 'Who filled thy countenance with rosy light? / Who made thee parent of perpetual streams?' For him the answer was obvious enough, but for anyone too dim to understand he introduced his poem with a quite detailed prose description of the Chamonix area and asked in the course of it, 'Who *would* be, who *could* be an Atheist in this valley of wonders?' Certainly Coleridge feels he couldn't, and extends his injunction that Mont Blanc should praise its maker to the glaciers which were (and are) such an important feature of the Chamonix region:

> Ye Ice-falls! Ye that from the mountain's brow
> Adown enormous ravines slope amain …
> Who made you glorious as the Gates of Heaven
> Beneath the keen full moon? Who bade the sun
> Clothe you with rainbows? Who, with living flowers
> Of lovliest blue, spread garlands at your feet? –
> GOD! let the torrents, like a shout of nations,
> Answer! and let the ice-plains echo, GOD![8]

Wordsworth was not keen on Coleridge's poem, calling it an example of the mock sublime. His own thoughts on the relation of the individual to Nature had been blatantly unorthodox – more animistic than Christian – and in a poem such as 'Tintern Abbey', to choose the most famous example, there was an originality of language and rhythm which could not but make 'Hymn before Sunrise' appear leaden and conventional, driven on as it is by exclamations and rhetorical questions. Yet the source of his dislike could also have been the knowledge that part of the hymn was an unacknowledged adaptation of a German poem (the notes to which provided Coleridge with the local details about the vale of Chamonix which appear in his prose introduction[9]), and that Coleridge had never been to Chamonix, or anywhere near it. He himself, on the other hand, *had* visited the Alps and would soon be writing much better verse about their effect on him in what became *The Prelude*. This visit had taken place in 1790 when, with a friend from Cambridge, he walked all the way through France in order to reach them. It was the kind of walking tour Rousseau had made popular and Wordsworth had chosen a good moment for embarking on it. The French king had recently accepted changes which would have transformed his country into something like a constitutional monarchy on the English pattern, so that France seemed then, in Wordsworth's well-known words, 'standing at the top of golden hours'.[10] But events moved rapidly and there followed the execution of the king, the Terror and then a period of instability before Napoleon seized power. For much of the time after Wordsworth's visit, and until the fall of Napoleon, Britain and France were at war. This meant that the continent was mostly closed off to British tourists or visitors. At the beginning, it was still possible to go to Germany, as both Wordsworth and Coleridge did in 1798; and in 1802, after the treaty of Amiens, British visitors flocked once again to Paris. But that peace lasted only a year and, with the resumption of hostilities, some British tourists found themselves interned in France until the fall of Napoleon eleven years later, and travelling to any part of Europe became even more difficult than it had been.

One effect of the war with Napoleon, and his increasing stranglehold on continental Europe, was that all those young British aristocrats who were in the habit of taking the kind of 'grand tour' which meant spending months in various European capitals found they had to think again. Since Byron was born in January 1788, the period when he was beginning to consider his own grand tour coincided with that when Europe was at its least accessible. When he left England in 1809 he therefore went first to Portugal, where the Duke of Wellington was installed and trying to push the French back out of Spain. From a Cadiz still free of French control, he sailed via Gibraltar to Malta (both of which were in British hands), and then on to Greece. This was a country ruled by the Turks, who were neutral in the Anglo-French wars. Byron had always had a strong interest in the Levant, as it was often called, and what he saw and experienced in Greece, Albania and on a visit to Constantinople gave an exotic flavour to his poetry which helps to explain its immense popularity; yet he may have had some regrets at not being able to visit the great cities of Europe. The defeat of Napoleon allowed him, and thousands of his compatriots, to view sites most of them had been starved of for over twenty years. In 1814, after Napoleon had been exiled to Elba, hundreds of the British, deprived for so long of French culture, flooded into France. The Emperor's unexpected return, and his resumption of control for what are known as 'the hundred days', caught them unawares. Remembering the fate of some of their compatriots after the breakdown of the Peace of Amiens, many hurried to get back home or scuttled off French territory into Geneva. Yet with Napoleon's final and definitive defeat at Waterloo in 1815 the floodgates could finally open and the continent was accessible once again.

In heading for Geneva in 1816 Byron was leaving behind a triumphant nation. Russia, Austria and the German states may have wavered in their opposition to Napoleon, sometimes allying themselves with him and sometimes not, but the British government had been hostile more or less throughout. It could now enjoy the fruits of victory, except that the social unrest which had been rumbling away during the last years of the war had become more acute. There were bad harvests, Napoleon's continental blockade had damaged trade, the price of bread was kept high by protective legislation, and the political system of which the British were so proud was no longer well adapted to the country's changing needs. The war had made it relatively easy to stifle cries for reform, but once it was over an entrenched Tory administration showed no greater disposition to listen to them, because it had by no means lost its fear of violent revolution. Some of the most repressive legislation the country had seen since the arrival of the Hanoverian kings belongs to the few years after 1815. Firmly anti-Tory as Byron was, and conscious that there was no political role he could easily play, the political climate might have provided him with a motive for leaving the country had he not, as it happens, had reasons which were much more personal.

Napoleon on St Helena was a major topic of interest for the chattering classes in the early days of 1816 but an almost equally important one was the separation of Lord Byron from his wife, or rather his wife's separation from him. Annabella Milbanke, who had been Lady Byron for just over a year, had left him on 15

January 1816, taking with her a newly born daughter called Ada. It is impossible to say quite how badly Byron treated his wife because nearly all the evidence comes from her side and was brought together at a time when she needed to prepare the strongest possible case to avoid his claiming custody of the child; yet there is more than enough circumstantial detail to suggest he certainly did not treat her well. Apart from total temperamental incompatibility, there were two major problems which dogged the marriage from the start. One of these was money. To settle the massive debts he had accumulated during his minority, and which he continued to accumulate thereafter, Byron had felt obliged to put on sale his family estate at Newstead in Nottinghamshire. He thought he had found someone who was willing to purchase it for £140,000 but the buyer reneged on the deal, forfeiting in the process £25,000. That this large sum was not enough to solve his financial problems shows how severe they were. Marriage hardly helped because most of his wife's wealth was in the expectation she had of inheriting from a childless uncle, and in fact it made things rather worse in that Byron felt nobly obliged to rent for himself and his new wife a house in Piccadilly which cost £700 a year (or would have done, had he been able to pay this rent). Throughout the year of the marriage his financial difficulties increased until, towards its end, bailiffs were often in the house. Byron seems to have dealt with the humiliation of not being able to provide properly for his family by drinking yet more brandy and spending a good deal of his time at Drury Lane theatre, where he was a member of the management committee, and where he had a brief affair with an actress.

Bad as this situation was, it was not so unfamiliar among the more disreputable members of the Regency aristocracy, for whom marital infidelity was not so important and owing large sums of money a way of life. But Byron had brought to his marriage a second major problem rather more unusual. In the months before it took place, his already warm relationship with his half-sister, Augusta Leigh, had become intermittently sexual. He and Augusta had the same father but had been brought up quite separately and it was not until he was a young man, and she a married woman with children, that they had got to know each other well. Byron's marriage put a stop to any sexual contact with Augusta but, with Annabella innocently encouraging her sister-in-law's visits, being in the company of both women at the same time seems to have put pressures on him which he was incapable of handling, even with large amounts of brandy. In one of the versions of the Midas legend, the barber who has found out that the king has asses' ears feels obliged to relate his discovery to the reeds on the river bank, which then disseminate it. This is a story which might have been composed specifically for Byron, who was the least secretive of individuals and had enormous difficulty in keeping anything to himself. Inhibited nevertheless from explaining bluntly to Annabella what had happened with Augusta, he took refuge in dark hints, enigmatic remarks and behaviour so bizarre and cruel that she thought him mad and contrived to have him observed by a friendly doctor. Only gradually did the light dawn. Since she was a pious woman she may have been horrified at the mere fact of incest; but since she was astute, she may also have perceived, and resented bitterly, that Byron had used marriage with her to extricate himself from a relation which was socially unacceptable in the form it had taken and could therefore have no future.

The period between his wife leaving him in January and his departure for Switzerland on 25 April was a difficult one for Byron. Annabella may not have intended a definitive break, but back with her doting parents (she was a late, only child), and surrounded by advisors, going back to the house in Piccadilly became increasingly impossible. The law of the time was heavily and unreasonably weighted in favour of husbands and fathers, so that Annabella had to provide Byron with strong disincentives against contesting the legal separation she sought, or reclaiming his child. A campaign of rumour began, or was begun, and it was at this time that Byron's former mistress, Lady Caroline Lamb, came to Annabella with allegations about his active homosexual past which, as far as they related to his time in Greece, were almost certainly true. Although he had supporters, the tide in the newspapers ran against him and there were signs of ostracism in the circles in which he was accustomed to move. At a fashionable ball given by Lady Jersey, to which he had been invited with Augusta, a number of former friends or acquaintances ostentatiously refused to speak to him.

It was not quite that Byron was 'driven abroad'. He had been thinking of a trip to the continent before his marriage and had even made one or two plans for getting away during it; but the separation was a profound psychological shock and the publicity it caused provided a strong additional incentive for leaving the country. When he came back from the Levant, he had been an obscure, indebted aristocrat with few friends among the rich and powerful. The poems he then published transformed him into what, in modern terminology, would be described as a major celebrity. Scores of young women sent him enthusiastic fan mail and London's leading society hostesses vied with each other to secure his presence at their gatherings. The scandal surrounding his separation from his wife turned this fame he had so quickly acquired into notoriety. Proud and defiant by nature, he was also highly vulnerable to insult ('skinless in sensitivity' is how one observer described him[11]), and suffered acutely from having to read what were sometimes violently defamatory descriptions of himself in the newspapers, or from having reported to him malicious gossip. Crossing the Channel meant a qualified escape from all that. Although on arriving in Ostend he headed for Geneva, his intention was to stay there only a few weeks and wait for the arrival of his close friend, John Cam Hobhouse, so that the two of them could then move on to Italy together.

2

The Shelley Party

Making its way to Switzerland at roughly the same time as Byron was what it is convenient to call the Shelley party.* This consisted of the young poet himself, still only twenty-three, and Mary Wollstonecraft Godwin, who would not become Mrs Shelley until the former Harriet Westbrook, Shelley's abandoned first wife, had made that possible by committing suicide later in the year. With Shelley and Mary was their baby son William, who had been born in January, and also Mary's sister Claire. To many the four adults were an object of scandal, and not merely because Shelley and Mary were as yet unmarried. Sent down from Oxford for publishing a pamphlet provocatively entitled 'The Necessity of Atheism', Shelley had then added insult to injury, as far as the political establishment was concerned, by privately publishing a poem called *Queen Mab* in which he trumpeted his belief in revolutionary politics, reaffirmed his hostility to Christianity, and also declared himself an opponent of marriage and an advocate of free love. He was a married man when he made this declaration but his first wedding had been a reluctant concession to social pressures (as indeed his second would be). Shelley's libertarian approach to sex, and the fact that he was travelling with two young women rather than one, inevitably caused questions to be raised about sleeping arrangements; and since the two women concerned were sisters, there were also whispers of incest, that word having a loose meaning in his time. But as Byron, who had reasons of his own for being particularly sensitive on the incest issue, was later to insist, there was

---

* For lack of suitable alternatives, I have in this book reluctantly followed the convention of calling Shelley and Byron by their last name and Claire Clairmont and Mary Shelley by their first. An expedient sometimes adopted is to refer to Shelley as Percy or Bysshe, but since it would be so unusual (and therefore confusing) to call Byron George, no-one ever does it.

in fact no blood relation between Mary and Claire. Mary was the result of a union between William Godwin, whose *Enquiry Concerning Political Justice* was for several years a Bible among many of those on the left of British politics, and Mary Wollstonecraft, the author of *A Vindication of the Rights of Women* (because both of them had publicly attacked the institution of marriage, they had some difficulty in justifying their own). When Mary Wollstonecraft died, shortly after giving birth to the future Mary Shelley, Godwin quite quickly married again, this time a woman called Mary Clairmont. She brought to the household two children, each by different fathers, and Claire – Claire Clairmont as she is usually known – was one of these. Throughout her childhood she was called Jane, but changed her name to Claire after she had become the travelling companion of Shelley and Mary. This may have been for the sake of alliteration only (although she was legally Claire Godwin rather than Claire Clairmont); but she may also have been thinking of the Claire who is the faithful friend of the two socially oppressed lovers in *Julie, ou la Nouvelle Héloïse*, Rousseau being one of the major reference points in the radical circles in which she grew up.

The Shelley party knew the way to Switzerland because they had already made more or less the same trip in the summer of 1814, shortly after Napoleon's abdication. This was when Shelley had eloped with the sixteen-year-old Mary, rescuing her from what he imagined was parental tyranny – to the fury of her father, who, in spite of his radical principles, was enraged to find his already married disciple taking away a daughter to whom he was particularly attached. There was no baby William then, but what made them already a party was Claire's presence. The second Mrs Godwin followed them as far as Paris, anxious that at least her own daughter should return home and not be drawn into what she feared might be a *ménage à trois*. But Claire preferred the excitement of Shelley's company and new sights to a dull life with her parents, and knew that she was useful to the young lovers because she spoke French much better than they did. She would claim with some justification that in any case the Switzerland towards which they were all travelling was the home of her ancestors. Her grandfather on her mother's side was a citizen of Geneva, and her brother's father was Swiss, although her own paternity is not known.[1]

The Shelleys (Mary and Percy Bysshe) published an account of their 1814 trip in 1817. Because they had had so little money, this often sounds like a nineteenth-century version of 'Europe on $5 a day'. It gives vivid glimpses of occupied France after the defeat of Napoleon, with whole villages devastated by the Cossacks, widespread poverty and a cowed, resentful population. Emulating

Wordsworth, and before him Rousseau, the three of them set out to walk from Paris into Switzerland but, partly because of an injury to Shelley's foot, they had to buy or hire more donkeys and carriages than they anticipated and arrived at their destination with very little money. After only a week in Lucerne, where they had thought of settling, they suddenly decided that they had had enough and chose in their impoverished state the cheapest route home via the Rhine and then the Low Countries. This meant travelling by boat in the company of some unsavoury characters, one of whom, Shelley felt, was insulting in his behaviour to Mary. Tall but slight and with a fair, boyish or even feminine appearance, Shelley then showed that his days at Eton had not been entirely unprofitable by knocking the man down[2] (the many fellow pupils who bullied or tormented him at school had soon learnt that he combined pacific principles with a murderous temper which could make him formidable). When the three travellers finally arrived at the Belgian coast they were penniless and had to promise the owner of a boat which could take them across the Channel that he would be paid on arrival. This proved a difficult promise to fulfil and led Shelley into the expedient of borrowing money from the wife he had abandoned in order to elope with Mary. For most this would have been a devastating experience, but Shelley could often persuade himself that he was acting from the highest principles, whatever he did.

By the time of the second trip to Switzerland in 1816, the state of Shelley's finances had improved. Expulsion from Oxford and marriage to the sixteen-year-old Harriet Westbrook had seriously alienated his rich father, so that the most which could be coaxed from him was £200 a year (with another two hundred coming from Harriet's family). But by 1816 his father had increased the annual allowance to £1000 and the Shelley party could therefore travel in rather more comfort and style than on the previous occasion, bringing with them from England their own carriage. They were held up in Paris over the issue of essential travel documents, the new French government having become ultra-cautious after a group of British officers had in January sprung from jail a leading light of the Napoleonic regime, the Count de Lavalette, who had been about to follow Marshal Ney to the firing squad.[3] They then went to Troyes as before (although this time not on foot), but from there headed via Dijon for Geneva rather than Lucerne. This slight change of route was entirely to accommodate Claire, who in April had begun an affair with Byron and knew that he was on his way there.

Like most young people of the period, and especially those of a radical persuasion, the three adults in the Shelley party were very keen on Byron. When in July

1814 Mary had written at the back of her copy of *Queen Mab* that she loved its author 'beyond all powers of expression', she backed up this claim by quoting twice from one of Bryon's love poems, 'To Thyrza', without realising (how could she?) that the name referred, not to a female, but to the adolescent chorister with whom Byron had been in love while he was at Cambridge.[4] Many of the lyrics clearly delighted them, but so too did Byron's adventure stories in verse, in particular *Lara*. For Claire to have become intimate with him was therefore an exciting development and it was one for which the chief initiative was entirely and quite spectacularly hers. Consciously or not, she had chosen what was in many ways an opportune moment to approach him. Throughout March and the first part of April he was reluctantly moving towards the final signing of a separation agreement. His wife's advisors believed that whisperings of incest and homosexual affairs, together with a suggestion that he had sodomised her, would make him want at all costs to avoid the publicity of court hearings and sign quickly. But Byron never shirked a challenge and was prepared to argue his case in public while he still believed that the decision to leave him permanently was not really Annabella's but rather that of those who surrounded her. Once she had made it clear that this was not the case, he felt even more depressed and humiliated than he had before. It was in this period, and while Byron was still dodging the bailiffs, that Claire, who had had no previous contact with him, made a bold and determined attempt to capture his attention and sent him her first letter.

She began by calling herself E. Trefusis and appears at first to have received no response. Byron was used to his young female readers insisting they were in love with him, if not to Claire's plea, weirdly anticipatory of *Frankenstein*, that he should not ignore her because 'the Creator ought not to destroy his Creature'.[5] Her second letter, which she mysteriously signed 'G.C.B.', had more success and led to an initial meeting. Her first ploy was to seek Byron's advice about the best way of becoming an actress but after he had made some practical suggestions she changed tack, sent him some of her writings, and asked him to tell her whether he thought she had any future as an author. The two great advantages she had, and which she exploited to the full, were her relation to Godwin, whom at one point Byron had tried to help financially, and her connection with Shelley. She must have reminded Byron that he had already been sent a copy of *Queen Mab* and she alerted him to the publication of *Alastor*, Shelley's second volume of poetry, which appeared in March. About both she was comically critical, saying of the first that 'the style is so unpoetical & unpolished that I could never admire it', and of *Alastor* that, though it showed 'most evident proof of improvement', she thought that its author's merit lay rather in translation.[6] These were phrases which Shelley himself no doubt never saw, although he appears to have been fully aware of Claire's contacts with Byron and, according to one of his biographers, may have actively encouraged them.[7] A young poet desperate to be heard, he had until then failed to make an impact other than by the political radicalism of his views. Meeting Byron through Claire might well have seemed to him a way of establishing a potentially advantageous relationship with a figure whom he not only admired but who had also become the most popular and bestselling poet in England.

Given the age in which they lived (most familiar to us from the novels of Jane Austen), Mary and Claire Godwin were remarkably enterprising young women. When it became clear to Mary that Shelley was in love with her, she seized the occasion of a visit with him to her mother's tombstone in Old St Pancras churchyard to declare her own love and offer herself to him body and soul.[8] With much less knowledge of Byron than Mary had of Shelley (who had been a frequent visitor to the Godwin household), Claire could be said to have far outdone her sister when, after only one or two meetings, she wrote Byron a letter in which she made specific suggestions about how they could take a coach out of town and spend the night together. There is no doubt that Byron ought to have detected in Claire's letters, and probably in her behaviour, a good deal of naivety and youthful instability and refused what was on offer. It would have been far better for all concerned if he had. But self-denial in sexual matters was not one of his strengths, he was in an unusually vulnerable state, and Claire was a woman who would prove sexually attractive to many men in the future. He had already discovered that she had a difficult temperament, calling her a 'little fiend' at one moment in this early part of their relationship;[9] but in addition to her youth she had one attribute he found especially appealing. This was that she could sing very well. A poem he wrote at the time may refer to her and begins: 'There be none of Beauty's daughters / With a magic like thee; / And like music on the waters / Is thy sweet voice to me'.[10] It is a reminder of the gift for simple lyrical expression which would help to ensure Byron's continuing presence in the anthologies throughout the nineteenth century. In the following year Shelley wrote two poems which do certainly evoke the effect of Claire's singing and which have been described as 'among his most sensuous love lyrics'. In one of them there are suggestions that, however much Shelley might have encouraged Claire's approach to Byron, he was sorry to lose her love, although whether that means that the two of them were sexually involved in the period before March 1816, or when the poems about her singing were written, cannot be established with any certainty.[11]

Claire Clairmont and Byron spent their night together on 20 April (he signed the final separation agreement on the 21st), but it was according to his arrangements rather than hers. On the following evening, in what seems like an obvious gesture of one-upwomanship, she brought Mary to meet him: her sister may have been able to land Shelley but here was a much bigger fish. The two women were very different in temperament and never really got on. Announcing to Byron that Mary would be accompanying her on her evening visit, Claire used the occasion to make a complaint. Her sister, she warned, was 'accustomed to be surrounded by her own circle who treat her with the greatest politeness'. Byron therefore needed to warn his servants because 'on Thursday evening I waited nearly a quarter of an hour in your hall, which though I may overlook the disagreeableness – she, who is not in love, may not'. Once the visit was over she claimed that Mary was delighted with Byron and had entreated her to obtain his address abroad 'that we may if possible have again the pleasure of seeing you'.[12] There is plenty of evidence that Mary was indeed charmed by Byron, but that it was Claire who was desperate to have his address in Geneva is clear from the way she continued to pester him for it later ('pray give me some explicit directions … it will break my heart if I do not know where you are'[13]). He at that stage had probably no idea where in Geneva he would be staying and no more precise postal address than 'poste restante'; but that she would see him abroad seems to have been roughly and (on his side) rather casually agreed and fully explains why, after Troyes and Dijon, the Shelley party slightly altered the trajectory of their previous 1814 journey.

They arrived in Geneva on 13 May and put up at the Hôtel d'Angleterre. This had the reputation of being the town's best hostelry and was where most of the travelling British stayed. Viscount Castlereagh had stopped there in 1814 when he was on his way to represent Britain at the Congress of Vienna (a fact that Shelley would not have been pleased to learn), and it was the usual choice of passing royalty. Full of enterprise, its owner bolstered his clientele by running a coach service all the way from Calais for those who did not want to take abroad their own transport. Well to the east of where the Rhone divides present-day Geneva into two, the hotel stood back from the lake on the road out to Lausanne but had gardens, or perhaps merely fields, which ran down to the water (they are now a public park). The Shelley party took the cheaper rooms at the top of the hotel from the windows of which, Mary recorded, they had a clear view of the lake, with details of the mountain range which includes Mont Blanc reflecting in the water.[14] They then settled into a routine. There was always a strong pedagogic element in Shelley's relations with young women. As a boy he had tried to lead his sisters forward into areas of arcane knowledge and he had indoctrinated Harriet Westbrook with his own advanced ideas. Mary needed no such indoctrination, but Shelley guided her in her efforts to master Italian and improve her French, while he complemented her comparatively 'light' reading (novels and plays) with his own study of a good many books of history and philosophy in Latin or Greek. At about six they would stroll down to the lake with Claire, hire a boat and, when the weather allowed, drift dreamily over the water's surface until nightfall. They did not have to hurry because although Geneva was a walled town and closed its gates firmly at ten in the evening, as well as on Sundays during religious service, the Hôtel d'Angleterre lay well outside them in a suburb known as Sécheron (that it could escape the curfew may well have been an additional reason for its popularity). All three of them were waiting for Byron to turn up but Claire much more anxiously than the other two. From Paris she had written him a remarkable letter in which she had repeated that Mary admired him and then added,

> you will I dare say fall in love with her, she is very handsome & very amiable & you will no doubt be blest in your attachment; nothing can afford me such pleasure as to see you happy in any of your attachments. If it should be so I will redouble my attentions to please her; I will do every thing she tells me whether it be good or bad for I would not stand low in the affections of the person beyond blest as to be beloved of you.[15]

Apart from their indication that Claire knew Byron was not in love with her, there is a hint in these words about Mary of how competitive she felt towards her stepsister. There is also perhaps in them a faint memory of how, at the beginning of 1815, Shelley had tried to establish a *ménage à quatre* with his friend from Oxford, Thomas Jefferson Hogg. He had encouraged Hogg to sleep with Mary while he spent most of his time with Claire, an arrangement which had collapsed chiefly because Mary had a much more conservative, possessive nature than his own and resented her sister's presence in the household. Claire appears to be envisaging some similar kind of arrangement in which Hogg would be replaced by Byron who would then be taken from her by Mary (although in that case Shelley would revert to her). The spirit of sweet self-sacrifice in which she accepts this possible outcome sounds too good to be true, and certainly it did not prevent her from being irritated when she arrived in Geneva to find Byron not yet there, even though he had left England a good week before she had. Could he have changed his travel plans en route or deceived her as to what they really were? She was, however, reassured a little when she went to the post office in Geneva and managed to glimpse, not only the letter she had written to Byron from Paris, but also one addressed to Dr John Polidori, whom she knew had been hired as a private physician by Byron shortly before he left England.

3

On the Road

There were reasons for Byron's late arrival in Geneva beyond his habitual, temperamental preference for a leisurely mode of travel. By going through France, the Shelley party had taken the direct route to Switzerland. Byron seems to have made enquiries about doing the same but learned that, although he could obtain travel documents for France in general, it would be on condition that he did not set foot in Paris. The authorities may have discovered that he was acquainted with one of the British officers involved in Lavallette's escape; they must have known that a book about France in 1815, which his friend Hobhouse had published and which dealt with the hundred days in a manner sympathetic to Napoleon, was mostly in the form of letters addressed to Byron; or perhaps he was just on the list as one of Britain's more notorious liberals. Always quick to take offence, the likely refusal of the necessary documents for Paris was why he chose to sail from Dover to Ostend, make his way to Cologne, and then follow the Rhine down to the Swiss border. That way he could avoid France altogether and the pain of seeing Napoleon's former people subjected to another of what he had called those 'stupid, legitimate-old-dynasty boobies of regular-bred sovereigns'.[1]

Choosing a longer route slowed Byron down but so too did the fact that he rarely travelled light. There was quite a large group to accommodate. With him was William Fletcher, who had worked on the Newstead estate, been converted into a valet and then accompanied Byron on his trip to the Levant. Also from Newstead was Robert Rushton, the son of one of his tenants. Because he was a boy at the time, he had set out on the Levantine tour in the capacity of a page but then been sent back home from Gibraltar by Byron, who was anxious about what might happen to a good-looking adolescent in those territories which were controlled by the Turks and where it was presumed – and not without good reason – that pederasty was rife. According to Caroline Lamb, in the testimony she eagerly passed on to Annabella Milbanke at the time of the separation crisis, this anxiety was needless because Rushton had already been 'corrupted' by Byron himself.[2] There is no doubt that as he developed Byron was strongly drawn to attractive adolescents just a few years younger than himself. This was a pattern of relationship which had been established at Harrow and then at Cambridge, where he had fallen hopelessly in love with John Edleston, the chorister who was the inspiration behind 'To Thyrza'. Whether these intense friendships with other young males were fully physical relationships seems doubtful, given that Byron could, for example, speak very openly about his passion for Edelston to a wholly respectable female friend five years older than himself.[3] Only during his second stay in Athens, in the winter of 1810–11, when his previous travelling companion Hobhouse had returned to England and he was living in the company of young boys, is it as certain as these matters can usually be that he had full sexual relations with other males.

Apart from the two male servants he knew well, Byron had taken the precaution of hiring before he left London a Swiss called Berger to smooth the way and reduce the chances of being cheated. As Claire Clairmont knew, he was also travelling, in the most aristocratic of fashions, with his own private physician. John Polidori had been recommended to him by one of his own doctors as a young man of promise. A handsome twenty-year-old, Polidori had completed his Edinburgh medical degree in record time the year before. This meant that he was still inexperienced in medical matters but what probably told in his favour was his literary background. Before moving to London to make a decent living from teaching and translation, Polidori's father had been secretary to the poet Alfieri at a time when – to cite the kind of detail which always appealed to Byron – Alfieri was living with the Countess of Albany, widow of Prince Charles Edward Stuart, the Young Pretender. Young Polidori harboured literary ambitions himself and had already written several plays. When in 1823 Byron was preparing for his second visit to Greece and again looking for a private doctor to travel with him, he wrote:

> I want a Surgeon – native or foreign – to take charge of stores and be in personal attendance – salary – a hundred pounds a year – all expenses paid – and his treatment at our table as a companion and a Gentleman.[4]

Apart from having to watch over the accounts rather than the stores, these were more or less the terms on which Byron engaged Polidori, who, anxious to establish his superior social status, refers to his employer in his diary as his friend or companion and to the other members of the group, not by name, but as indistinguishable 'servants'.

When he arrived in Ostend on 26 April, Byron would have had to shepherd his group through customs. Immediately he had slipped away from his house in Piccadilly, the bailiffs had moved in, so that it is possible he had taken as many valuable items as it could with him and that his luggage was correspondingly bulky, especially as he had no clear idea about how long he would be abroad. It would take him years to become reconciled to the idea that his exile would be permanent. He travelled from Ostend in a new coach which had been built for him before he left England. This was a copy of one that had belonged to Napoleon and had been captured at Waterloo. The equivalent of one of today's stretch limos, it contained a day bed, dining facilities and, by the time Byron had fitted it out, a small library. Having cost £500 it was one of his final, major extravagances. From his time at Cambridge onwards, Byron had spent money like water, on himself but also on others. When a friend was killed in a duel he visited the grieving widow and surreptitiously left behind a £500 note. This was such an inappropriately large sum that it led the woman to assume that he must be madly in love with her and meant that she gave him a hard time afterwards.[5]

It was in his Napoleonic coach and another, hired vehicle that Byron and his entourage headed for Ghent and then Antwerp. The landscape which surrounded the route struck him as so flat that he said 'a molehill would make the inhabitants think that the Alps had come here on a visit'.[6] In Antwerp, he was more impressed by the alterations Napoleon had made to the port facilities in order to resist the English ('poor dear Bonaparte!!!') than by any of the art he saw – 'florid nightmares' is how he described Rubens' paintings.[7] On leaving that town the brand new coach broke down and to have it repaired he had to drop down to Brussels. It does not seem that this town had been on his initial itinerary but once he was in it there was no avoiding a visit to the nearby battlefield of Waterloo. The area was full of British tourists, anxious to inspect the site of such a recent historic event, and among them Byron met Pryse Lockhart Gordon, who had been a friend of his mother and had known him as a boy.[8] It was with Gordon therefore that he went to Waterloo. 'I detest the cause & the victors', he told Hobhouse after his visit,[9] but at the same time he could not help being intensely interested in the details of the battle and collected various memorabilia (helmets and the like) which he sent back to his publisher, John Murray, for safe-keeping. He also began writing some stanzas about the conflict and its aftermath which could go into his new poem.

To Murray's delight, this was to be a continuation (canto 3) of *Childe Harold's Pilgrimage*, the first two cantos of which Byron had published after his return from Greece. Quite why these had been such an extraordinary success is not now easy to understand, but one possible reason was that they made up a kind of travel diary in verse with effective descriptions for the travel-starved British of numerous foreign locations, many of them exotic. Another, perhaps more important reason was the figure of Childe Harold himself, whose travels the poem recounts. In an obvious projection of his own temperament, Childe Harold is described by Byron as a young man of aristocratic lineage who has run through all the physical pleasures very early in his life, and who finds himself, while still young, disillusioned, world-weary and alone. He is someone who needs the stimulus of travel to distract him from an obscure feeling of predestined doom. Part of the appeal of this brooding and aloof figure lies in the sense of a better nature which could be revived by the right circumstances, or the right woman (and many female readers certainly lined up to do its creator that favour).

The same general posture which Byron had adopted in the first two cantos of *Childe Harold*, and which had been so successful, was again apparent as he began canto 3. 'I am as a weed, / Flung from the rock, on Ocean's foam, to sail / Where'er the surge may sweep', he writes in stanza 2; and he describes himself in the fifth stanza as one who has 'grown aged in this world of woe, / In deeds, not years, piercing the depths of life, / So that no wonder waits him.'[10] These words are all spoken *in propria persona* but the difference between the poet's feelings and those of Childe Harold himself is hard to distinguish, and does not become any easier as the poem progresses: 'Lord Byron,' Walter Scott wrote after having read canto 3, 'has more avowedly identified himself with his personage than upon former occasions, and in truth does not affect to separate them.'[11] The accuracy of this remark is suggested by the similarity between the terms Byron uses to describe himself in stanzas 2 and 5 and the way he refers to his protagonist in stanza 8, where he is called, 'He of the breast which fain no more would feel, / Wrung with the wounds which kill not, but ne'er heal'. This is a posture which went down very well with the general public, but there is no reason to believe that it was not also genuinely informed by Byron's own deep unhappiness at this time. After these lines he then comments sadly, in one of those striking phrases with which his poetry abounds, 'life's enchanted cup but sparkles near the brim'.[12]

Because the locations which Byron was offering to describe in the third canto of his poem were much more familiar to his British readers (either from their reading or from their personal experience) than those depicted in its two predecessors, the way he continued to foreground his own feelings under the cover of those of Childe Harold was both a necessary and an effective move. It was especially effective because curiosity about the poem's author had been enormously increased by the storm of publicity provoked by his separation from his wife. The hostility of public opinion had been made much worse for Byron by the publication in the newspapers of two poems which he had written chiefly to relieve his feelings, although also perhaps to further his own cause among a select few. The first of these was addressed to his wife and had been composed on 18 March, the day after he had reluctantly signed what was only a preliminary separation agreement. 'Fare thee well!', it began, 'and if for ever / Still for ever, fare *thee well* / Even though unforgiving, never / 'Gainst thee shall my heart rebel.'[13] The second, written a fortnight later, was entitled 'A Sketch from Private Life' and was a vicious attack on Annabella Milbanke's personal maid, whom Byron blamed for fomenting trouble in his household. The two poems need to be considered together because, after his wife had left him, Byron tried very hard not to allow himself to hate her. Resentment seeps through 'Fare thee well!' (it is not entirely clear who is supposed to be 'unforgiving' in the third line, and in later lines Byron asks whether no other arm could be found to inflict 'a cureless wound' than the one which had once embraced him); but in attacking her maid he could let loose more directly his seething anger. She had previously been Annabella's nurse and governess and was called Mary Clermont – an unfortunate fact which persuaded Claire of the same name but different spelling to have herself referred to as 'Clairville' when she first arrived in Geneva. 'With eye unmoved, and forehead unabash'd, / She dines from off the plate she lately wash'd', Byron wrote, 'Quick with the tale, and ready with the lie / The genial confidante, and general spy.'[14] The verse is lively but it was uncharacteristic of Byron to criticise someone for social origins they could not help (how would he like it, one newspaper retorted, if he were to be criticised for his club foot); and the mean-spiritedness helped to turn the tide further against him and make his final days in England all the more uncomfortable.

After Byron had written his two poems he had fifty copies printed to circulate among his friends. It was his enemies (and the supporters of his wife) who made sure that they had much wider distribution, although it has to be said that he was never shy about discussing private matters in public. He opened canto 3 of *Childe Harold*, for example, with a direct address to his daughter: 'Is thy face like thy mother's, my fair child! / Ada! sole daughter of my house and heart?',[15] and only after a long autobiographical section, parts of which have just been quoted, did he then describe the arrival of his protagonist on the battlefield of Waterloo and the feelings it aroused. The stanzas which evoke the preliminaries which led up to the decisive encounter are well known ('There was a sound of revelry by night' ...). They demonstrate that gift for narrative more fully displayed in the romantic verse novellas such as *The Giaour*, *The Bride of Abydos*, *The Corsair* or *Lara* which had quickly followed the first two cantos of *Childe Harold* and solidified his position as England's most successful poet. The contrast between the ball in Brussels where 'Youth and Pleasure meet / To chase the glowing Hours with flying feet', and the panic which ensues when noise of a battle is first heard and there are 'cheeks all pale, which but an hour ago / Blush'd at the praise of their own loveliness', is very effectively managed.[16] However, in the ensuing reflections on the outcome of Waterloo, and on the downfall of Napoleon, some of the difficulties and ambiguities inherent in Byron's political thinking begin to appear. If his first ambition had been to become a statesman, dazzling his fellow peers with his oratory, he soon discovered that he lacked the necessary qualities for the nitty-gritty of politics. In addition to which, no period could have been less propitious to someone of his views than the one in which he entered the House of Lords. If he belonged anywhere on the official political spectrum, it was with the small and often beleaguered group of the so-called Foxite Whigs who had applauded many of the principles of the French Revolution and refused to feel obliged to abandon them by either Robespierre's terror or the seizure of power by Napoleon. Byron admired Napoleon as a great man who, in the process of destroying corrupt old regimes in Europe, had helped to spread enlightened principles round the world; yet he had to disprove of him as a military despot and a man dangerously lacking in warm fellow-feeling. There was nevertheless one point on which Byron could be clear. However many perversions there had been of the original motives which sparked the revolution in France, anything was better than that return to the old values and institutions which Waterloo – a 'king-making Victory' – made possible, and which the Congress of Vienna had tried to set in train. 'What,' he complained, 'shall reviving Thraldom again be / The patched-up idol of enlightened days?'[17]

Once his own carriage had been repaired, and he had decided to buy an additional lighter and smaller 'calèche', instead of having to hire vehicles as he

went along, Byron set out for Cologne, taking with him a present from Pryse
Gordon which was to have an important effect on English literary history. This
was a copy of Giovanni Casti's *Novelle Galanti*, a late-eighteenth-century series
of comic tales in verse in which the author often addresses the reader in a conver-
sational and humorous manner. Thanking Gordon for this gift later, Byron said
that he had already enjoyed Casti's *Animali Parlanti* but that the *Novelle* were
much better and he longed to 'go to Venice to see the manners so admirably
described'.[18] The significant feature of the gift was that Casti wrote in the Italian
verse form known as *ottava rima*, which Byron would adopt for the great comic
poems of his later career: *Beppo*, *Don Juan*, and *The Vision of Judgement*. In 1816,
however, although he had previously written some satire, it was only in his letters
that he was comic. He may already have begun reading Casti as he and his party
followed the Rhine down to Koblenz, where he was impressed by the ruined
fortress of Ehrenbreitstein and, close by, monuments to two French heroes of
the recent wars, Generals Marceau and Hoche. A conscientious tourist, he had
only a mild interest in architecture, 'churches & so forth',[19] and often confessed
he knew nothing about art. What delighted him were impressive landscapes –
and there were plenty of those as he moved down the Rhine – but also, and
perhaps more importantly, places where memorable events had taken place. At
this stage in this life, he seems to have liked landscape best of all when it was an
aide-mémoire to history. Noting in *Childe Harold* how the banks of the Rhine
presented a 'blending of all beauties' with 'streams and dells, / Fruit, foliage,
crag, wood, cornfield, mountain, vine', he then added,

> And chiefless castles breathing stern farewells
> From gray but leafy walls, where Ruin greenly dwells.

Saying goodbye to this region later in canto 3, he claims that although there may
be 'more mighty spots', none could unite in 'one attaching maze / The brilliant,
fair, and soft', but also 'the glories of old days'.[20] Byron's feeling for history was
very strong, so that it is no surprise to find that the contemporary writer he most
enjoyed reading was Walter Scott.

As they had journeyed further down the Rhine and approached a French
segment of territory around Strasbourg, Byron and his group had crossed over
the river 'as we have not French passports – and no desire to view a degraded
country – & oppressed people'.[21] But it was not only in holding views like
this that he was by no means an ordinary traveller of his time. Before leaving
London, Polidori had been told by John Murray that if he kept a diary while

he was with the great poet it might be worth a lot of money. Describing their arrival in Ostend, the young doctor reported that Byron 'fell like a thunderbolt on the chambermaid'. The diary Polidori intermittently kept proved too self-centred and sketchy for publication in his lifetime (he does not seem to have understood that Murray was interested only insofar as it related to Byron), but in 1911 it was edited by his nephew William Rossetti, the brother of Dante Gabriel and Christina. Unfortunately, it had previously been in the possession of one of Polidori's sisters (William Rossetti's aunt rather than his mother), who had written out a fair copy which omitted all the phrases she thought improper and then destroyed the original. 'Falling on the chambermaid like a thunderbolt' was one of these phrases. Rossetti rescued it because he claimed to have remembered these words from having read them before the original diary was destroyed.[22] That he was right to do so is suggested by the letter which Byron wrote to Hobhouse from Karlsruhe on 16 May in which he described how the red cheeks and white teeth of the chambermaid at their inn had made him 'venture upon her carnally'.[23] He had the sexual morality of his age and class although he always prided himself on paying handsomely for his pleasures. The servants he slept with at Newstead were richly rewarded, as no doubt were the chambermaids in Belgium and Germany. It would take a revolution in attitudes before those in a position comparable to his could be made to feel as uneasy as they ought to have felt about casual sex as an exploitation of social privilege and power.

Travelling at the beginning of the nineteenth century was not easy. The roads were often bad and there were many more difficulties with poor accommodation and officialdom than anyone is likely to encounter today – it is striking how often Polidori reports in his diary that his own group's travel documents were inspected. Hardened by his experiences in Greece, Turkey and Albania (a country he was almost alone among his compatriots in having visited), Byron was proud of the way he could rough it when he had to, and accepted discomfort and irritation as part of the travelling experience. His young doctor was not cast in the same mould and also turned out, as they moved on, to be hasty and hot-tempered, someone who easily flared up. There were, in addition, some indications that he was not especially robust. Reporting from Karlsruhe, Byron said that up until now on their journey Polidori had treated two patients. One was a blacksmith ('I dare say he is dead by now'), and the other was not his employer but himself. 'Devilish ill' is how Byron described 'poor Polidori' at Karlsruhe, but he appears to have doctored himself effectively enough to be able to press on into Switzerland with the rest of the group after only a brief delay.[24]

Basel was the first Swiss town they visited and, after passing through Berne, they then stopped at Murten, or Morat as the French-speaking Swiss call it, the pretty town on its own small lake just south of Neufchâtel. There had once been there a huge ossuary of bones from the army of the Duke of Burgundy which the original members of the Swiss confederation had defeated so decisively, and so bloodily, in 1476. The battle of Murten was an important encounter in what Gibbon, who once thought of writing on the subject, calls 'The History of the Liberty of the Swiss', 'that independence which a brave people rescued from the House of Austria, defended against a Dauphin of France, and finally settled with the blood of the Duke of Burgundy'. 'From such a theme,' he went on, 'so full of public spirit, of military glory, of examples of virtue, of lessons of govern-ment, the dullest stranger would catch fire.'[25] Byron was not dull and for him the battle at Murten was a particularly moving triumph of republican endeavour. Although the bones of the fifteenth-century Burgundian mercenaries had been scattered by an invading French army in 1798, he managed to acquire a few to send back to Murray, explaining that otherwise they would only be used by the locals for penknife handles.

From Murten, Byron must have taken the road to Lausanne and then made his way towards Geneva along the lake, arriving at the Hôtel d'Angleterre on 25 May, exactly a month after he had set out. If he went there rather than to any other hotel it was almost certainly because everyone else did and not because he knew that Claire Clairmont was already one of its residents. Filling in the usual details then required in the register, he facetiously recorded his age as 100 (the punctilious Swiss manager quickly requested him to change it). This was no doubt a result of fatigue after the day's journey but it also indicated a constant feeling he had that, just like Childe Harold, he had already run through most of life's experiences and was old before his time. Travelling with the youthful Polidori might have encouraged him in this feeling, and he would find no discouragement for it in the 23-year-old Shelley and his two female companions, both still in their teens. In 1816 Byron was only 28, but in Geneva he would be the old man of the party.

4

First Meetings

With all his luggage, and his fellow travellers, Byron's arrival at the Hôtel d'Angleterre could hardly have been discreet and Claire Clairmont, on the *qui vive* as she must have been, was very quickly aware of it. She saw his entry in the hotel register and sent him a note saying that she was sorry he had grown so ancient although, from the slowness of his journey, she might have concluded he must be *two* hundred years old. 'I suppose your venerable age,' she wrote, 'could not bear quicker travelling'. This was late on Saturday. Instead of getting in touch with her immediately, Byron spent the period after his breakfast on the following day swimming in the lake with Polidori and he then took the calèche he had bought in Brussels into Geneva where he picked up his mail – he was disappointed not to have heard from Hobhouse about when he would be coming to join him – and did a little preliminary house-hunting. This explains an angry note which Claire wrote early on Monday morning. In the letters she sent to Byron in London, she had been keen to stress that she would make no demands and to assure him that 'in all things you have acted most honourably'. But now she asked how he could be so inconsiderate. She had waited, she said, 'in this weary hotel for a fortnight & it seems so unkind, so cruel, of you to treat me with such marked indifference'. What he should do, she continued, was go up to the landing on the top floor of the hotel at 7.30 that evening and she would make sure she was there to conduct him to her room.' In a letter Byron wrote to Augusta Leigh towards the end of his stay in Switzerland he assured her that, in spite of all the rumours which had been circulating in England, he had had only one mistress during the summer and that he had done all he could to discourage the relationship with her; but, he added, 'I could not exactly play the Stoic with a woman – who had scrambled eight hundred miles to unphilosophize me'.²

Claire had asked Byron to send replies to her notes via Shelley but there was an awkwardness in that procedure while the two poets had still not met. By either accident or Claire's design, the first meeting took place on the Monday. Byron had already heard about the possibility of renting a house at Cologny, a village out along the shore to the east of Geneva. Since Sécheron was out along the shore to the west, a convenient way to get to Cologny was to row or sail almost directly across the lake. This was what he and Polidori did and it was on their return, as they were disembarking, that they ran into the Shelley party, and Claire was able to introduce her sister's lover to her own. Byron dealt with the initial awkwardness by inviting Shelley to dine with him. Around four or five o'clock, therefore, the three men met again, and it would be interesting to know what was on the menu at the all-male meal which then took place. In *Queen Mab* Shelley had envisaged a brave new world brought about by four major changes to society: the abolition of monarchy, the defeat of Christianity, the elimination of marriage, but also the cessation of meat-eating. For a long time he had been a convert to vegetarianism. Byron's position was somewhat similar but he had reached it by paths which were distinctly less ideological. A famously handsome man, he had darkish curly hair (often described as auburn), attractive features, only slightly impaired by one of his blue-grey eyes being bigger than the other, and white, even teeth of which he took great care, badgering his friends while he was abroad to keep on sending him from London a special powder for cleaning them. Just over five foot eight, he was powerfully built apart from his withered lower right leg and deformed foot. This was a physical disadvantage about which – as years of painful quack treatments during boyhood eventually proved – nothing could be done, but the same was not true of the tendency he inherited for very easily putting on weight. While he was at Harrow his mother had rented out Newstead and gone to live in nearby Southwell. One of her neighbours there (the same intelligent young woman to whom Byron spoke so openly of his love for Edelston) said that the first time she saw him he seemed a 'fat bashful boy'.[3] When he went up to Cambridge at seventeen and a half, Byron was still fat and weighed in at fourteen and a half stones. Deciding that this would not do, he took medical advice and worked out a regime which he followed with such zeal and rigour that at one point he was able to bring his weight down to ten stones and six pounds. It may not only have been concern for his appearance which made him so determined to avoid being fat, although his congenital deformity had made him always acutely self-conscious about how he looked; there was also the fact that the more weight he carried, the more painfully it bore down on his club foot.

There were four major features of Byron's regime, one of which was violent, sweat-inducing exercise. His favourite pastime of swimming was not much use in this regard but fortunately he also enjoyed exerting himself vigorously in the practice of swordplay or boxing, and became highly proficient in both. His second method for losing weight was hot baths and the third an extensive use of purges or emetics. These latter were of course at this time many doctors' first port of call when their patients fell ill, but Byron seems to have believed that they helped him to get thinner, as indeed they may have done in the short run. His fourth method was the more familiar one of highly disciplined dieting. Byron did not always diet but whenever too much extra weight threatened to reappear he could be remarkably abstemious. There is a famous story of his dining for the first time at the house of the wealthy poet Samuel Rogers, refusing all the elaborate food which was available and finally making a meal of mashed potatoes, drenched in vinegar to give them added flavour. Thomas Moore, who knew him well, described how at times his daily intake consisted of 'a thin slice of bread, with tea, at breakfast – a light vegetable dinner, with a bottle or two of Seltzer water, tinged with vin de Grave, and in the evening, a cup of green tea, without milk or sugar'. 'The pangs of hunger,' Moore noted, 'he appeased by privately chewing tobacco and smoking cigars.'[4] The 'vegetable dinner' which Byron probably shared with Shelley after their first meeting in Geneva did not indicate any particular prejudice against meat on his part but rather against heavier foods in general, because they might be fattening but also because the use of purges, and years of intermittently living in the way Moore describes, had left his digestion in a delicate state and unable to cope easily with them: later in his life he would accurately describe himself as 'a weakly stomached gentleman'.[5] Yet that he often starved himself did not mean that was reluctant to indulge other people and he would no doubt have ensured that, whatever he and Shelley ate, the hotel provided the twenty-year-old Polidori with plenty of examples of its usual fare.

The exclusion of the two women from the dinner on 27 May was characteristic of Byron. When he was again living in close contact with Shelley in Pisa and the women also present included his own long-term mistress Teresa Guiccioli, Mary Shelley, and the wife of one of the Shelleys' friends, Jane Williams, he organised a series of dinners which were also all-male. This was in tune with the conventions or perhaps more accurately the prejudices of the time, but they suited Byron who, unlike Shelley, was conservative in many of his social practices but also had an aversion which he himself recognised as irrational (we might say, pathological) to watching women eat.[6] Not being present at the dinner must have made Claire anxious to know how it would go. If Byron and Shelley had decided they did not like each other, her situation would have been even more delicate than it already was. For her especially, therefore, it was fortunate that the two men established a close bond at once. Why this should have been so cannot be entirely attributed to vegetable dinners, or to similar social backgrounds. Shelley's aristocratic lineage was distinctly minor in comparison with Byron's, as well as far less ancient; but they were both English gentlemen who had been to public school (Eton in Shelley's case) and Oxbridge. In one way therefore they spoke the same language, inhabited the same field of reference. Yet this would in itself have been insignificant had they not both rejected many of the usual standards of their class and, partly for that reason, become social pariahs. If there was immediate sympathy between the two, one reason was that both of them knew only too well what it was to be ostracised and even persecuted. Later in the summer Shelley would translate for Byron parts of Aeschylus's *Prometheus Bound* and it was during this time that Byron wrote his short ode entitled 'Prometheus'. The figure of the Titan who breaks the rules of his clan in order to benefit mankind but remains defiant in his loneliness and suffering meant a lot to them both. Byron and Shelley were destined to be outsiders because they both held radical political views and they shared a despair over the restoration of the old regimes after Waterloo, which was an obvious unifying factor. Since the older man was someone with a largely instinctive hatred of any kind of oppression, whereas the younger had very specific ideas about how society could be reorganised, there were major differences in their political thinking which would only emerge later. On many topics they were not at one, especially over the role religion should play in any well-organised state – often anti-clerical and a sceptic on crucial questions of dogma, Byron nevertheless found the militant atheism of his friend not at all to this taste. Yet from the first he warmed to Shelley and felt that, whatever disagreements they might have, they were broadly on the same side.

It no doubt helped the friendship to develop that Shelley admired Byron deeply and regarded him as the greatest poet among his more immediate contemporaries. If his own work – the privately published *Queen Mab* and more recently *Alastor* – had dropped still-born from the press, Byron was a publishing phenomenon although one which Shelley felt was richly deserved. This disparity in success between the two of them would become troubling later, especially as Shelley's chances of catching up a little were hindered by the feeling he developed that his own creative spirit was impaired or inhibited by the fluency of his prolific friend. There are clear signs that he could not help resenting this a little. Byron, on the other hand, never gave any indication that he minded that Shelley was also a writer. Of his several vices, professional envy was not one and he was always genuinely pleased when an author friend did well. This is a tribute to his good nature but also an indication that he did not rely exclusively on his writing for his self-esteem ('no one should be a rhymer who can be anything better', he once said[7]). An anecdote which exists in three different forms has an exemplary force here. The most convincing version of the story goes that during their journey to Geneva Polidori, who had been reading an article which praised Byron's poetry, asked him what it was, apart from writing verse, that he himself could not do better than his employer (all the available information about the young doctor suggests that he was prone to making remarks as tactless and aggressive as this). Looking at the Rhine which they could both see from their hotel window, Byron replied tartly that he could swim across that river, hit the keyhole of the door with a pistol shot, and knock Polidori down.[8] Although his writing fulfilled a vital therapeutic role for him and he was pleased when it did well, he had a confidence in himself which did not depend on being a poet. He was nonetheless deeply interested in poetry and literature in general, as well as in history and philosophy, and was delighted to find in Shelley someone who could talk so enthrallingly, and in such an informed way, about all four. A friend of Shelley's left an interesting record of his conversation when he reported that 'to talk with a man of undoubted genius, who felt such a devout reverence for what he believed to be the truth that he laid his whole many-thoughted mind bare before you, was indeed a treat',[9] and it is clear that Byron was impressed in a similar way. Since Polidori had imagined that talking to Byron was to be his role, he must have felt his nose considerably out of joint. In his diary he insists on how clever he thought Shelley was and how many beauties he had found in *Queen Mab*, and he seems to have got on well with Mary, helping her in her efforts to learn Italian; but there may have been some anger at being supplanted behind a fierce quarrel later in the summer which led to his challenging Shelley to a duel. It was then that Byron quietened the situation down by telling Polidori that although Shelley had scruples about duelling, he had none and would always be ready to take his place.

To see Byron making it clear that he wanted to spend his time with Shelley must have been both a delight and a relief to Claire. It also meant that the Shelley party as a whole was a little less isolated. When she first arrived in Geneva, Mary wrote to a friend that 'we do not enter into society here'.[10] It might have been difficult for her, and the others, to do so. Although Polidori says that she was known as 'Mrs Shelley', there would be many amongst the expatriate community ready to sniff out the truth, and to make what mischief they would of Claire's presence. According to one scholar, there were over a thousand British men and women staying in Geneva at this time and in the canton de Vaud, that stretch of country along the lake to Lausanne and beyond, twenty-five villas were rented out to British people. The consequence was a 'colonie britannique' which formed an important component of Genevan society.[11] Byron dipped his toe in this world but it was not to his liking. Polidori remembered his accepting an invitation to a gathering organised by Lady Dalrymple Hamilton but 'upon approaching the windows of his ladyship's villa, and perceiving the room to be full of company, he set down his friend [i.e. Polidori himself], desiring him to plead his excuse, and immediately returned home'.[12] What would have discouraged him was not so much the possibility of being 'cut' (although that was certainly present) as the danger that people would stare and whisper. But if they did that to him, they would have been more than likely to have done it also to the Shelleys.

A second and to a large extent separate component of Genevan 'society' was indigenous and made up of the town's notables. This was notoriously difficult to penetrate but Byron had his entrées there from the beginning. Hobhouse had recommended to him a young banker called Charles Hentsch who turned out to be not only accommodating, efficient and interested in literature – he wrote poems himself and would translate into French verse Byron's farewell poem to his wife – but well connected and influential. Another influential figure to whom Byron had a letter of introduction, and who made contact with him immediately, was Marc-Auguste Pictet, the brother of Charles Pictet de Rochemont who was one of Geneva's leading citizens and the man who, at the Congress of Vienna, had helped negotiate his town's adhesion to the Swiss confederation and persuade the major powers to guarantee Swiss neutrality. Marc-Auguste was chiefly a scientist and distinguished enough to have been made a member of London's Royal Society; but his interests were also literary and he was associated with Geneva's *Bibliothèque Universelle*, formerly the *Bibliothèque Britannique*, in which there had recently been, and later would be, various accounts and translations of Byron's poetry. It was Marc-Auguste who introduced Byron to Madame Eynard-Chatelain, one of Geneva's leading hostesses. In her salon he met Pellegrino Rossi, a still young Italian who after teaching law in Bologna had fought against the Austrians in the army which Joachim Murat, the former king of Naples and Sicily, had gathered together after Napoleon (his brother-in-law) had escaped from Elba. The failure of that enterprise had forced Rossi to flee to Geneva where the success of his university teaching helped him to achieve the difficult feat of very quickly becoming a naturalised citizen. At the other end of the age scale from Rossi was Charles Victor de Bonstetten, author of *Researches on the nature and laws of the imagination* but more interesting to Byron as a man who had been a close friend of Thomas Gray and who had once travelled to Cambridge to stay with the author of the *Elegy in a Country Churchyard*.

There were many interesting people in Geneva and Byron met several of them in his first few days there. But, like his own Childe Harold, he was not in the mood for society. Wherever he went in those early days he made a point of taking Polidori with him, helping him to make contacts which might be a help in his future career. When they were first introduced in the salon of Madame Eynard-Chatelain, the doctor was unhappy that only Byron's name was mentioned: 'mine, like a star in the halo of the moon, invisible' (in a similar situation in Brussels he had described himself as a mere 'tassel to the purse of merit');[13] but once Byron had withdrawn he seems to have established himself as an independent fixture in several social circles. In May or early June Byron could have used the fact that Geneva's gates closed at ten as an excuse for an early escape from houses within the town; but later in the summer Polidori regularly let them close and stayed the night at a hotel, very probably at his employer's expense. To the contacts Byron provided for him he added a few, medical ones of his own: a Dr De Roche, for example, who spoke with apparent knowledge about the illness which had laid Polidori low on the journey to Switzerland, and a Dr Odier at whose house he listened to a paper on the interesting topic of how much a doctor should tell a man about his fiancée's state of health. All the signs are that Polidori flourished in Genevan society and, if that were so, one of the reasons would have been that he was an accomplished linguist. Byron, on the other hand, did not speak French, although he could and indeed did read it with ease. Pictet and Bonstetten would certainly have understood his English and he could have chatted away with Rossi because he had learnt to speak Italian fluently while he was in Athens, where it was the lingua franca of the expatriates. But with many others there must have been difficulties. Polidori remembered that the husband of Madame Eynard-Chatelain solved the problem by speaking to Byron in 'bad Italian',[14] although as a native speaker himself his 'bad' may have been a trifle harsh.

Yet it was not so much language difficulties which made Byron prefer the company of the Shelley party to a more varied social life when he first came

to Geneva. Battered and bruised psychologically after the separation crisis, he
needed some quiet and the company of a small group in the midst of which
he could feel comfortable yet stimulated. In his later descriptions of his mental
state at this time he would say he had been close to suicidal despair: 'I should,'
he wrote, giving the expression of his feelings a characteristic comic turn, 'have
blown my brains out, but for the recollection that it would have given pleasure
to my mother-in-law.'[15] His unhappiness was not, however, very evident to
someone like Mary, who noted that he had periods of gloomy abstraction, and
that there was an occasional 'waywardness' in his behaviour, but was otherwise
struck with how genial and amusing he could be. She always remembered his
'good humoured smile' whenever he met them and, in a fictional portrait, noted
not only his sexual attractiveness but the 'wit, hilarity and deep observation ...
mingled in his talk'.[16] But then Byron was a life-long depressive who had always
made considerable efforts not to seem depressed in ordinary social intercourse.
If he woke up most mornings feeling gloomy, he tried not to let it show.[17]

It was in his writing that he expressed without restraint his more morbid
feelings, but the problem there is that what he says often sounds stagy or melodramatic. Canto 3 of *Childe Harold* is very loose in structure but its dominant
concern is with the protagonist's rejection of society and his search for forgetfulness and comfort in Nature. 'I have not loved the world, nor the world me,'
Byron writes towards its end, 'I have not flattered its rank breath, nor bowed /
To its idolatries a patient knee'; and at the beginning of the following stanza he
repeats the same phrase, 'I have not loved the world, nor the world me; / But
let us part fair foes'.[18] This is only one of several attitudes Byron strikes in the
poem and they all seem unconvincing, like the postures adopted by a bedridden
invalid in a vain effort to alleviate the pain (and in any case, it is hardly true that
Byron had not loved the world and certainly not that the world had failed to love
him). He was an admirer of Coleridge but largely because of *The Ancient Mariner*
or *Christabel*. He does not seem to have paid much attention to those poems
in which Coleridge had, like Wordsworth, developed ways of talking about his
more painful feelings in a natural and intimate way (the obvious example in this
context being 'Dejection: an Ode' which was printed in the *Morning Post* in 1802
although it did not appear in book form until 1817). When Shelley published
his long poem *Alastor* he accompanied it with a number of not at all cheerful
short pieces, including a sixteen-line poem entitled 'Mutability' which deeply
impressed his future wife. There is in several of these pieces less rhetoric and
more of a sense of communing directly and sincerely with the reader than Byron

usually managed in what is known as his 'serious' poetry. 'If a writer has not the language to express feelings they might as well not exist', T. S. Eliot once wrote in an essay on Byron.[19] 'Might as well not exist' as far as the readers of the writer's poetry are concerned perhaps, but that people do not always express their unhappiness as well as they might surely does not mean that it is any the less genuine.

5

Diodati

Neither the Shelley party nor Byron felt happy at the Hôtel d'Angleterre. Apart from being full of inquisitive compatriots, it was also expensive (especially for someone with Byron's entourage). They had all begun house-hunting immediately after Byron's arrival and it can hardly have been an accident that they soon found places to live only a few hundred yards from each other. The focus for them both was on Cologny, which during the late eighteenth century had been the semi-permanent home of at least three rich English families. They lived there, according to one observer, 'in the greatest cordiality with the citizens of Geneva, and one another', and they made 'the hill of Cologny the most delightful place perhaps at this moment in the world'.[1] Without expecting quite this degree of felicity, Byron had been attracted in Cologny by a particularly handsome house known as the villa Diodati, but there were complications over the lease and it seemed too dear. It may well have been thanks to his influential banker Charles Hentsch that he was able to negotiate a satisfactory deal. He signed an agreement to rent the property on 6 June and moved in there four days later.

Ten days before his move the Shelley party had, with the help of Polidori, found a house almost directly down the hillside from Diodati and much nearer the lake. It stood in the area called Montalègre and was known as the Maison Chapuis, presumably from the name of its owner. Mary describes it in a letter as a cottage, but it was in fact a quite substantial, square, two-storey building and only cottage-like in comparison with Byron's residence. Dating from the beginning of the seventeenth century, the villa Diodati was at least three times as big and full of handsome rooms. Pillars which ran round three sides of the first of its three storeys supported a wide and handsome terrace from which there were (as there still are) magnificent views. From the shorter part of the terrace on what, looking from the lake, is the right-hand side of the house, it was possible to see the cathedral on top of the hill around which Geneva was built; and from its main part, which runs along the building's lake-facing façade, there were views across the continually changing waters of the lake to the hills and mountains of the Swiss Jura. There was no better prospect in the immediate area. In Byron's day, access to the villa Diodati was difficult and it was therefore very private. A further reason he had for liking it was that it was still in the hands of the descendants of the great Giovanni Diodati, who had come to Geneva from Lucca in Italy as a religious refugee and was famous for being the first person to have translated the Bible into Italian. It was this Diodati's nephew who had been a friend of Milton and had invited him to stay in Geneva.[2] The Shelleys could not boast of any comparable historical associations still clinging to their more modern building, but it was comfortable and spacious enough. On leaving it, they had only to cross over the road to Evian, which ran closely in front, and in two minutes they were at the lake. It took them less than ten to climb the steep hillside through the vineyards to Diodati. Everything was therefore set for an experiment in communal living, although in conditions of far more ease and independence than this term usually suggests.

Wherever he went, Byron liked nothing better than to establish a routine: wild Romantic poet though he might have been, he was also a creature of habit. Some of the habits he had were unusual, chiefly because he preferred to write his poetry in the middle of the night. This is what he had begun to do at the hotel and it meant that he did not go to bed until four or five in the morning. He would then get up around twelve and have his breakfast. The period between that meal and his dinner at four or five would usually be spent in business, exercise and the occasional excursion or visit. After dinner, when the weather allowed, he would go sailing or rowing on the lake with the Shelleys and Claire. Sometimes they would have joined him for one of the two main daily meals, or invited him to share it with them. Once the light had begun to fail, it was back to their rooms or, later, one of their houses for a drink, supper and more conversation. This was a regime he had begun to establish in May and he had kept it going in the first ten days of June, when he would sail across to Montalègre from Sécheron to see the Shelley party. Once installed in Diodati, he looked forward to making it more permanent.

The passion Shelley had for being on the water is expressed in *Alastor* where the protagonist, a solitary unworldly poet, who is seeking the ideal female companion he has encountered in a dream, spends most of the poem in a boat, sometimes allowing himself to drift wherever the winds and waves take him, quite indifferent to his own safety. Byron, whose grandfather had been an admiral known as 'Foulweather Jack' because of his tendency to run into it, had a similar if rather more practical passion. Early in their stay in the Geneva area, the two poets decided to buy a boat together, not one of the local variety which tended to be light and flat-bottomed, but a sturdily built English craft with a substantial keel. Just below the Maison Chapuis at Montalègre was a sheltered indentation in the lake shore where the boat could be kept. In the long run this may have been an economy. While they were still in the hotel, and on their own, the Shelley party had provided for their lake excursions by hiring a boat and once Byron had arrived he would do the same. Shortly after his arrival, the boatman with whom Shelley had been dealing came to him with a request. In Polidori's words, he wanted him 'as a favour not to tell Lord Byron what he gave for his boat, as he thought it quite fit that Milord's payment should be double'.[3] Shelley of course did not grant the favour and Byron's Swiss servant, Berger, was sent to give the boatman what was no doubt a piece of his lordship's mind.

Byron was evidently regarded in Geneva as the rich English aristocrat abroad and in many respects that is precisely what he was. This might seem strange given that as soon as he had left his house in Piccadilly, it had been ransacked by the bailiffs. Going abroad to avoid one's debts was, however, a classic manoeuvre. It explained why there were so many well-bred British people living in Calais and Boulogne (although also, of course, many who were not so well-bred); and why Byron's own father, whom he had last seen when he was two and half, had left Scotland to spend the final months of his short life in Valenciennes (he died there at 35, just a year younger than his son would be at his death). Being abroad meant that Byron had untrammelled access to his own income, which was considerable in spite of the relatively modest amounts of money he needed to give his wife as part of the separation agreement. There was in the first place the rents from the still unsold Newstead, where there were sixteen farms, other incomings from property and bequests and then, in addition, his writings. When he first began to publish poetry he refused to take anything for it, giving the copyrights away or trying to arrange that the money Murray offered was diverted to less well-born writers such as Godwin or Coleridge, who needed it more than he did. But later he abandoned that stance and would be pleased that Murray was persuaded to pay him 2000 guineas for canto 3 of

Childe Harold (more than twice Shelley's annual income). Any financial difficulties Byron might still have had in the second half of 1816 would disappear
when, at the end of the following year, his lawyers found someone willing to
buy the Newstead estate for close to £100,000. This was the time, one might
have thought, for ridding himself completely of all his debts. That he did not
do so but remained a slow and reluctant payer can appear unethical or even
immoral, and his recalcitrance may well have led to financial difficulties, or even
ruin for some; but a word needs to be said about his two major kinds of debt.
One was to the money lenders in whose toils Byron had become embroiled
when he was still under twenty-one and at Cambridge (at twenty he already
owed about £12,000[4]). Their rates of interest were so grotesque that it is not
surprising to find most of their victims waited to be squeezed rather than paying
up spontaneously. The second kind of debt was to tradesmen. Shelley had
exactly the same attitude to their bills as Byron, settling many of them as late as
he could. This was such a familiar habit among the wealthy that built into the
prices they were charged was often the expectation that the money would come
in slowly, if at all. Although his motives may have been different, the boatman
in Geneva was not the first person to have thought of charging Byron double
because he was a rich lord.

A quiet life and doing more or less the same things every day suited Byron, as
it did Shelley, but not everyone was happy. Polidori increasingly found compen-
sations elsewhere for the feeling that he was undervalued, and Claire was not
having such a good time either. Her expectation or fear of a *ménage à quatre* did
not materialise, but then neither did her aim of establishing herself firmly as
Byron's recognised mistress and companion. Quite why this should have been
so is impossible now to establish. Afterwards, in letters she sent to Byron from
England, she portrayed herself as entirely composed of selfless devotion and
referred to the 'cross unkind things you used to say to me', or the 'impertinent'
way he had of looking in the face of someone who loved him and telling her that
he was tired and that he wished she would go away.[5] It is highly likely that Byron
did say unkind things but then the unnaturalness of the selfless posture Claire
adopted may have irritated him and whether it was consistently maintained is
doubtful. Mary often complained how moody and temperamental her sister
could be and there are signs in other letters Claire wrote that it took very
little to make her confrontational. In many of his dealings with women Byron
himself was not especially aggressive but rather acquiescent and passive. His
valet Fletcher remarked with puzzlement that Annabella Milbanke was the first

woman he had met who did not know how to 'manage' his employer;[6] but in that case, Claire was the second. Her failure may in part have been because, although Byron did not mind advanced views on sexual matters in friends such as Shelley, it made him nervous to find them in young women. Yet why relationships fail is a topic on which it is very difficult to form a judgement when all the information is available and which becomes impossible when the record is as incomplete as it is in the case of Byron and Claire. The simple fact is that, although they began sleeping together in May, there are clear indications that, as time went on, they saw less and less of each other and that the prospect of any kind of permanent relationship quickly began to fade.

In spite of the deterioration of his relations with Claire, those which Byron enjoyed with Shelley continued to go from strength to strength. Writing to his friend and English banker Douglas Kinnaird in September, Byron would say, 'Pray continue to like Shelley – he is a very good – very clever – but a very singular man – he was a great comfort to me here by his intelligence & good nature.'[7] Byron was also of course a very clever, intelligent man but Shelley differed from him in being a full-blown intellectual, albeit a largely self-taught one. Their respective situations must have meant that in many ways Shelley deferred to Byron because the latter had more experience, wealth, and popularity; but there were nevertheless areas in which he was the dominant partner. One indica-tion of this is the way Shelley succeeded in making the older man temporarily change his mind about Wordsworth. Byron had never been a great admirer and found it particularly difficult to see the merit in Wordsworth's poems about simple people. After one of his own first collections (*Hours of Idleness*) had been savaged by the *Edinburgh Review*, he had retaliated by writing *English Bards and Scotch Reviewers*. In this lively satire in an eighteenth-century mode, the youthful Byron – he was barely twenty-one when it was published – laid about him both vigorously and indiscriminately, and with the apparent aim of making as many life-long literary enemies as he could, in the shortest possible time. Wordsworth he describes as someone 'who, both by precept and example, shows / That prose is verse, and verse is merely prose.' He accuses him of believing that 'Christmas stories tortured into rhyme, / Contain the essence of the true sublime', and he goes on:

> Thus when he tells the tale of Betty Foy,
> The idiot mother of 'an idiot Boy';
> A moon-struck silly lad who lost his way,
> And, like his bard, confounded night with day,

So close on each pathetic part he dwells,
And each adventure so sublimely tells,
That all who view the 'idiot in his glory',
Conceive the Bard the hero of the story.[8]

Shelley must have laboured hard to convince Byron that, amusing though jibes like this might be, his general view of Wordsworth was superficial. Both of them deplored the way in which the older poet had turned his back on his radical past and become a supporter of the Tory government, reneging on a time when, as Shelley had put it in a sonnet, 'In honoured poverty thy voice did weave / Songs consecrate to truth and liberty'.[9] When in 1814 *The Excursion* appeared, in all its nine books, Mary and Shelley were deeply disappointed and denounced its author as a slave to Tory prejudice and conventional opinion. But for Shelley at least, this apostasy did not mean that the revolutionary new voice which Wordsworth had brought to English poetry more than a decade earlier was any less worth listening to and he laboured to convince his new friend of that fact. 'When I was in Switzerland', Byron later told a friend, 'Shelley used to dose me with Wordsworth physic even to nausea, and I do remember then reading some of his things with pleasure'.[10] An early indication of this regime may be a poem which Byron wrote (or finished) in Geneva about a visit to the grave of the eighteenth-century satirist Charles Churchill, whose work had provided one of the models for *English Bards and Scotch Reviewers*. Churchill had died in Boulogne but his body had been brought back to be buried in Dover so that Byron had been able to pay his respects just before leaving England. His poem records finding the grave in scandalous disrepair and speaking to the sexton about it. The manner in which the episode is described is recognisably Wordsworthian, reminiscent of all those poems in which Wordsworth also chats with men or women of the people. Byron himself acknowledged the debt and said of the poem that it was a 'serious imitation of the style of a great poet – its beauties and defects'.[11] The difficulty is that it is hard to tell from any particular passage which of these last two qualities is being imitated and therefore whether, at any specific moment, Byron is trying to copy Wordsworth's style or merely parody it.[12]

'Churchill's Grave' is a strange performance; much more clearly indicative of the effect of Shelley's Wordsworthian campaign are four well-known stanzas in canto 3 of *Childe Harold*, the first of which begins,

> I live not in myself, but I become
> Portion of that around me; and to me,
> High mountains are a feeling, but the hum
> Of human cities torture.[13]

When Wordsworth read canto 3 of *Childe Harold*, he had no doubt that he had been crucial to its composition and complained of plagiarism. The whole of it was, Moore reported him as saying, 'founded on his style and sentiments – the feeling of natural objects, which is there expressed not caught by B. from Nature herself, but from him, Wordsworth, and spoilt in the transmission – Tintern Abbey the source of it all'.[14] As far as the lines above are concerned, Wordsworth was perhaps thinking particularly of the moment in 'Tintern Abbey' where he describes how 'The mountain, and the deep and gloomy wood, … were then to me / An appetite; a feeling and a love, / That had no need of a remoter charm'.[15] In both the poem and the *Childe Harold* stanzas a mountain is a feeling, yet the development of thought is very different in each. Byron moves on from his initial contrast between town and country in order to look forward to the time when he will be disembodied, no longer 'classed among creatures' and a 'link reluctant in a fleshy train'. Once he has spurned 'the clay-cold bonds which round our being cling', he wonders if he will not then merge into 'bodiless thought? the Spirit of each spot? / Of which, even now, I share at times the immortal lot?' How can being 'reft of carnal life' mean extinction, he implies, when the mountains, waves and skies are 'a part of me and of my soul, as I of them?'[16] There may well be echoes in this solipsistic development which are Wordsworthian, but the general effect is of Wordsworth filtered through Shelley who, militant atheist though he might have been, was in no way a materialist but rather a firm believer in the spirit world.

One of Byron's early complaints about Wordsworth is that he was a mystic, an 'Arch-Apostle of mystery & mysticism' as he once put it;[17] but in these four stanzas of *Childe Harold* he briefly became quite mystical himself. The author of 'Tintern Abbey' was of course no more a materialist than Shelley and writes in that poem of 'A motion and a spirit, that impels / All thinking things, all objects of all thought, / And rolls through all things'; yet his treatment of the matter/ spirit or body/soul dilemma is complex and he always seeks to give due weight to the material world. As he describes revisiting the banks of the Wye neither his present nor his former self is made to seem a 'link reluctant in a fleshy train'. Byron was conscious that in dealing with these same matters he was venturing on what was for him unusual ground and becoming, if not mystical, then at least metaphysical. He was proud of what he achieved, telling his sister in January 1817 that he thought canto 3 the best he had written, and that there was a 'depth of thought in it throughout and a strength of repressed passion which you must feel before you find; but it requires reading more than once, because it is in part *metaphysical* ....'[18]

The four stanzas which begin with the claim that mountains are a feeling do require reading more than once, but that is less true of another group of stanzas, later in canto 3, which are also 'Wordsworthian' in a similarly general way. They begin with an evocation of Byron alone on Lake Geneva (alone, one must assume, with his thoughts, since he would almost certainly have had a boatman with him), and addressing it by its alternative name.

> Clear, placid Leman! thy contrasted lake,
> With the wild world I dwelt in, is a thing
> Which warns me, with its stillness, to forsake
> Earth's troubled waters for a purer spring.
> This quiet sail is as a noiseless wing
> To waft me from distraction; ...[19]

Byron goes on to describe the sights and smells of a summer twilight, and also the sounds as 'on the ear / Drops the light drip of the suspended oar' (an echo of a very similar line in Wordsworth's 'Remembrance of Collins').[20] It is in moments of solitude and relative quietness like these, he explains, that he feels '*least* alone' and most aware of 'The Spirit, in whose honour shrines are weak, / Uprear'd of human hands'. The place to celebrate that spirit is not in churches but in 'unwall'd temples', among 'Nature's realms of worship'.[21] Since nothing quite like this had ever appeared in Byron's poetry before, one has to marvel at Shelley's success in temporarily transforming him into a Wordsworthian worshipper of Nature, although perhaps we should also remember that he was in an unusually susceptible state. Disgusted with the celebrity status he had once been happy to accept, and which had turned out so disastrously for him, and both recognising and deploring aspects of his own character which had contributed to his troubles, he was looking for a new start, a way of remaking himself in accordance with his present circumstances, and with what he deluded himself into thinking were his real needs.

6

Frightening Tales

The pleasant routine which Byron and the Shelley party had established towards the end of May, and in the first ten days of June, and which they all hoped to continue once they were living close to each other, was hampered by the weather. On the journey to Geneva the Shelley party had been dismayed to find that Les Rousses, one of their stopping places in the French Jura, was still snowed up. The climate improved once they were out of the mountains and in Sécheron, but there are indications that it was hardly set fair. Mary remembered being out with the others on the lake and finding that the water had become distinctly choppy. A strong north-easterly wind had begun to blow which, together with the current of the out-flowing Rhone, was driving them back into Geneva. It was then that Byron, in what was perhaps an effort to distract his companions from some danger, said he would sing them an Albanian song (he was very often heard singing to himself). To their surprise he let out what Mary describes as a 'strange wild howl' and then laughed at their disappointment.[1] It might have been from then on that he was known affectionately by them all as 'Albé', although another possible derivation of this nickname is the contraction of his title to 'LB'. Albé was less imaginative than the teasing names Byron would later find for Shelley, one of which was Shiloh. Now associated for most of us with a battle in the American Civil War, this was the biblical name which the 64-year-old Joanna Southcott, a well known English visionary and mystic, had said she would give to the new Messiah when she gave birth to him on 19 October 1814, an event of which there had been no further news by the time she died three months after it was supposed to take place.

By the middle of June what had been uncertain weather had given way to the frankly bad. Summer storms are not unusual in the Geneva area but that year there were an exceptional number of them, and it was often cold as well as wet. The summer of 1816 is in fact famous in meteorological history because there was so little of it, not only in Switzerland but elsewhere in the northern hemisphere. The phenomenon of bad weather was world-wide, and has been attributed by some specialists to a volcanic eruption of unprecedented size which had taken place in Indonesia the year before. This had sent millions of tons of dust into the upper atmosphere, forming a barrier between the earth and the sun. It did not help the general mood that, as the weather continued to deteriorate, various astronomers around Europe observed an unusual number of dark blotches on the sun. News of these spread and when one astronomer in Italy concluded that they heralded the end of the world, there was a good deal of panic, especially among those on whom the rain and cold were having a direct effect.[2]

That the bad weather should have economic consequences was inevitable. In Geneva, where the mean summer temperature would turn out to be the lowest since 1753, there was flooding in the bottom part of the town, which caused considerable distress. Meanwhile, in the region as a whole, the expectation of a ruined harvest caused the price of flour to rise and soup kitchens had to be opened (a section in a book which attributes the apparent world-wide climate change at this time to the Indonesian eruption is entitled 'Famine in Switzerland'[3]). The slopes to the west of Lausanne which Byron would gaze on from the terrace of Diodati were covered in vines, but in the canton de Vaud the grape harvest would be later than it had ever been. Byron and Shelley had to walk through vines to see each other in Cologny, and they made periodic trips to Geneva, but in none of their writings of the period, nor in those of the others, is there much indication of how hard the times were for the people amongst whom they were living. In *Queen Mab* Shelley refers to the 'gilden flies' who bask 'in the sunshine of a court' and are 'the drones of the community'. They are the people, he wrote, who 'feed on the mechanic's labour; the starved hind / For them compels the stubborn glebe to yield / Its unshared harvests'; and he then adds, 'many faint with toil, / That few may know the cares and woe of sloth'.[4] Neither he nor Byron was a 'gilden fly', and they were certainly not slothful; but they were able to live their lives largely insulated from the surrounding economic realities.

The favourite time for going on the lake was after dinner, but that was not possible if it was pouring down. The beginning of what was at least a week of cold and rain was probably the violent thunderstorm which Byron observed from his

terrace at midnight on 13 June and described in four stanzas of *Childe Harold*:
'How the lit lake shines, a phosphoric sea, / And the big rain comes dancing to
the earth!'.[5] From then on sailing became difficult and the Shelley party took to
going up to Diodati in the early evening and sometimes staying the night there
rather than tackling the short but also wet and muddy track back home. There
was never any lack of subjects to discuss, Mary recorded, and one of these was
prompted by a French translation of a number of German ghost stories entitled
Fantasmagoriana. It was after considering these that Byron suggested that a good
way to pass the time, and an appropriate one given the frequent lightning and
thunder outside, was for everyone to try to write something along the same
lines. What those lines might be they all knew from the enthusiasm they shared
for what is known as the Gothic novel. Horace Walpole is generally considered to have launched this genre in 1764 with his *Castle of Otranto* and other
notable, later contributions included William Beckford's *Vathek*, Ann Radcliffe's
The Mysteries of Udolpho and *The Monk* by Matthew Lewis. Everyone at Diodati
would have been familiar with these works, as well as with many others like
them, and Shelley, young as he was, had already written and published two
Gothic novels of his own. As the term implies, the settings for the Gothic novel
were often medieval and the plots full of sinister foreigners, murderous intrigues,
and strange or supernatural episodes; yet since they differ so much in detail, a
useful way to characterise them is through one of their intended effects. What
every Gothic novelist tried to do was to give the reader a pleasurable fright, and
in that sense the works they wrote were the ancestors of our own horror films.
This makes it likely that one initial driving force behind the discussions which
developed was Shelley, since it was a peculiarity of his temperament that he liked
to terrify others. He had done this to his sisters when he was a boy with tales
of a giant serpent living in their house's grounds, and there was a time when he
also did it to Claire. Richard Holmes has described very well the short period
when Mary would retire reluctantly to bed while Shelley and Claire worked each
other up with talk of the uncanny, eerie or supernatural until Claire fell into a
hysterical fit and had to be calmed down by her sister. As Holmes suggests, the
feelings Claire and Shelley aroused in each other may well have included a trans-
posed sexual element.[6]

   Byron had challenged them all to produce their own frightening tale, but it is
not certain that everyone complied. It has been suggested that a novel by Claire
for which Shelley was trying to find a publisher in 1817 could have had its origins
in these evenings at Diodati but, if it did, no trace of it now remains. Mary talks

of Shelley having proposed something based on his childhood but there is now no way of knowing what that was. His full and continuing participation in the discussions could have been hampered by an episode recorded by both Byron and Polidori. The conventions of the Gothic novel were a powerful influence on them all but so too was Coleridge's *Rime of the Ancient Mariner*. Byron had been very impressed by an unfinished poem by Coleridge in a somewhat similar vein called 'Christabel', in which the lady of the title invites into her castle the mysterious and sinister Lady Geraldine. At some point Byron read out loud a manuscript version of this poem (it was not until August that the Shelleys were able to read it in book form). One of the features which Mary, and many other women, found especially attractive about him was his voice, and at various stages of his life he showed himself to be an accomplished amateur actor. His reading of the creepy moment in 'Christabel' when Geraldine is alone in the heroine's bedchamber and undresses to reveal a withered torso, 'hideous, deformed and pale of hue',[7] in startling contrast to her youthful features, was so effective that Shelley became hysterical and rushed out of the room. It was a question of the biter bit, and suggests how far from mere cold exploitation his sessions with Claire had been. Later he said that while listening to Byron, and looking at Mary, he had had a vision of a naked woman who had eyes where her nipples ought to have been.

As the doctor in the house, Polidori treated Shelley by throwing water in his face and giving him ether to sniff. He was interested in abnormal mental states, having completed his degree in Edinburgh with a thesis on somnambulism, a disorder from which Shelley happened to suffer. The strange or uncanny was therefore of special interest to him and he certainly made his own contribution to the story-telling at Diodati; yet precisely what that was is not easy to work out. He later said it was the germ of the novel he published in 1819 entitled *Ernestus Berchtold*, but this story has little of the supernatural or uncanny in it. The ghost of the hero's mother appears occasionally to give him obscure warnings of what is about to happen and, in a feeble re-enactment of the Faust theme, it transpires that the man whom he eventually discovers to be his father, Count Doni, has become very rich by calling up an evil spirit. In exchange he can either sell his soul or accept that every invocation of this spirit (for more funds) will entail some domestic tragedy. He accepts this second option, with the result that his first two children, Louisa and Olivieri, become separated from his second two, the twins Ernestus and Julia, and that later Olivieri seduces Julia and Ernestus marries Louisa. The way these situations are treated suggests a routine indulgence in the incest theme beloved of the Romantics (the subtitle of the novel is 'The Modern Oepidus') rather than any direct reference to Byron and Augusta; but it is this theme which predominates and not anything particularly ghostly.

Which preliminary parts of his future novel Polidori offered to the others at Diodati is likely to remain a mystery, although Mary Shelley had what was possibly a vague and distorted memory of a scene from the novel in which Julia spies on her father as he conjures up the evil spirit. In the figure of Olivieri there are hints of Byron himself, particularly when he is described as someone who, though usually charming, could suddenly become disconcertingly abrupt (both Mary and Claire complained of the same trait). But Olivieri is summed up as a 'gambler, and a libertine',[8] and it was Polidori himself who later took to gambling and, if some of those close to him are to be believed, also committed suicide because of a gambling debt. Byron had at least one friend who was an inveterate gambler and once praised gambling because, whereas 'women – wine – fame – the table – even Ambition – *sate* now and then', 'every turn of the card – & cast of the dice' keeps the gambler alive and excited;[9] but he gave it up fairly early in his life. The picture Polidori presents in his novel of his ingenuous hero, Ernestus, being led into gambling, and dissipation generally, by Olivieri can hardly have reflected the situation in Geneva. What perhaps did are the few passages in which Ernestus is mocked by Olivieri because he insists on retaining his religious beliefs. These have a liveliness lacking from most of the rest of a lacklustre book and suggest something of the discomfort which Polidori may have felt at Diodati because he was a Catholic. Yet although Byron may well have teased Polidori about his faith, he would have been very unlikely to mock him for it. Interested in religious matters, and impressively knowledgeable about the Bible, he was usually tolerant of other people's views. It was Shelley who was the hater of Christianity. If anyone was going to make life difficult for Polidori because of his Catholicism, and provide therefore one of the sources for Olivieri, it would have been him.

More impressive than *Ernestus Berchtold* is the novella which Polidori also published in 1819 entitled *The Vampyre*. The starting point for this was Byron's own contribution to the evenings in Diodati. Because he rarely threw anything away, a manuscript of what he then wrote still survives and is dated 17 June 1816.[10] It tells the uncompleted story of a young man who is travelling in Greece with a fascinating but mysterious English aristocrat, slightly older than himself, called Augustus Darvell. The latter is slowly losing strength for no clear reason.

They stop in a Moslem cemetery where Darvell prepares to die and extracts from his companion a solemn oath that he will not tell anyone else about his death. Cunningly placed details warn the reader that something very peculiar and unnatural is going on. It is possible that Byron had already decided that Darvell was a vampire and very probable that he had explained to Polidori and the others how, once his narrator returned to England, he would be shocked to discover his resurrected former companion circulating in London society (in the story as Polidori continued it, the Darvell figure begins to pay court to the narrator's sister). The reason for the probability is that such a reappearance can be associated with an episode in Byron's own life. In 1810 he was lying very ill of a fever in Patras but at more or less the same time, he later worked out, various people in London, including his former school friend at Harrow, Robert Peel, were convinced that they had seen him walking around there. A natural sceptic, it was one of the paradoxes of Byron's nature that he was at the same time a superstitious man with a half-reluctant interest in prophesies or coincidences, and he puzzled over these apparently strange sightings of himself without being able to dismiss them entirely as obvious cases of mistaken identity.

The way Polidori built on Byron's initial idea in *The Vampyre* was quite skilful and in the process he made a lasting contribution to British and also European culture. Before his story appeared, vampires had almost always been represented as ugly and repulsive creatures. Lord Strongmore, as Polidori eventually called the Darvell figure, is a sophisticated English aristocrat and after him – although thanks chiefly of course to Bram Stoker – it has become difficult not to associate vampires with elegant upper-class manners and fine clothing. Yet if *The Vampyre* was an initial success, this had less to do with its originality in this respect than with the way its publisher suggested to the public that it had been written by Byron. In reclaiming his own authorship, Polidori vehemently denied that he was a party to this deception and he certainly does not seem to have profited much from it.[11] He was an unsuccessful author. Had he written in diary form an intimate and comprehensive account of living with Byron as Murray wanted him to, he could have done very well; but he seems to have needed fiction to express the tangled feelings of attraction and repulsion which his employer evoked in him, and he had great difficulty in making those clear. Like Olivieri, Lord Strongmore has several traits which appear to rely on his creator's memories of Byron. One of these is a pallor which many observers noticed in Byron and which may have been a consequence of either a naturally thick skin or his dieting. Another was an impassivity which sometimes gave the impression, to use Polidori's words in *The Vampyre*, of his being 'above human feelings and sympathies'.[12] This was probably no more than a touch of aristocratic *hauteur* (although most people were struck by how friendly and approachable Byron could be), or a manner which he had picked up from his time among the Regency dandies. But a story which Mary tells suggests that it disconcerted the volatile and demonstrative Polidori. Once when they were all in the boat together he happened to hit Byron hard on the knee with an oar. After the injured party had turned away his face in pain and remonstrated, Polidori remarked that he was glad to see Byron was not after all dead to all feeling. He was then told that it was not a good idea to tell people you were glad you had hurt them and that, but for the presence of the women, he might have found himself thrown out of the boat.[13]

Byron, Polidori and perhaps Claire and Shelley made contributions to the evening entertainment at Diodati but, insofar as what had been proposed was a competition, the undoubted winner was Mary Godwin. Byron was later to say that he thought *Frankenstein* 'a wonderful work for a Girl of nineteen – *not* nineteen indeed – at that time'.[14] Her idea for it arose from lively discussions about the possibility of reanimating dead matter, in which Polidori, with his scientific education, and Shelley, who was fascinated by science and had been in the habit of conducting scientific experiments in his rooms at Oxford, no doubt played important parts. As with *Ernestus Berchtold*, it is impossible now to discover the original short form in which Mary presented *Frankenstein* to the company. Over the succeeding months, and with Shelley's help, she worked hard on it, filling out or adding details, but the finished novel, published in 1818, bears obvious marks of its origin. Her young scientist Victor Frankenstein, for example, is a native of Geneva and the crucial encounter with the monster he has created takes place on one of the glaciers above Chamonix, which the Shelley party visited in July. When in defiance of his Creature's threats Victor foolishly decides he will marry his childhood sweetheart Elizabeth, a house is secured for them 'near Cologny',[15] and after the wedding ceremony they row over the lake to Evian where they vainly hope to spend their first night together. These details recall the circumstances in which *Frankenstein* was first conceived; yet it is not really a ghost story and there is little in it which might now be called supernatural, although plenty which seems improbable. The crucial improbability lies not so much in the way the monster is created, his speedy acquisition of remarkable linguistic skills, or his ability to cover huge distances on foot, but in the psychology of the protagonist. The intelligent and apparently sensitive Victor has to become at moments incomprehensively obtuse so that the plot can

be driven forward and his tragic fate sealed. He treats his Creature with bewil-
dering stupidity and, even though he has been deprived by him of his brother
and best friend, cannot seem to work out that, on the night after his marriage,
it will be Elizabeth who is attacked rather than himself. But all this is necessary
because *Frankenstein* is one of those frightening tales which do not depend on
surprise for their effect but on the dramatic irony of the reader clearly seeing the
blow about to fall well before its victim does. In its final version, it is both well
written and skilfully constructed, and raises a number of serious issues which its
first critics, considerably helped by Mary's dedication of the novel to her father,
identified as 'Godwinian'.

One of these is criminality. Victor's Creature kills all those who are closest
to him, but he is shown to have been in the first instance a noble savage in a
Rousseauesque mould, full of generosity and warm feeling, and someone who
only turns to crime after his rejection by his creator and the realisation that his
hideous appearance causes people to shy away from him in horror. *Frankenstein*
is complex enough to be read on several different levels but its enormous success
has nevertheless been dependent on the original idea Mary Godwin had on that
June evening in Diodati, and on the way the progress of science has continually
made that idea more rather than less relevant. Of course, no one now believes
that creating life could ever be a matter of collecting various body parts from
the local morgues or graveyards and reanimating the resulting conglomeration
with electricity, as Victor does; but the phenomenon of cloning does sharpen
the interest in Mary's treatment of the unexpected consequences of scientific
advance, one of many questions on which she was temperamentally far more
conservative than her future husband. She was in Cologny a quiet, reserved
young woman, over-awed by her brilliant lover and by a figure as celebrated and
charismatic as Byron; but the story she told the others in the villa Diodati, by
the flickering firelight, while the wind howled outside and the rain continued
to pour down, would result in a work eventually far more widely known than
anything the two men ever wrote.

7

A Narrow Escape

By 22 June the weather had cleared sufficiently for Byron and Shelley to feel that they could set out on an expedition which they must have been thinking about for days. In normal circumstances, they might well have felt obliged to take Polidori with them but on the 15th he had sprained his ankle, jumping off a wall, and three days later the injury was much worse, incapacitating him. The two poets could therefore go off on their trip without having to experience any unease about leaving him behind. What they had planned was a literary pilgrimage in honour of Rousseau. When they first arrived in Geneva both the Shelley party and Byron had made independent visits to view the statue of Rousseau which then stood in the Planpalais, a small park or walking area just outside the city walls. Looking at the figure, Byron caustically suggested that it must have been constructed from the stones which Rousseau's fellow citizens had thrown at him.[1] Familiar with the *Confessions* as he was, he probably knew that it was not in Geneva that the stones were thrown but in the tiny principality of Neufchâtel which, in the eighteenth century, was controlled by the King of Prussia and therefore a safer haven for Rousseau than most others in the region. Yet there was a metaphorical truth in what Byron said in that the Genevan authorities had banned *Emile* and made it clear that its author would not be welcome should he ever decide to return to his home town.

As Byron and Shelley set out on their trip, *Emile* was hardly in the forefront of their minds and neither were Rousseau's *Confessions*. The work that principally concerned them was *Julie*, which is set on the shores of Lake Geneva and celebrates the beauty of the local countryside. They carried copies of this novel with them and marvelled at the effectiveness of its descriptive prose as they visited various sites which are important in the action. Although only Byron had read the novel before, both men were enthusiastic about it yet, in Shelley's case especially, this is strange. *Julie* tells the story of the passion which develops between the heroine and her tutor. The two young people sleep together, with the result that Julie becomes pregnant and then has a miscarriage. They want to marry but Julie's father is appalled at the idea of uniting his daughter to someone so far beneath him in social standing and, besides, he has promised her to an old friend. The lovers are separated and Julie eventually feels constrained to give up St. Preux (as the tutor is called) after her mother has discovered the letters he has written to her daughter, fallen ill, and died. All this might seem to illustrate a belief in the evils of contemporary institutions and social conventions similar to Shelley's. Yet in fact once Julie has been pressurised by her father into marrying his friend, she becomes a convert to the sanctity of marriage. Her elderly husband turns out to be an improbable paragon of tolerance and wisdom and not only easily forgives Julie for her previous indiscretion, but also works to reunite her with St. Preux, so that the two of them can re-establish their relationship on the basis of warm but platonic friendship. On the shores of the lake he establishes with Julie an ideal community run on highly conservative, patriarchal lines while she herself continually makes it clear that she now regards her previous physical relationship with St. Preux as a sin. Since Shelley expresses keen admiration for *Julie* it may be that in June 1816 he was not only reading it for the first time – in spite of its extraordinary European success – but in bits, only paying attention to those parts which were directly relevant to the sites he was visiting. A painfully long novel, it certainly benefits from that approach.[2]

To accommodate Byron's sleeping patterns, the two men set sail from Montalègre at 2.30 on the afternoon of Saturday 22 June, in the company or the care of two boatmen. They made their leisurely way eastwards along the coast, sleeping first at Nernier, twelve miles away, and then at Evian, sixteen miles further on. The consequence was that they had moved out of Switzerland into Savoy and, by one of the peculiarities of that *ancien régime* which the defeat of Napoleon at Waterloo had partly restored, were in territory which was technically Sardinian. This was because at the Congress of Vienna it had been handed to Victor Emmanuel I, someone described by one English liberal of the time as 'the silliest man now practising royalty'.[3] He was a scion of the house of Savoy, but principally known as the King of Sardinia. During the Napoleonic wars, this island had somehow managed to stay out of French control, so that Byron had been able stop there when he was sailing from Spain to Malta and could recall having seen his 'Cagliari majesty' at the opera in his own capital city.[4] Now as he arrived in Evian and was once more in the land of his Cagliari majesty, he discovered that he had left crucial travel documents behind him in Cologny. Yet he managed to either bluff or bluster his way through a potentially awkward situation with local officials. Shelley recorded that at Nernier they saw a crowd of children who were partially crippled and disfigured with goitres. The impression of general poverty and ill health was even stronger at Evian, where the inhabitants appeared to him more wretched, diseased, and poor than any he had ever recollected seeing. 'The contrast indeed between the subjects of the King of Sardinia and the citizens of the independent republics of Switzerland,' he wrote, 'affords a powerful illustration of the blighting mischiefs of despotism.'⁵ A similar political point is made rather less forcibly when in *Frankenstein* Victor's fiancée, Elizabeth, tells him: 'The republican institutions of our country have produced simpler and happier manners than those which prevail in the great monarchies that surround it.' It would appear from this that Mary and Shelley held very similar views on the virtues of Swiss republicanism. No doubt they did, although, as it happens, the sentence from the novel is one of the many corrections or additions which Shelley made to *Frankenstein*.⁶

By the time Byron and Shelley left Evian on the 24th, the weather was again unpleasant. They were going to Meillerie, an important first step on their Rousseau itinerary. When, early in *Julie*, St. Preux is temporarily banished from the heroine, he settles for a while in Meillerie where, by looking diagonally across the lake, he can longingly observe Julie's home in Vevey with the aid of a telescope borrowed from the local priest. Meillerie is where the mountains come closest to the lake shore, leaving only a very narrow living space. It is the middle of winter when St. Preux finds himself there, but he scrambles up steep slopes to a favourite high spot suitable for his observations and writes another of his many letters to his mistress (like Richardson's *Clarissa*, *Julie* is an epistolary novel) 'on a boulder which the ice had detached from a neighbouring cliff'.⁷ Bad as the summer of 1816 was, there would have been no ice easily visible from Meillerie when Byron and Shelley disembarked to dine there. It was then that Shelley learnt how Napoleon's second wife, the Empress Marie Louise, had chosen to spend a night in Meillerie, before the inn in which they were eating was built and when 'the accommodations were those of the most wretched village'; and all this 'in remembrance of St. Preux'. It seemed to him beautiful that 'the common sentiments of human nature can attach themselves to those who are most removed from its duties and enjoyments, when Genius pleads for their admission at the gate of Power'. He thought that a 'Bourbon dared not even to have remembered Rousseau' (Marie Louise was a Habsburg), and that the Empress owed her ability to do so to 'that democracy which her husband's dynasty outraged, and of which it was, however, in some sort, the representative among the nations of the earth'.[8] Here was one, not entirely satisfactory way of meeting the difficult challenge which Napoleon set liberals such as Byron and Shelley. He may have been a despot himself but he had built his regime on a careful selection of revolutionary principles and then carried those principles into the whole of continental Europe. As for the violence which those principles had initially produced, the bloody events of the Terror which might be said to have laid the foundations for Napoleon's despotism, Byron was at this time their eloquent apologist just as Shelley would have been, writing in canto 3 of *Childe Harold* (of the French population before 1789):

> But they,
> Who in oppression's darkness caved had dwelt,
> They were not eagles, nourish'd with the day;
> What marvel then, at times, if they mistook their prey?[9]

In the latter part of *Julie*, St. Preux finds himself again in Meillerie but this time with his former lover, now a wife and mother. Together they visit the spot from where he used to attempt to see her house on the other side of the lake, and so many memories are revived that their passion for each other is rekindled (although it is then heroically suppressed). In the novel, they are described as starting out on this boating expedition from the Vevey area and, as the wind strengthens and the weather deteriorates, finding themselves in serious trouble near the opposite shore and being forced to land in Meillerie until conditions improve. It is ironic that as Byron and Shelley left Meillerie for St Gingolph, only a short distance along the shore, they too were caught by the weather and probably the same currents which Rousseau (who knew the lake well) had imagined giving St. Preux and Julie so much trouble. A fierce storm began to blow, the waves rose higher and higher, and soon their cabin-less, open boat was shipping water, in imminent danger of capsizing. Byron explained afterwards that it was over-loaded. Apart from himself, Shelley and the two boatmen, there was also his servant, by far the most probable candidate being Berger. That would make a boatload of only five and with Mary, Claire and Polidori it had been at least that full before. What was likely to have made a difference is Byron's luggage, of which there appears to have been always plenty. One of the reasons for this is that, during his time in London, Byron had adopted a modified version of the

Dandy code, with its insistence on personal hygiene and very frequent changes of clothes (especially underwear). It was also true that he enjoyed dressing up. Like the stutterer who becomes an actor, his natural shyness was complemented by a strong tendency to exhibitionism. He gave early and neat expression to this further paradox in his nature when he was a student at Cambridge and entitled, as a lord, to a special form of dress. 'Yesterday,' he told his lawyer, John Hanson, 'my appearance in the Hall in my State Robes was *Superb*, but uncomfortable to my *Diffidence*.'[10]

The boat which was about to sink may have been overloaded, but Byron also describes its sails as having been 'mis-managed'.[11] Shelley said that a foolish boatman held them in too tight and then let them go completely, only later, after they had almost sunk, re-establishing control. That may have been the case, although it is possible also that the boat was carrying too much sail. A sketch of it by a member of the Hentsch family[12] – when Byron moved on to Italy the boat was left in the care of his banker – shows it to have had two main sails attached to the two main masts, with additional small sails fore and aft. Like the boat in which Shelley would drown in Italy, it seems to have been built more for speed than safety. The fact that it had a substantial keel may not have helped either, since there are conditions in which that is not an advantage. But whatever the reasons for their difficulty, it was considerable. They were still near the shore, but one which was so rocky that, with the waves running high – 'at least 15 feet high' according to Shelley[13] – and the wind blowing very hard, they had to contemplate either their boat or themselves being smashed against it. It was a life-threatening moment in which the two men found themselves in very different situations.

Byron was an exceptionally strong swimmer who had leant to swim early in his life in Aberdeen and quickly become proficient. A powerful incentive was no doubt that in the water he could compete on equal terms with other boys. At school, participating in as many of the usual sports as he could, he had been proud at having played a not inglorious part in the Eton/Harrow cricket match, even if he had to bat with the aid of a runner. In swimming, his disability disappeared altogether, although he always wore long trousers for those moments of getting in and out of the water. When he was in Portugal, he had swum across the river Tagus in difficult conditions. This meant being in the water for just under two hours, but eight years later, in Venice, he won a swimming competition which involved his staying away from dry land for almost four. His most celebrated exploit in the swimming line, however, occurred when in 1810 he was on a ship which was delayed in the Dardanelles on its way to Constantinople. It was then that, together with a lieutenant from the marines called Ekenhead, he emulated the feat of Leander who, in Ovid's account of the myth, swam not once but every night across the Dardanelles, or the Hellespont as it was formerly called, in order to be with his mistress Hero. This meant crossing over from the Asian shore at Abydos to the European side at Sestos (to use the old names), a distance of not much more than a mile – although the strong as well as cold currents meant that, when Byron tried it, he had to swim a total of about four miles. This was sufficiently taxing for him to wonder whether 'Leander's conjugal powers must not have been exhausted in his passage to Paradise'.[14] Yet he was mightily pleased with himself and wanted everyone to know what he and Ekenhead had done. In his letters of the time he boasts repeatedly about this swim, not so much because of the physical prowess involved – he hardly ever mentions his swim across the Tagus, although that appears to have been at least as difficult – but because he could associate his feat with an episode from the mythical past with which every classically educated schoolboy would be familiar. That he had done what Leander was reputed to have done made all the difference. So excited was he by his exploit that he was in danger of sounding foolish and it was perhaps only in the second canto of his *Don Juan* that he found a satisfactory form for broadcasting the news widely without sounding too conceited. Of Juan he writes there,

> A better swimmer you could scarce see ever,
> He could, perhaps, have pass'd the Hellespont,
> As once (a feat on which ourselves we prided)
> Leander, Mr. Ekenhead, and I did.[15]

As the wind blew harder near Meillerie, Byron was confident of being able to save himself, but Shelley, in spite of his obsession with boats and what almost amounted to an addiction to being on the water, could not swim at all. He was not a particularly athletic person and, as Byron had been made to realise when he had read 'Christabel' aloud, he had a highly nervous temperament. What therefore impressed Byron immensely, and strengthened the friendly feelings he already had towards his companion, was the calm with which Shelley faced his difficult situation. They had both taken off their coats and, with the boat 'filling fast', Byron had begun explaining that he thought he could rescue the other man once they were in the water, as long as he did not struggle. But Shelley felt humiliated at the thought of risking someone else's life to save his own and, with his arms crossed, calmly insisted that no-one was to bother about him and that he would take his own chances. It was the *sang froid* he exhibited in this moment of danger which so impressed Byron – who was himself far from being the kind of person an uninformed observer might infer from both his interest in sports and his practice of them. Prone to the occasional hysterical fit himself, he told his sister in November that he had recently been 'subject to casual giddiness and faintnesses … so like a fine lady'.[16] With his own highly nervous temperament, he was in a position to form a good idea of what Shelley's impressive self-control might have cost. Had the boat sunk he would no doubt have attempted to save them both, but fortunately the situation improved after the boatman had regained control of the sail and, with much frantic baling by all, they struggled into St Gingolph at last. Such was the fury of the storm that the locals were amazed to see them and Byron noticed later that, in the high land above the village, the wind had been strong enough to uproot several huge trees.

Once he was safely installed at the inn at St Gingolph, and after his close shave with death, Shelley drafted a will and sent it off to his lawyer to be formally drawn up. He made Byron one of his two executors, along with his close friend Thomas Love Peacock. Since Byron was a relatively recent acquaintance, he would hardly have done this without consulting him. What is impossible to say is whether he also discussed with his future executor the terms of the will. Shelley was disposing of assets he would only have on the death of his father, an event which he wrongly assumed would occur before his own demise: he would die while he was not yet thirty whereas old Sir Timothy Shelley soldiered on beyond ninety. The estate which he expected to inherit he left to Mary, with a bequest of £6000 to his wife Harriet and £5000 to each of the two children he had had by her. But the interesting item concerned Claire. When Claire had decided to leave her parents and throw in her lot with him and Mary, Shelley had promised that he would always look after her. In the will he drafted at St Gingolph he left her £6000 and a further £6000 'to be laid out in an annuity for her own life, or that of any person she may name if she pleases to name any other'.[17] These rather puzzling words have been convincingly interpreted as a reference to a child and an indication therefore that he probably already knew that Claire was pregnant. A daughter was in fact born to Claire in January 1817. The assumption was that Byron was the father and that the baby had therefore been conceived in April 1816 before he left England, perhaps on that solitary occasion on the 20th when he and Claire had spent the night together. If this were indisputably the case it is a little surprising that, in his will, Shelley should imply some doubt about Byron's willingness to accept financial responsibility for the coming child (a matter which, in Evian, the two men could easily have discussed). If, on the other hand, he felt that there was some faint possibility of the baby being his own, the bequest would make better sense. Pondering the matter at the time of the child's birth, and wondering if the little girl was indeed his, Byron said that he had reason to think so, 'for I know as much as one can know about such a thing – that she had *not lived* with Shelley during the time of our acquaintance – & that she had a good deal of that same with me'.[18] The word 'lived' is here obviously a euphemism for sexual relations. By saying that Claire had not slept with Shelley during the time he knew her, Byron appears to imply that they had been lovers previously. As far as the birth of the child was concerned, the crucial question would then be quite how previously that had been.[19] The dates strongly favoured Claire's claim on him rather than his friend and, on the whole, it was a responsibility he accepted. Shelley's bequest of an extra £6000 to Claire may therefore only have been a failsafe, just in case he hadn't.

8

Chillon, Clarens and Ouchy

After nearly capsizing in their efforts to enter the port of St Gingolph, it was a relief to Byron and Shelley to find that the weather was much calmer the next day and there were no difficulties about continuing their journey. They were heading for Villeneuve, at the head of the lake, and back into Swiss territory. As they passed beyond St Gingolph, and saw where the Rhone entered the lake, Shelley noticed that the powerful currents of the river caused the colour of the water to change in exactly the way St. Preux describes before the storm which forces him and Julie to land in Meillerie. Looking more or less directly down the lake towards Geneva at its far western end, Villeneuve was then, according to Shelley, 'an old wretched town';[1] but very near is the château de Chillon with its splendid towers and imposing battlements. Built on a flat rock, and far more in the lake than out of it, Chillon had for several centuries belonged to the counts of Savoy but in 1536 had been captured by the Bernese Swiss. By the time Byron and Shelley visited the château, it had been transferred to the canton de Vaud (or Léman), which had long been under Bernese control but had been able to join the Swiss Federation as an independent unity in 1803 (the French invasion having had some positive democratic effects). The château de Chillon figures importantly in *Julie* in that it is after dining there that one of the heroine's children slips and falls into the lake. Plunging into the water to save him, Julie catches the chill from which she then dies.

The two poets were shown round the château by someone Shelley describes as a 'gendarme'.[2] It was characteristic of Byron that he should be especially struck by two features of the visit. One of these was a black and rotten beam in one of the dungeons, from which, he and Shelley were told, State prisoners would be hanged in secret. A detail such as this appealed to Byron's liking for the macabre –

not as pronounced as Shelley's, whose early work is full of suppurating carcasses, but definitely present. Back in Newstead his gardener had once brought him a human skull discovered in the grounds. Byron sent it to the local jeweller's so that it could be elaborately mounted and transformed into a drinking cup, and he had inscribed on it:

> Start not! – nor deem my spirit fled:
> In me behold the only skull,
> From which, unlike a living head,
> Whatever flows is never dull. ...[3]

This could be dismissed as no more than the frivolity of a witty young man who had read too many Gothic novels; yet a sign of its being rather more was Byron's determination in 1812 to have a good view at the public hanging of Bellingham, the man who had recently shot the British Prime Minister, Spencer Perceval; and shortly after he had left Switzerland, he insisted on watching the beheading in Rome of three thieves, later describing the event in all its grisly detail to John Murray. 'The quick rattle and heavy fall of the axe,' he concluded with a certain degree of aesthetic relish, ' – the splash of the blood – & the ghastliness of the exposed heads – is altogether more impressive than the vulgar and ungentle-manly dirty "new drop" & dog-like agony of infliction upon the sufferers of the English sentence.'[4] Executions fascinated Byron, although the main focus of his interest seemed to have been how the victims behaved. It was as if, with his own nervous temperament, he was always wondering how he himself would comport himself in extreme circumstances.

The second feature of the visit which particularly struck Byron was a dungeon in the lower depths of the château, feebly lit through long narrow windows in the upper wall and with seven stone pillars supporting its vaulted roof. The waters of the lake lap continually against the outside of this elongated space, a pleasant sound in normal circumstances but not perhaps if you happened to have been chained to one of the pillars. This had been the fate of Bonni-vard, a figure to whom Byron and Shelley would have been alerted by a note in Rousseau's *Julie*, but about whom their guide now gave them many more details. François de Bonnivard was a sixteenth-century Protestant from Savoy who became well known as a preacher in Geneva but then had the misfortune to be captured by his Catholic fellow-countrymen and imprisoned in Chillon. Only when the château was taken by the Swiss in 1536 was he released. Stories of persecution always seized hold of Byron's imagination, and what the guide said about Bonnivard very quickly led to one of his most popular poems. In *The Prisoner of Chillon* Byron recreates the gloom of the dungeon – 'Dim with a dull imprisoned ray' – and adds the unhistorical but dramatic detail (perhaps suggested to him by the guide) of two brothers of Bonnivard who are chained to neighbouring pillars. It is his fate to watch these brothers die one after the other, and then to see the heartless jailors bury them in shallow graves on the very spots where they expired. The poem records how after several years there is an improvement in Bonnivard's circumstances so that he is able to move more freely around. Carefully avoiding the places where his brothers are buried, he finds he can peer through one of the narrow openings in the wall and observe the striking beauty of the surrounding mountains and lake. When he turns from this view, his dungeon is 'as a new dug grave' and yet his eyes 'too much opprest, / Had almost need of such a rest'. This minor subtlety prepares the way for the conclusion in which Bonnivard, at last released, has become so accustomed to captivity that he half regrets his own has ceased.[5] With its imaginative insight into the psychological effects of incarceration, and its protest against intoler-ance, *The Prisoner of Chillon* was a great success all over Europe although it earned much less for Byron than it did, throughout the nineteenth century, for the ever growing Swiss tourist industry. The numerous visitors it attracted to Chillon were shown, as they still are, Byron's name carved on one of the pillars in Bonnivard's dungeon, but there has been some dispute as to whether he himself put it there.[6]

The two poets sailed on from Chillon along the northern shore of the lake against what Shelley latter described as a contrary wind and a heavy swell. They were heading towards the culmination of their pilgrimage. The subtitle of Rousseau's *Julie* reads 'Letters of two lovers who live in a small town at the foot of the Alps'. Vevey is of course the small town in question and close by, nearer to Chillon, is Clarens, where the heroine goes with her family when they retire to 'the country', and where she and her husband later establish their ideal community. Landing at Clarens, Shelley claimed he had never felt so strongly that 'the spirit of old times had deserted its once cherished habitation. A thousand times I said have Julie & St. Preux walked on this terrassed road looking on the scene which I now see – nay treading the very ground which I now tread.' There is an indication here of how real the characters in *Julie* were for Shelley, and indeed a few sentences earlier he had written that they were created 'by a mind so powerfully bright as to cast a shade of falsehood on the records that are called reality'.[7]

Montreux, Clarens and Vevey are today on their way to forming one vast conurbation, crammed with villas and hotels, but in 1816 this cannot have been why Shelley felt that the spirit of the old times had disappeared. Whatever the explanation, his disappointment on his first landing at Clarens was short-lived. At the boarding house where he and Byron stayed, he discovered that Rousseau's characters were as real to its landlady as they were to him: pointing from the window, she told her two guests that it was in this direction they would find *le bosquet de Julie*. 'Julie's bower', as it is usually called in English, is where the novel's heroine prepares to receive St. Preux's first kiss. When Byron and Shelley went to look for it the next day, they found that it had been ploughed up by the local monks for their vineyard. In a note to some of the stanzas in canto 3 of *Childe Harold's Pilgrimage* which deal with Rousseau, Byron observed how remarkable it was that, 'though long ago cut down by the brutal selfishness of monks of St. Bernard, (to whom the land appertained), that the ground might be inclosed into a vineyard for the miserable drones of an execrable superstition, the inhabitants of Clarens still point out the spot where [the bower] stood'.[8] 'Miserable drones of an execrable superstition' is the kind of immoderate outburst his Tory publisher had learnt to dread. Every time Murray received a manuscript from Byron he would look nervously through it searching for those side-swipes at the Tory government, the monarchy or religion which might threaten to limit the sales of his remarkably popular author. A dig at Roman Catholics he would not, however, have minded at all, although this one might well have surprised those who remembered that one of Byron's speeches in the House of Lords had been in passionate support of Catholics in Ireland, and in favour of their emancipation from all the legal obstacles which prevented them playing their proper part in civic life. During that speech he had mocked those who denounced the 'damnable idolatry of the Papists'.[9] It may have been the immediate irritation of finding Julie's bower gone which produced a similar use of words in his note. But their tone is characteristic of the general way Shelley would talk about Christianity and therefore much more probably another indication of the powerful influence he had on Byron at this time.

The way in which Byron records the destruction of the bower – it may have disappeared but the locals still remember it – suggests how reluctant both poets were to accept disappointment for long. Reading *Julie* as they travelled, they were on the whole enchanted with the correspondence between what they saw and the descriptions in the novel. 'This journey,' Shelley later wrote, 'has been on every account delightful, but most especially, because then I first knew the divine beauty of Rousseau's imagination, as it exhibits itself in Julie.'[10] In what now seems a much more interesting work by Rousseau than his novel, he describes how he came to write *Julie* and throws out a challenge to the reader. 'Go to Vevey,' he writes in his *Confessions*, 'visit the countryside, examine the sites, walk by the lake and tell me whether Nature has not made this beautiful area for a Julie, for a Claire [Julie's intimate friend], and for a St. Preux.'[11] In his notes to *Childe Harold* Byron quotes this passage and says that from his own 'not uninterested nor inattentive survey of all the scenes most celebrated by Rousseau in his *Heloise* ... it would be difficult to see Clarens ... without being forcibly struck with its peculiar adaptation to the persons and events with which it has been peopled.' 'But this is not all', he goes on, amplifying thoughts already in the stanzas he is annotating:

> the feeling with which all around Clarens, and the opposite rocks of Meillerie is invested, is of a still higher and more comprehensive order than the mere sympathy with individual passion; it is a sense of the existence of love in its most extended and sublime capacity, and of our own participation of its good and of its glory: it is the great principle of the universe, which is there more condensed, but not less manifested; and of which, though knowing ourselves a part, we lose our individuality, and mingle in the beauty of the whole.[12]

This is very much as Shelley liked to talk and in another mood, or another phase of his life, the author of *Don Juan* would have found it fatuous. In 1816 it was, like the 'Wordsworthian' stanzas in canto 3 of *Childe Harold*, a sign of how taken Byron was with his friend's transcendentalism.

From Clarens the two poets made their way to Vevey, which Shelley thought a town 'more beautiful in its simplicity than any I have ever seen.'[13] The main purpose of their trip fulfilled, they then sailed on to Ouchy, the port which lies just below Lausanne. Already, on the way there, the weather had begun to deteriorate again. The poets were shown evidence of a recent rock slide when two huge boulders had thundered down from the mountain, tearing up a vineyard in their path, with one of them then coming to rest in a young woman's bedroom; and they were told how a boat had very recently capsized in the middle of the lake, with the resulting death of two local women, two cows and twelve black pigs. Once they had arrived in Ouchy, two days of violent wind and rain prevented them from heading home immediately and Shelley recalled walking on a pier near the lake while it was being lashed with waves. It was not a good summer. On the front wall of what is now the Hotel d'Angleterre in Ouchy (in Byron's day it was called the Hôtel de l'Ancre) there is a plaque which claims that he wrote *The Prisoner of Chillon* there. With time on his hands, that is almost certainly what he began to do, but what he also wrote from Ouchy on the 27th of June was a letter to John Murray in which he said: 'I have traversed all Rousseau's ground – with the Heloise before me – & am struck to a degree with the force & accuracy of his descriptions – & the beauty of their reality.'[14]

Byron and Shelley employed the free time which the bad weather gave them by visiting the house in Lausanne which Edward Gibbon had once occupied. Gibbon's massive *Decline and Fall of the Roman Empire* had first been conceived in Rome's Coliseum, but it was almost equally well known that it had been completed in the summer house of his Lausanne residence. As he explained in his *Autobiography*:

> It was on the day, or rather night of the 27th of June 1787, between the hours of eleven and twelve, that I wrote the last line of the last page … After laying down my pen, I took several turns in a *berceau*, or covered walk of acacias. … I will not dissemble the first emotions of joy in recovery of my freedom, and, perhaps, the establishment of my fame. But my pride was soon humbled, and a sober melancholy was spread over my mind, by the idea that I had taken an everlasting leave of an old and agreeable companion, and that whatsoever might be the future fate of my History, the life of the historian must be short and precarious.[15]

When Byron visited the house (perhaps on the anniversary of the event described here), a covered walk was still in existence and he collected from it some acacia leaves to send back to Murray. This was in the same spirit in which he had sent back to his publisher for safe-keeping swords and helmets from Waterloo, or whitened bones of Burgundians killed at the battle of Murten. In spite of his attack on the 'execrable superstition' of Catholic monks, he had a powerful feeling for relics – although he always had to believe that they were real relics and that, for example, the field of Marathon, which he had visited during his time in Greece, was where the battle had really happened. In his time there was a tradition that the Trojan war had taken place on a plain running south from the Hellespont, but in 1796 Jacob Bryant had published a book in which he claimed that there had been no such thing and that the whole episode was a myth. 'I have stood upon that plain *daily*, for more than a month, in 1810,' Byron wrote in 1821, 'and if any thing diminished my pleasure, it was that the blackguard Bryant had impugned its veracity. … But I still venerated the grand original as the truth of *history* (in the material *facts*) and of *place*. Otherwise, it would have given me no delight.'[16] One of Byron's fundamental traits was what Coleridge described in Wordsworth as 'a matter-of-factness, a clinging to the palpable'.[17] Temporarily influenced by Shelley though he was, he could never have praised a fiction like *Julie* because, in his friend's words, it 'cast a shade of falsehood on the records we call reality'.

Shelley watched Byron as he gathered the acacia leaves but refused to take any himself, 'fearing to outrage,' as he later explained, 'the greater and more sacred name of Rousseau; the contemplation of whose imperishable creatures had left no vacancy in my heart for mortal things. Gibbon had a cold and unimpassioned spirit.'[18] His refusal may have in part been motivated by the visit which he and Byron made to the local château when they were in Clarens. On its terrace they gathered roses, in the feeling, Shelley claimed, 'that they might be the posterity of some planted by Julie's hand'.[19] It must have seemed to him that it was a sacrilege to add acacia leaves associated with a historical figure to the roses perhaps originally planted by an imaginary one. But more significant in his refusal to take the leaves might have been his knowledge of a passage in Gibbon's autobiography in which the author describes how, in coming back for his second stay in Lausanne, he fell in love with Suzanne Curchod, a beautiful and talented young woman with a modest social background. When he asked his father for permission to marry Mademoiselle Curchod and his father refused, Gibbon rather meekly yielded to his fate: in the famous phrase which appears in the *Autobiography*, 'I sighed as a lover, I obeyed as a son'.[20] This capitulation had been censored by Rousseau himself and was in striking contrast to the intensity Julie and St. Preux initially display when they are struggling to defend their love against social pressures. For Shelley, the fact that Gibbon's account of the rise of Christianity in chapters fifteen and sixteen of the *Decline and Fall* had scandalised all true believers may not have compensated for his 'cold and unimpassioned spirit'. The more pragmatic Byron could have felt that things did not turn out so badly in the end, since Suzanne Curchod recovered from her disappointment at losing Gibbon and went on to marry the rich and powerful Swiss financier Jacques Necker, and thus became the mother of Madame de Staël.

After two nights in Ouchy, the weather finally cleared and Byron and Shelley could head home to Polidori and their waiting women. Stopping one further night at Rolle, a village further along the northern shore of the lake, they arrived back on Sunday, 30 June. Their trip had clearly gone very well and it strengthened the bond between the two poets. In the weeks and indeed months or years which followed, Byron always spoke well of the other man, but Shelley's verdicts on Byron could be more equivocal. He would continue to regard him as the finest poet of their generation, greatly admiring and indeed envying almost everything he produced. But admiration for the poet was one thing, feelings about the man rather different. 'Lord Byron,' Shelley wrote to Peacock in the middle of July, 'is an exceedingly interesting person, and as such, is it not to be regretted that he is the slave to the vilest & most vulgar prejudices, & as mad as the winds? I do not mean to say,' he went on,

> that he is a Christian, or that his ordinary conduct is devoid of prudence. But in the course of an intimacy of two months, & an observation the most minute I see reason to regret the union of great genius, & things which make genius useless. For a short time I shall see no more of Lord Byron, a circumstance I cannot avoid regretting as he has shown me great kindness, & as I had some hope that an inter-course with me would operate to weaken those superstitions of rank & wealth & revenge & servility to opinion with which he, in common with other men, is so poisonously imbued.[21]

When Shelley talks here of not seeing Byron again for a short time, he is refer-ring to the trip he was planning to take to Chamonix with Mary and Claire. The accusation that Byron retained many of the prejudices of rank and wealth was probably true. Shelley's own principles were more egalitarian, although when, in the following year, he was introduced to middle-class radicals such as Hazlitt and Keats, they took a dislike to him because they felt that, however much he would talk of equality, there was in his manner an unconscious assumption of social superiority derived from his privileged background. On the issue of 'revenge' he was no doubt right. Byron fiercely resented insult or injury, was very unhappy if he could not retaliate immediately, and always showed a most unchristian reluctance to turn the other cheek. As for his 'servility to opinion', that phrase could mean many things. Characteristic of one of these may have been the way that Byron, immediately after the stanzas in canto 3 of *Childe Harold* which deal with Clarens, talks of Gibbon. Linking this famous 'lord of irony' ('Sapping a solemn creed with solemn sneer') with Voltaire, and considering them both as enemies of religion, he says of their 'decayed dust': 'And when it shall revive, as is our trust, / 'Twill be to be forgiven, or suffer what is just'[22] – sentiments which ought to have made Shelley suspect that his friend might be some kind of Christian after all. 'Servility to opinion' could, however, be a reference to public opinion and gossip, in which case all one can say is that Byron might well have been more vulnerable in that area than his critic. Yet he was not so servile that he ever thought of giving up his friendship with Shelley, who was regarded with something close to horror by most of Byron's former friends in England. Their strong disapproval would have been confirmed by knowledge of the intellectual influence the younger man had already had on Byron by this time. For Shelley himself, who here displays his supreme confidence that intercourse with him would always bring benefit to the other person, that influence had been nowhere near profound enough.

Part Two

9

Coppet

While their lovers were away on the trip round the lake, Mary and Claire were left to amuse themselves. They had baby William to look after but this still left Mary plenty of time to pursue her own interests. She seems to have continued to work through what was clearly a long list of books in French and Italian, but also to have begun writing *Frankenstein*. In addition, she carried on making fair copies of Byron's verse (there is a version of canto 3 of *Childe Harold* in her hand). Claire was also heavily involved in this copying, a task for which at the time she was an eager volunteer but which in retrospect, and from our present point of view, inevitably looks like exploitation. It is a sad irony that she seems to have done more copying the more her relationship with Byron deteriorated. 'It would make me happy to finish Chillon for you,' she wrote to him in the middle of July. 'It is said that you expressed yourself decisively last Evening that it is impossible to see you at Diodati; If you will trust it down here I will take the *greatest* possible care of it ... Let me have Chillon then, pray do.'[1] Both women regarded it as a privilege to be the first to see verses by a poet they admired greatly; but for Claire, copying also seems to have represented a sadly unavailing method for keeping up a connection which Byron was clearly anxious to break. His not wanting to see her at Diodati any longer would have been the result of a dawning awareness of the gossip which was beginning to circulate in the area, some of it very wild indeed. A certain Lord Glenbervie, for example, who arrived in Sécheron in July, reported that Byron was 'now living on the Savoy side of the lake with that woman, who it seems proves to be a Mrs Shelley, wife to the man who keeps the Mount coffee house' (it was Shelley's first wife, Harriet Westbrook, whose *father* owned a coffee house); and friends of George Leigh, the husband of Byron's sister, told him that while they were in

Geneva they had heard that Augusta was with her brother there, disguised as a page.[2]

Polidori's diary shows that, during the absence of Shelley and Byron, he dropped in on Mary and Claire daily, and that he often dined with them. But as his ankle improved he also began making visits again, to Geneva but also to Genthoud, an area a few miles northward along the lake shore from Sécheron where he had many friends. On his return from his trip Byron showed no more inclination to join Polidori in these visits than he had before he left, yet there was now a major change in his social life. This was because in June Germaine de Staël had returned from Italy to her château at Coppet, which lay diagonally across the lake from Montalègre. She had inherited this building from her father Jacques Necker, a man who, although born in Geneva, had become a key figure in the final days of France's *ancien régime* and been Louis XVI's last serious finance minister. Born and brought up in France, his daughter and only child was old enough when the Revolution broke out to play an active part in organising those who advocated a constitutional monarchy on the British model and was therefore fortunate to escape imprisonment, or even execution, during the Terror. Once the Jacobins had been crushed, she became politically active again and tried hard to convert the rising young general, Napoleon Bonaparte, to the constitutional cause. But he never liked her, saying on one occasion that he was no more fond of masculine women than of effeminate men, and, once he had seized control, took a dim view of the way Necker's daughter, or Madame de Staël as she was by this time, became a focus for liberal opposition wherever she went. Banished from anywhere in France which was within forty leagues (about a hundred and twenty miles) of Paris, she kept trying to creep back until, by 1812, she was restricted, and not for the first time, to Coppet.[3]

The conditions of de Staël's exile to Coppet in 1812 were more draconian than they had been previously, and it was not in any case a place where she felt particularly happy. Her opinion of mountains and glaciers was the same as that of her mother's old flame, Gibbon, and she was never much interested in Nature: one of her friends claimed that, although as a child she had been able to recite James Thomson's *Seasons* by heart, she could never tell one flower from another. But the real trouble with Coppet in 1812 was that the new prefect in Geneva, which was by then part of France, refused to allow her to move about freely in the immediate vicinity, and that Napoleon's secret police punished anyone who paid her a visit. Slipping away from her château before the local authorities had noticed, de Staël made her way through Germany and Austria to Eastern

Europe and then pressed on to Moscow, where she arrived only a few weeks before Napoleon's invading army. She moved from there to St Petersburg from where she could sail to Stockholm. Sweden was a good place for her to retreat because her husband had been a Swede: the Baron de Staël-Holstein, who for much of the time between his marriage to her in 1786 and his death in 1802 had been the Swedish ambassador to France (he was far from being the best match her remarkably wealthy parents might have found for their daughter but they had narrowed the field by insisting on a Protestant, and a Protestant resident in Paris). Sweden was also comfortable for Madame de Staël because she had once known well Jean-Baptiste Bernadotte, the Napoleonic general who by an extraordinary twist of fate had been designated Sweden's Crown Prince and successor to the country's childless king. On her way to Stockholm she had engaged in numerous discussions with important political figures, including the Russian Tsar; and she now laboured hard to convince Bernadotte that he ought to abandon Napoleon and join what would be the sixth great European coalition against the French Emperor. At the heart of this coalition, in the sense that they picked up many of the bills, were the British, so that it seems natural that, after nine months in Sweden, Madame de Staël should have decided to move on from there to England.

Familiar with England from previous visits, de Staël arrived in London on 17 June 1813 as a major European celebrity. She owed this status to her father's fame, her reputation as a heroic victim of Napoleon, and her own political activity. But it was also a consequence of the fact she was a highly successful writer: her novels *Delphine* and *Corinne* had both been, and continued to be, very popular all over Europe (Byron had complained at one moment of not only Lady Caroline Lamb's 'wild way' but also her '*Delphine* language',[4] and *Corinne* would be one of the favourite novels of his future mistress, Teresa Guiccioli). Over four hundred visiting cards were delivered to de Staël's London hotel but, if there were any recalcitrants among those in London with influence or talent, she was not slow in chasing them up. She was anxious to meet, for example, the leader in Britain of the anti-slavery movement, William Wilberforce, since that was a liberal cause in which she took a strong interest; but he was a deeply religious man and, after seeking heavenly guidance, refused the first of her invitations to an evening party. Yet she pursued him with characteristic vigour and eventually secured not only his company but his friendship. It was inevitable that, socially active as she was, she should meet Byron, a London celebrity himself at this time. This was especially the case as one of her additional reasons for coming to England was

to have published there *De l'Allemagne*, a book aimed at persuading the French
to revise their low estimate of German life and culture. This had been printed
in France but then seized and banned by Napoleon's police, chiefly because
it implicitly urged all Germans to unite in order to throw off foreign domination. Byron would have known all about *De l'Allemagne*, not least because, in
November, it was published in both French and English by his own publisher
and friend, John Murray.

It was at a gathering organised by Lady Jersey on the evening after de Staël's
arrival in London from Sweden that Byron first met her, and he then dined with
her the next day at the house of Sir Humphrey Davy. His initial impressions were
not favourable. He would have been made uncomfortable by her frank dislike of
Napoleon and he looked with a jaundiced eye at the way she ingratiated herself
with members of the ruling Tory administration (which she had to do if she were
to continue the unofficial diplomatic work she had been engaged on in Sweden).
He also thought that she talked excessively. This was a widely held view: when
he met her in Germany Goethe had said that though she talked very well, she
also did so far too much. A general complaint among the men in England was
that, instead of retiring with the other ladies and leaving them to their port, she
would linger on and harangue them on political subjects. This was one aspect of
what one of her biographers calls her 'prodigious loquacity'.[5] She could also be
disconcertingly frank and was never restrained by ideas of decorum from saying
exactly what she thought. Madame de Staël apparently told the Prince Regent
precisely what course he should follow (as she had told the Tsar), and was not
therefore going to be restrained from telling Byron, as she did in the first uneasy
period of their relationship, that he had treated Lady Caroline Lamb barbarously
and must therefore be a man of no feeling.

All this got Byron and de Staël off on the wrong foot, but these first impressions of her in the flesh were offset for Byron by his admiration for her writings.
When she first arrived in England she was the recent author of a short pamphlet,
Reflections on Suicide, which had been published abroad but now appeared in
a London edition. This was a topic in which Byron took a special interest. He
was convinced that his maternal grandfather had killed himself, would say that
what was most desired in life was 'an easy passage out of it',[6] and always kept a
dose of poison close by for his own possible future use. De Staël's reflections
were intended to dissuade those with suicidal intentions and, shortly after
their publication was announced, Byron told his future wife that he had not
yet read the pamphlet for fear that the love of contradiction might lead him to

'a practical confutation'.[7] What he did eventually think of it is not clear but we know that he greatly admired *De l'Allemagne* when it appeared in November and that, making a reference to this book in a note on a line in his poem *The Bride of Abydos*, which he was then publishing, he called it 'the latest work of the first female writer of this, perhaps of any, age'.[8] De Staël was delighted and wrote him a flattering note of appreciation, to which on 30 November 1813 he replied in the same style, apologising for not having called on her more often. From then on their relations were much more cordial. Pondering the motives which lay behind the note she had written to him, Byron concluded that she was after all 'a very good-natured creature',[9] a view shared by almost all those who knew Madame de Staël well. It was perhaps because he came to like as well as to appreciate de Staël that Byron was not more annoyed when he learnt of certain criticisms of his behaviour which she had communicated to Matthew Lewis, author of *The Monk*, knowing that he was Byron's friend. One of these was that he would sit at the dinner table with his eyes half or completely shut. 'I wonder if I really have this trick,' he mused, 'I must cure myself of it, if true. One insensibly acquires awkward habits, which should be broken in time. If this is one, I wish I had been told of it before.'[10]

Once she was back in Coppet, in the summer of 1816, and had become aware that Byron was in her vicinity, Madame de Staël set out to draw him out of his social isolation. One ill-natured British observer suggested that this was because she could never 'resist a little celebrity – of what kind soever & with whatever vice or meanness allied';[11] but it was rather that she felt Byron was too gifted and interesting not to be in general circulation and was herself too powerful and secure to care much about gossip. She bombarded him with notes, as was her wont with those she had determined she wanted to see. He must have yielded to her insistence rather reluctantly, knowing that her salon would be full of the visiting English. It was rumoured that when he did finally appear there, several people made a point of staying away and, according to his own, later report, one elderly lady fainted when his name was announced. This was Elizabeth Hervey, a minor novelist and friend of his mother-in-law. The woman herself reported only that she had been 'quite disordered' on first seeing Byron enter the room, but then boasted that she had treated him with marked coldness, even though she had not been able to prevent him from taking her hand. One of the Hôtel d'Angleterre's rumour-mongers, she also said that Byron had been followed to Geneva by a young woman whom he had then kept shut up in his chamber for a week, and that this person was one of the two girls he had been seen running after 'in high frolic' in the garden of Diodati – as well, that is (she slyly added), as someone with his disability *could* run.[12]

What made Byron continue to visit Coppet, in spite of the occasional encounter with people like Elizabeth Hervey, was the warmth of de Staël's welcome and the ability she had – helped by her fluency in English – to make him feel entirely at home. There was a certain kind of older woman with whom Byron had always got on well – Lady Melbourne, who was his wife's aunt and Caroline Lamb's mother-in-law, being a striking case in point; and de Staël turned out more and more to be one of them. He quickly accustomed himself to the relatively short trip across the lake, often taking Polidori with him (the young doctor recorded in his diary that he dined in Coppet on at least three occasions). From the small port or landing place in the village, it was a walk of only three or four hundred yards up the slope to the château, although it appears as if his more usual method of arriving there was to sail to Genthoud and then finish his journey on horseback.[13] More impressive for its sheer size than for any distinctive architectural feature, the château at Coppet had space enough to host large parties and enough rooms to allow numerous guests to stay there in comfort. Although some of Necker's huge fortune had disappeared during the revolution, he had made wise investments in the United States which meant that, after his death in 1804, his daughter was never short of enough money to live very comfortably.

Apart from his compatriots, Byron met up again in Coppet with several figures from the local liberal intelligentsia to whom he had already been introduced when he first arrived in Switzerland (having spent several winters in Geneva, Madame de Staël knew everybody who was anybody in the region). One of these was Bonstetten, an old friend of both Necker and his daughter. Another was Pelligrino Rossi, but it was in Coppet that Byron met for the first time Ludovico di Breme, or the abbé de Brême as he was known in French-speaking parts. This young man had very quickly abandoned religion for literature and liberal politics and would be an important contact when Byron went to live in Italy. De Brême further stimulated Byron's interest in the Italian struggle for independence, a topic on which he would no doubt have liked to talk in Coppet with Charles de Sismondi, the nom de plume of the Genevan-born Charles Simonde, who in 1807 had published the first volume of his massive history of the medieval Italian republics (an important work for Italian nationalists). Byron bought this book and later said that he greatly respected its author, but although Sismondi had been for several years one of Madame de Staël's more devoted protégés, he was temporarily absent that summer.

If Sismondi was usually a semi-permanent fixture in Coppet, this was even more the case with August Wilhelm Schlegel, who by the terms of de Staël's will would be granted permission to occupy his apartment in the château for as long as he lived. She had found Schlegel in Germany in 1804 when she was beginning to research her book on that country and had brought him back to Switzerland in what became the largely nominal capacity of tutor to her three children. A leading opponent of the domination of French classicism in Europe, Schlegel was a gifted translator of Shakespeare and also an eloquent spokesman for the new Romantic drama. An English translation of his *Lectures on Dramatic Art and Literature* had appeared only recently and Byron echoed some phrases from them when he was writing his ode on Prometheus.[14] Schlegel ought therefore to have been someone with whom Byron could have had interesting discussions, but he was a vain man, universally described as difficult to get on with ('a presumptuous literato, contradicting *a outrance*' is how Polidori described him[15]). Byron shared the general feeling, but that scarcely diminished the rich variety of people he found he could talk to in Coppet, many of them in either Italian or English. It was now, for example, that Byron would have met for the first time Etienne Dumont, a leading local intellectual who had spent many years in England and had been so successful in introducing the ideas of Jeremy Bentham to the French-speaking world that they were at least as well known on the continent as they were in England. Passing through Lausanne in the following year, Stendhal was so impressed to learn of the number of distinguished people Madame de Staël had managed to gather together in 1816 that he described Coppet as 'the Estates-General of European opinion,'[16] the Estates-General being the rudimentary parliamentary system whose coming together had sparked off the French Revolution. He was perhaps sanguine in implying that the gatherings had any political importance. During what had been almost a year in England, Madame de Staël had laboured to convince important political figures that, after Napoleon, France should become a constitutional monarchy under Bernadotte; but she eventually became reconciled to the return of the Bourbons, which was after all a better solution than partition for the country she called her own.

When a Bourbon was restored to the French throne for the second time, after Napoleon's escape from Elba and the hundred days, the political climate became even more reactionary than it had been before, not only in France but all over Europe. Little as de Staël liked Coppet, it provided a useful temporary retreat and became a centre where the flame of liberal opinion could continue to flicker and new ideas about literature and art could be debated. The credit for making it so successful in that regard was down to its proprietor, who has been described as a woman who put her talent into her writings but her genius into her friendships. She talked a lot but she could clearly also listen and convince a wide variety of individuals of her genuine interest in their affairs. Byron was certainly convinced. On arriving in Switzerland he had more or less given up 'society' but, with her kindness and concern, Madame de Staël was able to remind him of its rewards and pleasures. Two months after Byron had left Switzerland, the *Gazette de Lausanne* reported that he would often sail on Lake Geneva in the middle of the night and while a storm was blowing, careless of the danger and enraptured by the majestic beauty of the spectacle. The unhappy author of *The Bride of Abydos*, the writer went on, having broken with great regret the bonds of matrimony, had now accompanied his dreamy and melancholic muse elsewhere:

> He seems to flee social intercourse and only appreciate in Nature what is sombre or awe-inspiring, seeking mountains, forests, torrents and bitter solitudes [*âpres solitudes*]. He is the enemy of society and the lover of deserts.[17]

This is a description of Childe Harold and the Byronic hero in general, as well as of how Byron occasionally liked to think of himself; but it is not an accurate description of his true nature. He was on occasions misanthropic but in general, as he often protested, he was a sociable individual who sought in intercourse with others relief from his gloomy thoughts. Madame de Staël reminded him of the social aspect of his nature and he was always grateful to her for doing so.

10

Romans à clef

In the Estates-General of France to which Stendhal refers, there were three houses: one for the aristocracy, one for the clergy and a third for everyone else. The tripartite division in Coppet was rather different. Apart from the members of Madame de Staël's immediate family, there were first of all the visiting English, to many of whom she was returning the hospitality she had enjoyed during her recent stay in their country. There were then the local intellectuals of a liberal cast and, finally, a fair sprinkling of princes, dukes, and titled dignitaries from continental Europe. The *châtelaine* of Coppet had a weakness for titles, to which she would readily admit – it cannot have harmed her warm feeling for Byron that he was a lord. Not having the same anxiety as her parents about an alliance with a Catholic, she had recently married her daughter, Albertine, into one of the most aristocratic families in France. Part of the reason she could do this was that, when in 1790 her father was forced to resign as French finance minister, he left behind in the Treasury a loan of two million francs as a gesture of confidence in the country he had served so conscientiously. Madame de Staël spent fifteen years trying to recover these two millions and only finally did so when Louis XVIII was restored to the French throne. Her daughter's most promising suitor, the Duke de Broglie, faded a little into the background during the hundred days but once Louis was again in Paris, and it was clear that the money would still be part of Albertine's dowry, he was ready to make her his duchess. The young couple had been married in February 1816 and were with Madame de Staël in Coppet when Byron was a visitor there. In his memoirs, the Duke de Broglie remembered his mother-in-law's English visitor far from fondly, complaining that his conversation was full of tiresome paradoxes and the truisms of a vulgar liberalism;[1] but his attitude may have been influenced by the fact that, when Madame de Staël had been in England, there had been some vague talk of Byron as a possible husband for her daughter.

Making part of this small family group was Jean Rocca, a handsome former army officer who had been born in Geneva, fought in Spain for the French, and was half Madame de Staël's age. In England, the common assumption that he was her lover, and the fact that she was thought to dress badly, had led to the suggestion that Rocca was the only proof the English had of her good taste. Repeating this joke with some disapproval, Byron had added, 'Monsieur l'Amant is remarkably handsome; but *I* don't think more so than her book'.[2] The rumour-mill in England was in any case mistaken in that Rocca and de Staël had been secretly married in 1811, an event of which Byron had become aware by 1816. Born in 1766 and widowed in 1802, de Staël had throughout most of her later life shown a weakness for handsome young men but also for those, not necessarily handsome, who could match her intellectually. Prominent among this latter class was the unprepossessing but highly gifted Benjamin Constant, who was probably Albertine's father and with whom Madame de Staël conducted an on-and-off affair for at least fifteen years. She was a person who hated to let go and was remarkably adept at hanging on to lovers, keeping them within her orbit even when she was sleeping with somebody else. As his ardour cooled, she would alternately threaten and cajole Constant, throw the occasional hysterical fit, shower him with letters and send her servants to fetch him back to Coppet, or wherever she happened to be, so that, conscious as he was of how much he owed her, he found it very difficult to break off. This was even true after he had contracted his own secret marriage with Charlotte von Hardenburg in 1808. It took a meeting at the Hôtel d'Angleterre in Sécheron, when Charlotte explained to de Staël how matters really stood, to initiate a final but still very gradual breaking-off. Much of his early experience of trying to separate himself from Madame de Staël was incorporated by Constant into *Adolphe*, the yet unpublished novel which he was reading aloud in Paris salons in 1815. That was the year in which he made the mistake of throwing in his lot with Napoleon who, on his return to Paris from Elba, had made some encouraging noises about constitutional reform (distrusting the old enemy, de Staël had wisely lain low in Coppet during the hundred days). This meant that, after Waterloo, Constant had felt it safest to retreat to London, where he arranged to have *Adolphe* published and where he met Byron: the soirée given by Lady Jersey in April 1816, at which Byron had been 'cut' by various ladies of fashion, had partly been held in Constant's honour. Although the circumstances of *Adolphe*'s heroine Ellénore were very

different from those of Madame de Staël, everyone in London assumed the
novel was about her, so that, in a preface to a second edition, Constant felt
obliged to issue a formal denial. Although it is doubtful whether she believed
him, de Staël praised the novel and early in July lent a copy to Byron, who had
left England before it appeared.

   Adolphe could not but have struck a chord with Byron. 'It is a terrible misfortune,' the narrator says at one point, 'not to be loved when one is in love; but
it is a much greater one to be loved with passion when one no longer feels the
same oneself.'[3] This was not his position with Claire Clairmont, from whom
he was now trying to distance himself, because he had never been in love with
her; but it was certainly what had happened to him with Lady Caroline Lamb.
His relationship with her had begun as a standard Regency affair, although with
passion on both sides, but had then spun out of control. In a sector of English
society where most marriages were still arranged by parents or at least largely
determined by questions of income and property, the extra-marital affairs of
women were often tolerated as long as they were conducted with discretion and
constituted no obvious threat to the established social order. But Lady Caroline's
behaviour, especially as she felt Byron slipping away from her, was increasingly
wild and eccentric and had included rushing off alone to his lodgings disguised
as a page (it was only with the help of Hobhouse that he was able to get her
back home before there was a scandal which would have made it very difficult
for her husband to continue to recognise her as his wife). She was clearly ready
to burn her bridges, but Byron was doubtful, partly because his feeling for her
was weakening much more quickly than hers for him, but also because he was
aware of how much more difficult it would be for a woman to live outside the
accepted boundaries of English upper-class life than it would be for a man. If,
however, she positively insisted on wanting to run away with him, and could not
be dissuaded from taking that irrevocable step by her mother or others from her
intimate circle, then he held himself ready to do the decent thing, but less out
of love than from a sense of obligation. Lady Caroline could therefore have said
to him very much what the heroine of *Adolphe* says to the narrator: 'You think
you are in love when all you really feel is pity',[4] words which the narrator goes on
to describe as fatal to his relationship with Ellénore because they were so true.

   Adolphe is now generally recognised as a minor masterpiece of acute psychological analysis. Writing to his old friend Samuel Rogers on 29 July, Byron claimed
that the novel made an 'unpleasant impression' but one 'very consistent with the
consequences of not being in love' (by which he must have meant 'no longer

being in love').[5] That Constant's work stayed in his mind is clear from his having made the mistake, once he was living in Italy, of giving it to Teresa Guiccioli as something interesting to read. It must have seemed to him an appropriate antidote for the high-flown sentiment in de Staël's *Corinne*, which his mistress so admired; but the result was that he had to spend almost as much time convincing Teresa that the situation described in the novel had no bearing on their own as Constant had on persuading Madame de Staël that there was no connection between her and Ellénore. If in 1816 the action of the novel would have reminded Byron of Caroline Lamb, she would have been back in his mind in any event given that a second book which Madame de Staël gave him to read, at more or less the same time as *Adolphe*, was *Glenarvon*, whose publication he had likewise missed by leaving the country. Published by Henry Colburn, who would later be responsible for the edition of Polidori's *Vampyre* falsely attributed to Byron, *Glenarvon* was Caroline Lamb's fictionalised account, in three volumes, of her affair with Byron, and many of the English he met at Coppet must have either read or been reading it. Madame de Staël knew Caroline who, at the age of six, had been dandled on the knee of Gibbon in Lausanne and whose husband William (a future prime minister of England) had re-translated parts of *De l'Allemagne* for Murray's English version. She had therefore been sent a complimentary copy of *Glenarvon* which she was able to pass on to Byron. This was a transaction of which Lady Caroline would have been overjoyed to hear. Revenge is never entirely sweet unless the victim is made fully aware of its origin and nature.

Whereas *Adolphe* is a modified *roman à clef* whose impressiveness is now in no way dependent on a reader's knowledge of its background, *Glenarvon* is a blatant example of the genre and one which, although it has impressive passages, is very far from being a masterpiece. Set in Ireland at the time of the rebellion of the United Irishmen against the British in 1798, it tells the story of Lady Calantha Deleval, an innocent, religious girl who is married to Lord Avondale. He is a kind husband but a sceptic with worldly values which shatter Calantha's naiveté and undermine her religious principles. The plot is complicated, not to say downright confused, and full of standard Gothic features such as old castles and villainous Italians. At the centre of the action is Lord Glenarvon, an Irish patriot who eventually turns his coat. He is a fascinating creature – 'When he smiled it was like the light radiance of heaven; and when he spoke, his voice was more soothing in its sweetness than music'[6] – but cold-hearted and full of disdain for others (there is much talk, not of his shutting his eyes at dinner, but of the way he curls his upper lip). In describing how Lady Calantha falls under the spell of this handsome aristocrat, Caroline Lamb is kind to herself, falsely suggesting that she had not had an extra-marital affair before meeting Byron and being very indefinite about the degree of physical intimacy her relationship with him involved (she is more explicit when she transfers some of her own experience from Lady Calantha and onto two other women whose lives have also been ruined by Glenarvon). That the seducer of all three is indeed meant to be Byron is very clear to the general reader (like the heroes of his narrative poems, Glenarvon has a 'horrid secret' which weighs upon his mind); and it was made doubly so to initiates by the way in which Lamb fictionalises well-known episodes from their stormy affair and quotes extensively from the letters they exchanged. One of Byron's weaknesses, to which most of his friends quickly accommodated themselves, was that he would casually show the letters he received to third parties. It is a major complaint of Calantha against Glenarvon that he does so with hers. Lamb was also furious to discover that her own letters had been read by others and she retaliated by giving to phrases he had both written and said to her the wider currency of a novel. They were a reminder, highly uncomfortable to Byron if not to a wider public, of how infatuated he had once been with Caroline Lamb. Her problem was that she had been even more infatuated with him and she struggles, in her presentation of Calantha, to explain and extenuate her own behaviour, hovering uneasily, and often incoherently, between the idea of her heroine as saint and sinner. She finally resolves her difficulties by having Calantha die penitent but also bitterly regretted by her husband and family. Glenarvon dies too but only at the very end of the novel and after being loaded with crimes, including the abduction of one small child and the murder of another. It is then that, in a Gothic phantasmagoria which recalls both the spectres at the end of *Richard III* and the finale of *Don Giovanni*, he is finally driven mad by remorse and glimpses the tortures of hell which lie in wait for him. If it is wrong to deceive one's husband, those who are decoding the autobiographical elements in the novel are encouraged to feel, how much worse is it to be the one who brings an end to a torrid affair.

The way in which Byron broke off with Caroline Lamb left her with understandably strong feelings of bitterness and resentment, and a determination to do Byron all the harm she could. Part of that determination had involved her in urgently requesting a meeting with Annabella Milbanke during the separation crisis so that she could reveal Byron's darkest secrets, but in *Glenarvon* she set out to tell not only one person but all the world what her former lover was really like. When he had been given some idea of the novel's contents by Madame de

Staël, but before he had read it himself, he told John Murray that if it was wrong to kiss and tell then it was worse to fuck and publish; but after he had given himself over three months to digest its contents, he wrote more soberly to Tom Moore:

> It seems to me that, if the authoress had written the *truth*, and nothing but the truth – the whole truth – the romance would not only have been more *romantic*, but more entertaining. As for the likeness, the picture can't be good – I did not sit long enough.[7]

Byron passed off *Glenarvon* as lightly as he could, but it must have been very painful to read, and he cannot have felt comfortable going into company where many people had recently read of his 'cold malignant heart' and 'demoniac smile', or been told that he united 'the malice and petty vices of a woman, to the perfidy and villainy of a man.'[8]

When in late July Byron first read *Glenarvon* he was already preoccupied with the disadvantages of celebrity, or notoriety as it had often become in his case. On the seventh of that month, Richard Brinsley Sheridan had died and, because Byron had been a friend of his, he was asked to write a 'monody' which could be read out at Drury Lane, the theatre of which Sheridan had once been in charge. He was a man who had had a remarkable career both as a successful playwright – *The Rivals*, *The School for Scandal* and *The Critic* are still deservedly in the repertory – and as a politician (the speech he made in the Commons at the time of the impeachment of Warren Hastings was regarded by Fox as the finest he had ever heard). He had also enjoyed a good deal of success with women and was at one time the lover of Lady Caroline Lamb's mother. Byron had only known him towards the end of his life, when he was debt-ridden and alcoholic, but the two became close, with Sheridan insisting that his young friend did have a future in politics and that same young friend relishing the wit and vivacity of someone who had known all the great men of his time. It often fell to Byron to take a drunken Sheridan home after a night on the town, a task he describes as 'no sinecure'; but he recounted with pleasure how once, when Sheridan was lying drunk in a gutter and was asked by a watchman for his name, he had the presence of mind to reply: 'Wilberforce'.[9]

The 'Monody on the Death of the Right Honourable R. B. Sheridan', faithfully copied out by Claire, is not very good: when Byron had to write to order, he rarely wrote well. The 'occasional' verse, which the eighteenth-century poets he admired were so adept at producing, was not his strong suit. The poem has an arresting beginning but quickly loses direction and, as with so much of his work, only gains interest when it becomes personal. Referring to the disreputable condition to which Sheridan was eventually reduced, Byron reflects,

> Hard is his fate on whom the public gaze
> Is fixed for ever to detract or praise,
> Repose denies her requiem to his name,
> And Folly loves the martyrdom of Fame.

Byron goes on to talk of secret enemies who spy on the famous, and of the envious who 'breathe in others' pain', and he concludes on this topic:

> Behold the host! Delighting to deprave,
> Who track the steps of Glory to the grave,
> Watch every fault that daring Genius owes
> Half to the ardour which its birth bestows,
> Distort the truth – accumulate the lie
> And pile the Pyramid of Calumny![10]

These are somewhat helpless gestures of protest about his own situation which he could not have allowed himself in prose and without the pretence of talking about someone else.

It was after his return from his trip with Shelley round the lake that Byron seems to have become properly aware of the rumours circulating in the area about his relationships with both Mary and Claire: a swapping of sexual partners which, since the two women were legally if not actually sisters, could be described by the malicious as a 'league of incest' (a term which he later became convinced Robert Southey had put into circulation). He may then have begun to believe what both Hobhouse and Shelley later reported – that there were residents of the Hotel d'Angleterre, directly across the lake, who were using spy-glasses to observe the comings and goings in Diodati (even today the villa is clearly visible with the naked eye from the lake shore below where the hotel used to be), and that the proprietor was willing to rent out such glasses for those who did not have any of their own. If Byron was feeling the pressure in this way, reading *Glenarvon* would hardly have helped. That was a novel which exposed him to the public gaze even more obviously than *Adolphe* did Madame de Staël. The dilemma in which they both found themselves was no doubt one minor factor in the growing warmth of their relationship. The de Staël who set out to rehabilitate Byron in society was after all someone who knew what a threatened or damaged social standing was all about and who had often demonstrated, long before Byron was known to the public, a personality strong enough to triumph over rumour and innuendo.

11

Chamonix

Byron took Polidori to Coppet with him, but not Shelley. It is very unlikely that the latter would have been unwelcome there, attractive and eloquent young poet as he was; or indeed that Madame de Staël would not have been interested to meet Mary. During her relatively recent stay in London, she had made sure not to miss seeing Mary's father, William Godwin, and she must have known that Mary's mother, Mary Wollstonecraft, had lived a precarious life in Paris during the early years of the revolution, just as she herself had. It would be anachronistic to attribute to de Staël the 'feminism' for which Wollstonecraft laid the foundations, but the heroine of *Corinne* is in many ways an emancipated figure and, at the beginning of chapter 3 of *De l'Allemagne*, de Staël writes: 'Nature and society impose on women a habit of suffering and it seems to me undeniable that today they are in general worth more than men'.[1] Much of her life was devoted to demonstrating that proposition and, by being herself so determinedly forceful and prominent, she did a great deal to assert women's rights.

What de Staël and the daughter of Wollstonecraft might have said to each other remains a matter for speculation because, for whatever reasons (the most powerful of which was probably Coppet's English visitors), Shelley decided against going there. 'Madame de Staël is here,' he told his friend Hogg, '& a number of literary people whom I have not seen, & indeed have no great curiosity to see, unwilling as I am to pay the invidious price exacted by all, to range oneself according to peculiar parties'.[2] As an alternative diversion he decided the time was ripe for the trip to Chamonix with Mary and Claire and he hired from Geneva a young Swiss woman to stay behind in Montalègre and look after William. Called Louise Duvillard, she was always known by the Shelleys as Elise, and she would play a very important role in their future lives.[3]

What the Shelley party began on the morning of 21 July was the quasi-
obligatory excursion for any Britons in the area and they had no doubt been
discouraged from taking it before by the bad weather. On that Sunday morning
in July, however, it was 'cloudless and exceedingly hot', although Shelley did note
that, as they made their way in a carriage along the valley of the Arve towards
Bonneville, the river was 'much swollen by the rains' and that, at the approach
to the town, the cornfields on each side of the road were flooded.[4] (A clergyman
who made the same trip a week later said that the Arve was swollen 'to a degree
not to be exampled in the memory of man'.[5]) From Bonneville they pressed on
to Cluses, from where the valley narrows and there are numerous waterfalls,
and then spent the night at an inn in St Martin, which is on the other side of
the river from Sallanches. The next morning the carriage had to be given up and
they hired mules and guides to take them to Chamonix, where they arrived at
seven in the evening, 'fatigued to death'.[6] It was after their arrival at the inn in
Chamonix, on the 22nd, that Shelley wrote to Byron, giving his first impressions of a landscape which he was shortly afterwards to say provided 'the very
excess of satisfied expectation where expectation scarcely acknowledged any
boundary'.[7] He wrote that no sooner had they entered 'this magnificent valley'
than they had decided they would stay there 'several days', and he urged Byron to
join them. 'I wish the wonders of these "palaces of Nature"', he went on, quoting
a description of the Alps which Byron was using in canto 3 of *Childe Harold*,[8]
'would induce you to visit them whilst we, who so much value your society,
remain yet near them'.[9] But the weather soon turned nasty once more, so that
by the morning of the 26th they were all on their way home again. Writing to
Samuel Rogers on the 29th, Byron said that he would go to Chamonix 'with the
first fair weather – but really we have had lately such stupid mists – fogs – rains –
and perpetual density – that one would think Castlereagh had the foreign affairs
of the kingdom of Heaven also'.[10] The recurrence of the bad weather prevented
Byron from going to join the Shelleys in Chamonix, but it is likely that he would
have been reluctant to do so in any case since that would have meant making up
a public foursome with Claire.

Curtailed though it was, the Mont Blanc excursion had important literary
consequences for both Mary and Shelley. On the 23rd, the two of them, accompanied by Claire, were taken further along the valley beyond Chamonix to
where, near the village of Les Praz, they could view the sources of the Arveiron, a
small mountain river which is fed by the *mer de glace* and is, as its name suggests,
a tributary of the Arve. This was a regulation visit at the time because, in the

days before global warning, the famous glacier was still moving steadily forward and could be clearly seen and inspected as it stretched far down into the valley. So disturbed were the locals by its progress that, several years later, they invited a local bishop to pray that it might halt. Anyone who visits the sources of the Arveiron today and sees the bed of rocks and boulders which the no longer visible glacier has left behind might well feel that in this case prayer has proved all too powerful.

On the 24th, the Shelley party made its first attempt to climb to the high point on the Montenvert where the *mer de glace* can be seen in all its majesty, sweeping between the mountains in wide curves and filling what Shelley called a 'flat valley'.[11] This is now a comfortable twenty-minute trip on a cog railway but in 1816 the ascent, first on mules and then on foot, was immeasurably more difficult. When the Shelley party attempted it on the 24th, there was a continual sound of avalanches in the near distance and the rain which began to fall was eventually so heavy that the three travellers were 'wetted to the skin' and felt obliged to turn back.[12] They had better luck the following day and, as a reward for their efforts, were able, when they did arrive at the *mer de glace*, to inspect its surface closely. Although Mary complains that on setting out on their trip there was '*beaucoup de monde*', the experience of standing on the glacier, surrounded by high mountains, clearly made a great impression on her and she soon incorporated some of its details into *Frankenstein*. It is after he has crossed the *mer de glace* and can then look back, not only at the Montenvers, but also at Mount Blanc towering up behind, that Victor meets his Creature again. The details of the glacier's surface which Mary gives then are similar to those in her diary, or in the long letter Shelley wrote to Peacock at this time, with frozen waves rising ten or fifteen feet high and deep crevices where the ice shone with an intense blue. In our day, the surface of the *mer de glace* is so brown that it can look like a huge motorway waiting to be resurfaced. In hers, it was nearer to white. With the knowledge that it was advancing inexorably, one extra foot each day according to Shelley, the impression that she and no doubt her two companions had as they stood on the glacier, with the cracking and crashing of avalanches all around, was not of some static monument but of forces of nature slowly but irresistibly edging forward. It was, Shelley wrote, as if 'Mont Blanc was a living being & that the frozen blood forever circulated slowly thro' its stony veins'.[13]

This sense of the threatening aspects of the landscape around Chamonix is apparent in 'Mont Blanc', the well known poem which Shelley was inspired by his visit to write. Quite a long piece in five sections or stanzas, this was not quite the only literary consequence of his stay in Switzerland. During his trip on the lake with Byron, he had sketched out a similarly philosophical composition entitled 'Hymn to Intellectual Beauty', 'intellectual' being a word of the time for spiritual or non-material. His concern in this poem is why the 'unseen Power' which he is addressing, and because of which the world has not only beauty but also meaning and significance, should be as inconstant as a rainbow, or moonbeams 'behind some piny mountain shower': 'Why dost thou pass away,' he asks 'and leave our state, / This dim vast vale of tears, so vacant and desolate?' In posing this question he is engaging in his highly personal and distinctive way with issues raised by two of his great Romantic precursors. Coleridge had evoked in 'Dejection' the misery of a world deprived of what the psychologists would now call affect, and in 'Intimations of Immortality' Wordsworth had suggested that it is only when we are young that it appears 'apparelled in celestial light'. In his poem Shelley goes back to his own youth and recalls how, when he was desperately seeking what meaning life could have when we are after all destined to die, the shadow of Intellectual Beauty fell upon him, with the result that 'I shrieked and clasped my hands in extasy!'. Since that epiphany, he says, he has devoted his gifts as a poet to the service of beauty (in the widest sense) with consequences which he hopes will be beneficial to mankind.[14] Shelley's poem therefore concludes on an optimistic note, but the chief impression it leaves is of how transient and unreliable our positive experiences are and how constantly in flux are both our sense impressions and our feelings. This was a major preoccupation which he had expressed before leaving in England in his short poem 'Mutability', that favourite of Mary, who has Victor Frankenstein quote the eight lines which make up its second half, and which end 'Naught may endure but mutability', as he makes his way up the Montenvers to the *mer de glace*.[15]

The experience of Chamonix certainly helped to confirm Shelley's strong sense of constant flux but, if 'Mont Blanc' is anything to go by, it did much more than that. The features of the landscape evoked in the poem prompt Shelley into complex thoughts about the ultimate source of the immense natural power he sees around him (a topic on which Coleridge had offered a very simple answer in his 'Hymn before Sunrise'), and the relation to that power of the individual mind, or of 'mind' in general. Near its beginning, there is a description of the Arve as it rushes along the ravine at the bottom of the Chamonix valley, fed by the snows and glaciers above. This is a spectacle so overwhelming in its materiality that Shelley is led into comparing the contribution made to it by the perceiving human mind with the noise of a 'feeble brook' among torrents and waterfalls. What he feels he is witnessing is an endless cycle of destruction and creation as vast pines above are shattered by avalanches, the advancing glaciers destroy animal habitats, and waterfalls pour down into the Arve so that it can flow on and eventually provide 'the breath and blood of distant lands'. In speculating that there must be a first cause of all this prodigious activity, some 'unknown omnipotence' which has unfurled 'the veil of life and death', Shelley comes as close as he ever is to conventional religious thinking. But he goes no further than taking Mont Blanc itself as the epitome of some awesome impersonal and amoral power which 'dwells apart in its tranquillity', and he then concludes by asking what even such a mountain would be, 'If to the human mind's imaginings / Silence and solitude were vacancy?'[16] The implication here seems to be that the human mind is not such a feeble brook after all. Yet to give a brief general impression of 'Mont Blanc' is very difficult because critics are still arguing over the interpretation of many of its lines. There are within it memorable passages of description but, even more than the 'Hymn to Intellectual Beauty', it is primarily a struggle with difficult philosophical concepts and therefore often disconcertingly abstract. Shelley was distressed by his lack of public recognition in comparison with Byron, but then he had a much less straightforward mind.

There will be different views about the quality of the poems Shelley wrote in Switzerland when they are compared with those of Byron, but there can be no doubt that in quantity he fell well behind his friend. By the end of July Byron had not only more or less completed canto 3 of *Childe Harold* and *The Prisoner of Chillon* but also produced a good number of shorter works (he needed to write continuously in order to keep himself on an even keel). It was in this month, for example, that, in addition to the monody on Sheridan's death, he wrote three poems based on his own dreams, daytime visions, or haunting memories from the past. The first of these is called 'The Dream' and begins with reflections on the nature of dreaming; but he soon abandons general thought to focus on the particular dreams or visions which appear to have been obsessing him at the time. These concern the Mary Chaworth with whom he had fallen so hopelessly in love while he was still at Harrow. She lived on an estate which adjoined Newstead and was from the start an intriguing figure for the young boy since she was a descendant of the William Chaworth who, in 1765, had been killed in a duel by Byron's great-uncle, the man from whom he inherited his title. The difficulty was that whereas Byron was only 15 when he became infatuated with Mary, she was 18 and being courted by a neighbouring landowner. 'The Dream'

is divided into nine sections and in the third of them Byron recalls the moment
in Mary's home (Annesley Hall) when he was trying but failing to write a note to
her and, on her appearance, took her hand and then left her for good. The critical
event which gave Byron the strength to fight against an infatuation which had for
months stopped him returning to school may have been his having overheard
Mary say to her maid, 'Do you think I could care anything for that lame boy?'[17]
(Flattered though she may have been by his attentions, she did not want them to
damage her matrimonial prospects.) The fourth and fifth sections are flashbacks
to Byron's time in Greece and then to his return home and the discovery that
the marriage Mary had by then made with the neighbouring landowner was not
at all happy. In section seven he has a dream or vision of his own marriage and
reveals that as he stood 'before an Altar' – a piece of poetic licence, since at his
own insistence Byron married Annabella Milbanke in her own home and not
in church – memories of his final parting from Mary flashed across his mind.
'What business had they there at such a time?' he very reasonably asks.

   In the final sections of 'The Dream' the reader learns what was historically
true (this is not a poem in which Byron was making much up): that Mary
Chaworth had a nervous breakdown or, in the more direct parlance of the time,
went mad: 'her thoughts / Were combinations of disjointed things; / And forms
impalpable and unperceived / Of others' sight familiar were to her'. He contrasts
this kind of genuine madness with what he calls a deeper one, noting that

>   the glance
> Of melancholy is a fearful gift;
> What is it but the telescope of truth?
> Which strips the distance of its phantasies,
> And brings life near in utter nakedness,
> Making the cold reality too real![18]

In the letter to Peacock in which Shelley had said – after the trip on the lake
– that Byron was 'a slave to the vilest and most vulgar prejudices', he had also
claimed that his companion was 'as mad as the winds'; and Byron himself was
later to write that during his time in Switzerland, or at least during the composition of canto 3 of *Childe Harold*, he was 'half-mad'.[19] But although his behaviour
could sometimes seem bizarre, he was always lucid and what he seemed to suffer
from most was the Pascalian bleakness of vision described so effectively here, a
state of mind in which there is nothing to distract or divert one from the brutal
realities of birth, copulation and death. In the penultimate section of his poem

he recalls how recently in England he was 'compass'd round / With Hatred and Contention' so that he has been driven to seek his consolations away from mankind and in Nature; and he ends by observing that, although only one of the two young people he has been revisiting in his dream may now have gone mad, both of them have ended 'in misery'.[20]

'The Dream' is not a cheerful poem and neither is the fragment on death which Byron wrote about the same time, in which he claims that life itself is 'but a vision'. The most striking moment in this comes when he asks of the absent dead whom we shall all one day join 'in the dark union of insensate dust' whether they are in fact 'decomposed to clay',

> Or do they in their silent cities dwell
> Each in his incommunicative cell – [21]

This somewhat 'Gothic' speculation is developed a little before the poem peters out in an implicit confession of bafflement and ignorance. Even more 'Gothic' in character is the third (but this time completed) poem in the 'dream' sequence, the one which was eventually called 'Darkness'. Although this begins 'I had a dream', it is much more like a nightmare. Byron imagines in this poem what would happen if the sun were to be extinguished, so that there were no more heat and no more light. He was prompted to this morbid fantasy by the current controversy over the increasing number of sunspots which astronomers had observed, but also by the exceptionally bad weather: he wrote 'Darkness', he later said, on 'a celebrated dark day, on which the fowls went to roost at noon, and the candles were lighted as at midnight'.[22] He may also have discussed end-of-the-world scenarios with Shelley, who was inclined to take the fact that the glaciers in Chamonix were continually creeping forward as confirmation of the Comte de Buffon's view that they would one day take over the valley (it was Buffon who, in saying that 'every object in nature is subject to change and decay', also asserted that 'the sun itself will be extinguished'[23]). A consequence of darkness in Byron's poem is that all buildings are pulled down to feed beacons or watch-fires, including 'the palaces of crowned kings'. Forests are set on fire as men look up 'with mad disquietude on the dull sky'. Everyone retreats into a selfish struggle for survival with 'no love left' and each man sitting 'sullenly apart / Gorging himself in gloom'. Cannibalism sets in – 'The meagre by the meagre were devoured' – and dogs attack their masters, with the exception of one animal which protects its master's corpse until hunger ends its own life. The scarcity of resources occasioned by the absence of sunlight means that war has broken out, but Byron describes how eventually two sworn enemies, who are the last two men still living in a famished city, glimpse one another in the flickering firelight and are so appalled by each other's appearance that they too die. In the end all is destroyed, including sailorless ships 'rotting on the sea' (a faint echo perhaps of Coleridge's *Ancient Mariner*), and the triumph of darkness is complete.[24] Although there are no ghosts in Byron's poem, it would have made, with its lurid details and melodramatic atmosphere, a very effective contribution to those discussions in June at Diodati which gave rise to *Frankenstein*. But where it perhaps now has most effect is in giving some indication of Byron's state of mind at this period, all the more so in that it does this, not in an autobiographical form, but indirectly. However much the idea of a world from which daylight and warmth have been excluded was dependent on the absent summer of 1816, what 'Darkness' clearly provided is what used to be called an objective correlative for Byron's frequent black moods.

12

The Problem of Claire
and the First of the Visitors

By the time the Shelley party came back from Chamonix, the problem of Claire, now well into her fourth month of pregnancy, was becoming acute. On the evening of their return, all three of them dropped in on Byron at Diodati and talked with him until twelve, their fatigue after the journey making for a relatively early night. Mary records in her diary that on three of the five subsequent evenings they also visited Byron, but on the sixth (2nd August) she writes: 'S. & C. go up to Diodati. I do not for Lord B. did not seem to wish it.'[1] This has been interpreted as an indication of a council of war about Claire's future, from which it was thought best that Mary should be excluded. One possible reason for this interpretation is that Mary's entry is followed immediately by one in which she notes that Shelley had come back that evening from Diodati with a letter from his lawyer which suggested he ought to return to England. There seems little doubt that Shelley's financial difficulties did require his presence back home, but the arrangements made with, and for, Claire meant that he needed to be there quite soon in any case.

In the aristocratic circles in which Byron had often moved, attitudes to illegitimate children tended to be relaxed. When he himself had been married, in the home of the otherwise pious and strait-laced Milbankes, the officiating clergyman had been a bastard son of Annabella's rich uncle, Lord Wentworth. At the other end of the social scale, the disruption of children born out of wedlock could be smoothed over with money. Shortly after leaving Cambridge, Byron made one of the maids at Newstead pregnant and therefore settled on her £100 a year, which later became £50 for the mother and the same amount for the child. But Claire's case fell uncomfortably between these two social extremes. He could not marry her and legitimise the coming child because he was already

married; and he did not want to have her live with him because they did not get
on, or at least it appears that he increasingly found her company irritating. It may
be also that, at this stage in his life, he did not want to do anything which would
compromise the possibility of a future reconciliation with his wife. The arrangement all three came to was that Claire should go back to England and, under
Shelley's protection and with his help, have her baby as discreetly as possible.
After a suitable time had passed, Byron would then adopt it and give its mother,
posing perhaps as an aunt, no more than visiting rights. This was a sacrifice Claire
was willing to make because she thought that adoption by an English peer would
necessarily secure the child a bright future. What Byron seemed determined to
do in all this negotiation was to prevent Claire from using the baby as a means of
tying herself to him. To those who thought this hard he might have pointed out
that, as far as his affair with Claire was concerned, she had made all the running;
yet it is difficult not to feel sorry for her. In the letter she had written to him from
Paris, on her way to Geneva, she had said, 'I have no passions; I had ten times
rather be your male friend than your mistress';[2] and her subsequent career does
suggest that she had no very strong interest in sex. What she wanted was to be,
like her sister, the soulmate of a man of genius, but now that dream was about to
be shattered. There is an uncomfortable pathos in the letter she wrote to Byron
when in late August the Shelley party was on its way back to England. 'There is
nothing in the world I love or care about but yourself,' she declared, adding, 'I
make no account of Mary & Shelley's friendship so much more do I love you.'
At the same time she could not refrain from also saying, 'One thing I do entreat
you to remember & beware of any excess in wine'.[3] There are suggestions in his
relationships with Lady Melbourne and Augusta that Byron rather liked to be
mothered, but that is not the same as being nagged; and he might well have
resented, in this warning to him not to drink too much, an unjustifiable propri-
etary tone.

   The available documentary evidence is insufficient to indicate clearly quite
why Byron's relationship with Claire began to go seriously wrong or when, as far
as he was concerned, it broke down completely. Between the letter she wrote to
him complaining of his cruelty shortly after his arrival at the Hôtel d'Angleterre
in May, and the one in which the warning not to drink too much occurs, there are
only three short notes (if he wrote notes to her, they have not survived). In the
first of these three, she asks Byron to clear the decks for a late evening visit she
intends to make to Diodati by sending Polidori off to 'the lady he loves'. The news
that the young doctor had found someone in Geneva to fall in love with seems

to have become common knowledge in the group some time in July. Profiting from the entrée into Genevan social life which his association with Byron had given him, as well as from his own good looks, Polidori attended numerous balls in private houses and was involved also in the amateur theatricals which were then a major pastime of both the local and the expatriate circles he frequented. In the course of enjoying himself in this way, he saw a good deal of a Portuguese lady called Madame Brelaz and fell in love with her. He then made the mistake of confiding in Byron, only to find that, when the two of them next saw the Shelley party, the feelings to which he had confessed were immediately the subject of what Tom Moore calls 'jesting allusions'. (Mary must have described this episode to Moore, who, in his biography of Byron, went on to note an 'utter incapacity of retention' as one of his subject's weaknesses.[4]) It was because Claire had been present when Byron was teasing his doctor about Madame Brelaz that she could urge him to send Polidori off to visit his loved one so that her own entry into Diodati would pass unnoticed. Otherwise it would be, at such a comparatively late hour, she writes in her note, 'so extremely suspicious'.[5]

Aware as he was becoming of all the scandal which surrounded him, it may not be surprising that Byron wanted to keep his affair with Claire secret, especially as her pregnancy became more evident; but it is not so obvious why she herself was anxious not to be seen by Polidori on one of her late-night visits to Diodati when it is clear, from his diary, that he knew from the start she was his employer's mistress. Her notes suggest that she was at least as anxious as Byron to keep up appearances, although this may have been partly because his own anxiety had been transferred to her. In the second of the three surviving notes, she says that she is afraid to come up and see him 'for fear of meeting any one'; wonders whether he cannot 'pretext the copying'; and she then apologises for using Shelley as a messenger: 'S— says he won't look at my note so don't be offended.'[6] The third and final note was written shortly before the Shelley party set off for Chamonix and is the one in which Claire reports how she has been told that, on the previous evening, Byron had insisted that it would be impossible for her to come to Diodati any more. 'Shall I never see you again?', she asks him, 'Not once again?'[7] In fact she was up at the villa several times before the putative council of war to decide her future, as well as on a number of occasions after. There is no record of her having protested with any force about the arrangements which were made on her behalf either at that council or later, and certainly, at this stage, neither Shelley nor Mary recorded an objection. Neither do the two of them appear to have thought any the less of Byron for having helped to make them, or registered a strong sense that, in general, Claire had been treated badly. It seems nevertheless likely that Byron went on sleeping with Claire after he had ceased to have any feeling for her, saying to himself perhaps, as he puts it in stanza 53 of the third canto of *Childe Harold*, 'It is in vain that we would coldly gaze / On such as smile upon us'.[8]

One of Byron's suggestions which had been rejected by Claire during the discussions over her immediate future was that, at an appropriate age, her baby should be sent to Augusta and absorbed into her growing family of five. If, as seems possible, he believed that Augusta's fourth child Medora, born in April 1814, was his own, then this solution might have struck him as appropriate; but it was in any event very much in line with his feeling at this time that his sister could always be relied upon: that she was, in emotional terms, his one remaining support in a hostile world. This is a conviction which in July found expression in two poems, one described as simply 'Stanzas' to Augusta and the other as an ' Epistle' to her. There are six of the 'Stanzas' and the character of them all is fairly represented by the first:

> Though the day of my destiny's over,
>   And the star of my fate hath declined,
> Thy soft heart refused to discover
>   The faults which so many could find;
> Though thy soul with my grief was acquainted,
>   It shrunk not to share it with me,
> And the love which my spirit hath painted
>   It never hath found but in *thee*.[9]

The 'Epistle' is similar in theme but its rhythms are much less facile and it is significant in Byron's poetic career as his first attempt to use the *ottava rima* which he had so much admired in the book of poems by Casti (given to him in Brussels by his relative Pryse Gordon), and which he deployed so successfully in his later comic works. Nothing could, however, be less like *Beppo* or *Don Juan* than the 'Epistle to Augusta' as Byron once again reviews his recent troubles, confessing that they had made him contemplate suicide and admitting that he had been 'cunning in mine overthrow / The careful pilot of my proper woe'. He has found some consolation, he says, in 'Alpine landscapes' but still yearns for his sister's company: 'Oh that thou wert with me!' Since she is not, Nature will have to supply her place ''till I look again on thee'. In the meantime he can rest easy in the thought that in the heart of his 'own sweet Sister' – 'I know myself secure'.[10] It was an irony of his situation, far away from England and out of touch with what was happening there, that he was far less secure than he thought.

Public declarations of Byron's love for his half-sister were an embarrassment to Augusta: given a veto over the publication of these two poems she allowed the first but not the second. Her situation was very difficult. Her husband had been a friend of the Prince of Wales, or Prince Regent as he later became, but they had then quarrelled, so that all he was more or less good for at this time was the accumulation of gambling debts. The family was always in financial difficulties, the acuteness of which was only ever temporarily relieved by generous hand-outs from Byron. A bright spot had been Augusta's appointment in March 1815 as a lady-in-waiting to Queen Charlotte, whose husband, George III, had been declared irretrievably mad in 1810, the year which officially inaugurated the Regency decade. This brought a modest income, but it was a position threatened by the waves of rumour and innuendo which began to engulf Augusta at the time of her brother's separation from his wife. Lady Byron's willingness to keep seeing her – not to cut her off – provided some protection against the whisperings of incest which might otherwise have brought social disgrace, loss of her position at Court, and even more acute financial difficulty. Writing to Byron from England in September 1816, Shelley said that the news of Lady Byron being at that time with Augusta gave him great pleasure because he regarded it as 'decisive contradiction of the only important calumny that ever was advanced against you'.[11] Contradiction of this kind was bought by Augusta at a very high price. In an exchange of letters throughout the summer of 1816, Lady Byron manoeuvred her sister-in-law into implicitly admitting that the calumny to which Shelley refers was no such thing and then, in a meeting which took place at the beginning of September, she extorted from her a direct confession of incest. Yet she felt that Augusta displayed an insufficient sense of the gravity of her crime. In collaboration with a mutual friend called Mrs Villiers, she decided that it would be a Christian duty to make the sinner realise how deeply she had sinned, and how threatening to her repentance and eventual salvation was her continuing communication with Byron. The implied suggestion that Augusta should stop writing to her brother was one which even the thoroughly intimidated and chronically anxious victim of these two women felt she had to resist; but she did agree to do all she could to discourage him from expressing his love and, crucially, to show to Lady Byron anything he wrote to her. The latter was therefore able to observe closely how increasingly baffled her husband became by the equivocal and hesitant way in which Augusta responded to his effusions, and have the double satisfaction of both saving a sinner and revenging herself on the man who had done her so much harm.[12]

Claire Clairmont made a fair copy of at least the first of the poems to Augusta. In doing so, she was probably able to confirm how much Byron needed a woman in his life and regret again that it had not fallen to her to fulfil that need. Although he did not see much less of her immediately after the meeting on 2nd August, their contacts were set to become less frequent and they came to a virtual halt as the Shelley party slowly prepared to leave and Byron began to receive at Diodati a stream of visitors. The first of these was Matthew Lewis, who arrived on the 14th. 'Little Matt Lewis', as he was often patronisingly known on account of his physique, had been a friend of Byron's for some time and had already visited him at Newstead. The son of an important War Office official, he had himself been an MP for six years, having in 1796 succeeded William Beckford as the member for Hindon in Wiltshire, a pocket borough of 120 souls which would be swept away in the 1832 reform of Parliament. Since Beckford was the author of *Vathek*, this was a case of one Gothic novelist, and perhaps also one homosexual, replacing another, although whereas the evidence for Beckford's sexual orientation is strong, Lewis's case is much more uncertain and doubtful. By the time Byron saw Lewis in Switzerland, he had inherited a large fortune after the death of his father and, with a very different temperament from his host, had almost completely stopped writing. In his day – a period roughly corresponding with his time as a member of Parliament – he had been his country's leading popular dramatist and the author of a dozen works for the stage. Yet his fame rested more on his remarkable first (and only) novel, which he had written in his late teens and published in 1796, before he was twenty. *The Monk* has many of the usual Gothic features: exotic Catholic practices, abbeys and convents as well as ancient ancestral homes, murders, and of course ghosts; but Lewis gave his novel extra impact with liberal additional helpings of rape, transvestism, Satanism, torture and putrefaction. What makes it now so striking, however, is the analysis at its heart of sexual repression (not for nothing does the epigraph to the first chapter consist of the lines from *Measure for Measure* which describe Angelo as someone who 'Scarce confesses / That his blood flows'). Ambrosio, the monk of the title, is excessively proud of his reputation in Madrid for sanctity, but he is tempted from the straight and narrow by a beautiful woman in monk's clothing who turns out in the end to have been an agent of Satan. *L'appétit vient en mangeant* so that, having satisfied his lust with Matilda (as the disguised 'monk' is called), he then sets his sights on Antonia, an innocent young girl whose rape he can only eventually achieve by recourse to the black arts. It is Matilda who intro-duces him to these and they include a magic mirror which, in a notoriously erotic scene, allows him to watch Antonia undressing. The intricate description of Ambrosio's struggle with his unruly passions is remarkable for a nineteen-year-old author, as is the expertise with which he handles all the other elements of a complicated plot. The novel caused a scandal (Coleridge attacking it for its 'libidinous minuteness'[13]), but it was an international success and became so well known that its author was habitually referred to as 'Monk' Lewis. The friend whom Byron welcomed to Diodati had therefore been at least as preco-cious as he himself had been, or as Mary and Shelley then were; and all three of them would, along with Claire and Polidori, have known Lewis's work well. Before he went up to Oxford Shelley had published with his sister a collection of verse which had to be withdrawn almost immediately because it contained a direct plagiary of a poem by Lewis; and Byron was familiar enough with what his visitor had written to have made fun of it in *English Bards and Scotch Reviewers*, alluding ironically to 'chaste descriptions on thy page, / To please the females of our modest age'.[14]

Once Lewis was installed in Diodati, Byron and Shelley spent a good deal of time with him. Reports of the discussions between the three men suggest that the author of *The Monk* ought to have come two months earlier, when the competition as to who could tell the most terrifying tale had been kick-started by a collection of stories translated from the German. Because he wanted him to be a diplomat, Lewis's father had in 1792 sent his seventeen-year-old son to the Weimar court, where he rapidly picked up the language. Being fluent in German gave Lewis, who soon rejected diplomacy in favour of writing, easy access to a wealth of creepy stories, several of which would find their way into his various works. While he was at Diodati, 'Apollo's sexton' (as Byron had called Lewis in *English Bards*) entertained his company with stories of this kind, five of which so impressed Shelley that he recorded their details in Mary's diary. What he also recorded was a philosophical disagreement which he had had with the two older men over the existence of ghosts. Byron and Lewis were inclined to be sceptical on the matter and assumed that, since Shelley was an atheist, he would be sceptical also. They apparently took the commonsense view that denial of God implied a denial of the supernatural. But Shelley's atheism was of a complicated, non-materialist variety (it might have helped less sophisticated minds had he simply called himself anti-Christian), and he was someone who, as his poetry showed, firmly believed in a spiritual world. Byron and Lewis, he noted in protest, 'both agree in the very face of reason, that none could believe in ghosts without also believing in God'.[15]

This disagreement over ghosts might help to explain why, when on 16 August Byron and Lewis paid a visit to Ferney, Shelley did not join them. Ferney is the village where Voltaire had built himself a fine château and where he lived and wrote for almost twenty years. Since it lies only a dozen or so kilometres behind Sécheron, one might have expected Shelley to have already been there; but it could be that for him Voltaire had come to seem the same kind of dry stick as Gibbon, and he would have known that, when Rousseau was forced to retreat from Paris back into his native Switzerland, he had no fiercer enemy than the old but still alarmingly active lord of Ferney. Unlike Rousseau, Voltaire was a figure from the late eighteenth century who did not point forward to Romanticism. That may have been a problem for Shelley but, as time passed, it would become less and less of one for Byron. While he was living in Venice during the following year, he bought the ninety-two volumes of Voltaire's complete works and enjoyed dipping into them, amused rather than offended by their occasional hostile allusions to Rousseau. Some time later he came across a reference to Voltaire as 'a shallow fellow' which he attributed to a member of the so-called Lake school: Coleridge, Wordsworth or his particular *bête noire* in that group, Robert Southey. Suggesting that these writers were known as a school only because their education was incomplete, he claimed that their whole 'filthy trash of Epics, Excursions, etc.' was not worth 'the two words in *Zaire*, "tu pleurs", or a single speech of Tancred' (*Tancred* and *Zaire* being of course plays by Voltaire). An action for which Byron particularly admired Voltaire was his orchestration of a Europe-wide and eventually successful campaign for the rehabilitation of Jean Calas, a Huguenot cloth worker from Toulouse who in 1762 was executed for the murder of his son – the charge was that this son had been killed because he was about to convert to Roman Catholicism, whereas in fact he had committed suicide. In the 'apostate lives' of members of the Lake school, Byron asked, 'with their tea-drinking neutrality of morals and their convenient treachery in politics', was there anything 'to equal or approach the sole defence of the family of Calas, by that great and unequalled genius – the universal Voltaire'.[16] By the time he wrote these words, in a note to the fifth canto of *Don Juan*, the temporary enthusiasm for Wordsworth which Shelley had inspired in Byron was well and truly over.

13

Reconciliation

Matthew Lewis had been at Oxford with Fox's nephew, Lord Holland, and knew most of the people in that sector of the fashionable world Byron had frequented, as well as many other important figures outside it. It was therefore inevitable that he should have met Madame de Staël when she came to England, especially as he shared with her such a strong interest in German literature. Describing Lewis much later, Byron said that he was 'a good man – a clever man – but a bore' ('pestilently prolix' is a term he had used earlier to describe how boring he could be). 'He was a Jewel of a Man,' he went on, 'had he been better set – I don't mean *personally*, but less *tiresome* – for he was tedious – as well as contradictory to every thing and every body.'[1] It was no doubt the spirit of contradiction in Lewis which helped to ensure that on one of his meetings with de Staël in England (the same at which she complained that Byron would shut his eyes during dinner), the two of them had a serious disagreement. 'They fell out, alas!', Byron had lamented, 'and now they will never quarrel again. Could not one reconcile them for the "nonce"?'[2] It was perhaps with the idea of reconciliation that he accompanied Lewis to Coppet although, once there, he made sure he introduced a topic which he knew would set his guest 'by the ears' with Madame de Staël.[3] He was quite fond of this kind of mischief-making.

The topic Byron launched was slavery, and it was one on which Lewis had a right to feel expert since his father had not only left him a lot of money, but also two large plantations in Jamaica with hundreds of slaves. Unlike his father, Lewis had been a keen supporter of the 1807 Act which abolished the slave trade in the British Empire, but the quarrel was then over whether existing slaves should be freed (something which did not happen until 1833). He felt, as de Staël probably did not, that emancipation would be a bad thing in that it would destroy the economy of the plantations, leave the freed slaves destitute, and result in violence against the whites. Earlier in the year he had visited his properties and instituted a number of humanitarian reforms. These included prohibiting the whip (a measure British sailors would also have appreciated), giving his slaves a second day off so that they could cultivate their allotments more effectively, and improving hospital facilities, especially for expectant mothers (a self-interested action in that, with the trade in slaves abolished, any future labour force had to be self-generated). He introduced several other measures to make the lives of his slaves easier, not worrying that the immediate consequence appeared to be a huge drop in productivity. Lewis was aware that unless plantation owners who were resident in Britain made periodic visits to their properties, taking the long sea trip which, as the interesting diary of his own visits shows,[4] could often be difficult and dangerous, power would fall into the hands of paid subordinates and all the owners' good intentions might go for naught. While he was at Diodati he therefore drew up a codicil to his will in which he stipulated that those who inherited his plantations would have to pass three months on them in every three-year period, and also agree not to reverse any of his own reforms. This document was signed by Byron, Shelley and Polidori but, when he was back in England, Lewis had a consultation with Wilberforce which led to its cancellation. He seems to have decided that the codicil would not be effective and realised that a major problem with benevolent despotism is that it is impossible to guarantee the benevolence of the despot's successor.

Lewis's codicil was signed on 20 August and he appears to have left for Italy the next day. During his stay with Byron he had not only told ghost stories but also translated for him parts of Goethe's *Faust*. This is important because although Byron would already have been made familiar with *Faust* by the detailed account (with translations) which appears in Madame de Staël's *De l'Allemagne*, he later acknowledged the particular influence of Lewis's oral rendering on *Manfred*, the poetic drama he was now beginning to write. The origin of this 'Witch drama', as Byron at one point called it,[5] dates back some time, but it was in August 1816 at Diodati that he wrote the first scene. This takes place at midnight in a 'Gothic gallery' where a disillusioned Manfred, who has realised that 'The Tree of Knowledge is not that of Life', is attempting to raise spirits. Among those which eventually appear is the spirit of Mont Blanc, without whose authorisation 'The Glacier's cold and restless mass' would not move 'onward day by day'. Also raised are the tutelary spirits of five other aspects of the natural world, but the seventh and final apparition is of the spirit associated with the star which rules Manfred's own destiny. In words which reflect Shelley's rather than Byron's strong interest in contemporary astronomy, this is described as 'the burning wreck of a demolish'd world', 'a wandering mass of shapeless flame', and a 'pathless comet'. The spirits resentfully enquire of Manfred what he requires of them and he replies, 'Forgetfulness'; when they ask what he wants to forget, he tells them that they, with their supernatural powers, ought to know and demands again, 'Oblivion, self-oblivion'.[6] But it turns out that, although power and riches are in the gift of the raised spirits, allowing Manfred to forget is not (even though I may not be what I once was as a poet, Byron writes at the beginning of canto 3 of *Childe Harold*, I shall go on writing 'so it fling / Forgetfulness about me'[7]).

There are certainly in the first scene of *Manfred* faint echoes of the opening of Goethe's *Faust* but of several other texts as well (including *Macbeth*). Also at the back of Byron's mind might have been a particularly striking episode from the famous novel of his visitor. This is where Matilda, having thrown off her male disguise, shows the monk of the title how she can conjure up an agent of the devil. Byron would never have made a deliberate, unacknowledged borrowing from another writer (as Coleridge does in his 'Hymn before Sunrise'); but even more than most poets, he had a magpie mind and, as his relationship with Shelley clearly shows, picked up hints and suggestions everywhere, both consciously and unconsciously.

Two days after Lewis's departure Mary recorded in her diary that Byron was in 'ill spirits' because he knew that his wife was sick.[8] He had almost certainly heard this news via Coppet in that, as he explained in a letter to Madame de Staël, he had asked all his usual correspondents never to mention Lady Byron. Trying to describe how he felt about what he had heard, he went on,

> The separation may have been *my fault* – but it was *her* choice. – I tried all means to prevent – and would do as much & more to end it, – a word would do so – but it does not rest with me to pronounce it. – You asked me if I thought that Lady B was attached to me – to that I can only answer that I love her.[9]

This reply stimulated an ambition that de Staël may well have been nursing for some time. She had set out to rehabilitate Byron in society but now she felt she ought to try to reconcile him with his wife (when she first read 'Fare Thee Well', the poem he had addressed to Lady Byron before leaving England, she had wondered how any woman could resist such a moving appeal). Bringing about a reconciliation was a tough task, but not especially daunting for someone who had repeatedly tried to make Napoleon change his mind. She must have asked whether, in attempting it, she could make use of the note Byron had just sent her, since he replied that it was at her disposal but then gloomily predicted that her efforts would be useless.

Because Lady Byron had become adamantly opposed to reconciliation, that prediction turned out to be true; but matters were not helped by the fact that, staying at the Hôtel d'Angleterre at this time, and occasionally visiting Coppet, was Henry Brougham: he had arrived at the beginning of July and complained that in his first ten days, only two were free of constant rain. A successful lawyer and rising Whig politician who would eventually become Lord Chancellor, Brougham espoused causes to which Byron was also sympathetic and had defended Leigh Hunt when, in 1813, he was prosecuted with his brother John for attacking the Prince Regent in *The Examiner*. The similarity of their political views ought to have made Byron and Brougham friends but, on the latter's part at least, there was a history of antagonism. It was Brougham who had demolished Byron's *Hours of Idleness* in the *Edinburgh Review*, suggesting that in this early collection the author's effusions were 'spread over a dead flat, and can no more get above or below the level, than if they were so much stagnant water'. He had mocked the debutant mercilessly for the way that, in his preface, he had implied that his youth might constitute an excuse for the inadequacies of his writing; he had complained that there were too many references to the author's aristocratic lineage; and he had advised him to abandon poetry altogether.[10] Because Byron thought that this advice had come from Francis Jeffrey, Brougham escaped relatively unscathed from *English Bards and Scotch Reviewers*, although he did find himself referred to there as 'blundering Brougham' and had to read a sarcastic note on the pronunciation of his name (which was 'Broom').[11] More important perhaps than these pinpricks is that Byron had once made the mistake of referring in a disobliging way to the wife of George Lamb, who was Brougham's mistress and a main reason for his trip to Geneva in 1816 (she was staying there with her mother, the dowager Duchess of Devonshire). George Lamb was the younger brother of the William of that name and Brougham's mistress was therefore Lady Caroline Lamb's sister-in-law: it was not from this quarter that one was likely to hear much that was complimentary about Byron. His fondness for George Lamb's wife may have been one of the reasons why, during the separation crisis, Brougham played the major role in making sure that Byron's 'Fare Thee Well!', and his sketch of his wife's former governess, both of which were originally intended for private circulation only, appeared in the newspapers; and why he was more than willing to offer Lady Byron legal advice. Being part of the team which supported her, he must have heard enough scabrous details to reinforce his strong dislike of her husband.

Visiting Coppet as he did, Brougham would have heard of de Staël's wish to bring Byron and his wife back together. Without being asked to interfere, he took it upon himself to write to Lady Byron and keep her abreast of developments. In the letter he sent her from Geneva on 23 August, he says that he has hesitated to write for fear of giving her pain but feels he must apprise her of her husband's activities. Byron, he reports, is 'avoided by the numerous English who are here' and if Brougham himself has had to meet him two or three times, it is 'without taking any notice of him'. On all occasions the language Byron employs in public is 'that of despondency', but he imputes no blame whatsoever to his wife, apart from complaining that she is unforgiving. Recently he has been making it clear that he would like nothing better than a reconciliation. This is a matter on which Brougham feels only Lady Byron can make a decision ('you must judge and not I'), but his acknowledgement of that truth is followed immediately by a statement of his opinion. This is that Byron may be employing a device to put Lady Byron in the wrong and make people believe that blame for the separation rested with her; he may be trying to 'regain some footing of esteem in Society'; or he may be finding 'reports spreading & wish to give them a refutation, by having once more your countenance'. Whatever his motive, it cannot be a good one, 'especially considering the life he has been leading here'. Brougham had no sooner posted this letter when he learnt that Madame de Staël had sent the note in which Byron declared that he still loved his wife to a friend in England, Lady Romilly, with a request that it should be passed on to Lady Byron (whom de Staël herself hardly knew). He therefore immediately wrote again in order to warn Lady Byron against 'this new attempt against your peace (for such only I can consider it)', and hope that she would not 'take any notice of it'.[12] He need not have worried. Lady Byron replied to Lady Romilly by asking her to convey to Madame de Staël her thanks for the interest she took in her family affairs but also her determination not to be reconciled with her husband. To Brougham she said much the same thing, instructing him to tell de Staël, or anyone else prepared to listen, that although the 'expression of sentiment' in the letter from her husband which had been sent on to her was impossible to hear with indifference, it was also impossible to trust; and that she was not 'weak enough' to be shaken in a determination to stay separated from Byron which had been as much influenced by consideration for his well-being as for her own.[13]

Only later did Byron learn the full extent of Brougham's hostility. It was characteristic of him that he then wanted to 'call out' his enemy and thought of returning to England specifically for that purpose, or of trying to persuade Brougham to meet him in Calais where the two of them could duel in relative security. But the idea came to nothing, perhaps because his friends were uncooperative and thought that he had insufficiently precise grounds for a challenge; perhaps because it was clear that Brougham would never accept one (especially from a man who practised pistol shooting every day); or perhaps because Byron had begun to realise that the intensity of the fury he felt was at least in part a result of having to divert his anger away from his wife. He had assured Madame de Staël that he still loved Lady Byron, but even before the attempt at reconciliation collapsed there were the cracks in the façade. This is evident from one of the poems he seems to have written around September, the 'Lines On Hearing That Lady Byron Was Ill'. The tone at the beginning of this poem is sympathetic: 'And thou wert sad – yet I was not with thee; / And thou wert sick, and yet I was not near', Byron writes; but from then on it is a series of bitter variations on 'I told you so' and 'serves you right'. He wonders whether the illness of Lady Byron means that he has been 'too well avenged', but then: ''twas my right; / Whate'er my sins might be, *thou* wert not sent / To be the Nemesis who should requite'. In the *Oresteia*, Clytemnestra entangles her husband Agememnon in a robe and then stabs him. For Byron his wife has become a 'moral Clytemnestra' who with a 'cold treason of the heart' has destroyed all his hopes. He accuses her of having entered into 'crooked ways' and become less than truthful, full of deceit and equivocation. Although all this is perhaps with 'a breast unknowing its own crimes', she will nonetheless never sleep easy again because she is now 'pillow'd on a curse too deep'.[14] One has to feel that although Byron may have begun this poem on hearing his wife was sick, he must have completed it when the news had arrived, via his friend Hobhouse, that she was better, or at least in no immediate danger.

The 'Lines On Hearing That Lady Byron Was Ill' were never published in their author's lifetime, but this is not the case of the 'Incantation' which concludes the first scene of *Manfred*. This comes after the spirits which Manfred has called up have disappeared and he himself has fallen senseless to the floor. A disembodied voice is then heard intoning what turns out to be a curse in seven stanzas. Much of this seems to have been written in England, but the sixth stanza belongs firmly to August 1816:

By thy cold breast and serpent smile,
By thy unfathom'd gulfs of guile,
By that most seeming virtuous eye,
By thy shut soul's hypocrisy;
By the perfection of thine art
Which pass'd for human thine own heart;
By thy delight in others' pain,
And by thy brotherhood of Cain,
I call upon thee! and compel
Thyself to be thy proper Hell![15]

The dramatic context here (as well as the third line up) quite clearly indicate that these words should be directed against Manfred as he lies unconscious, but everything else in the play makes that seem impossible. He emerges as morbidly proud, defiant and deeply misanthropic, but never hypocritical or full of guile, so that it is hard to resist the suggestion of one of Byron's editors that what this passage represents is 'a barely concealed curse on Lady Byron'.[16] That is how it must have seemed to many readers of the day. It would have been painful for Lady Byron to have seen the lines when *Manfred* was first published in 1817, but the way they appear would have allowed her to feel she could ignore them. Unfortunately for her peace of mind, the 'Incantation' had already been published separately in the collection *'The Prisoner of Chillon' and Other Poems*, copied out by Claire Clairmont and published by the end of 1816. There is no distracting dramatic context in this version to prevent readers from concluding that its object was indeed Lady Byron.

Like many of those who lead intensely creative lives, crowded with imaginary scenarios, Byron was often tempted by what Freud calls the omnipotence of thoughts. When he hated someone his feelings had such strength that he found it hard to believe that they would not have some practical effect in the real world. There are hints of this belief in his response in 1818 to the suicide of Sir Samuel Romilly (the husband of the woman to whom Madame de Staël had somewhat misguidedly appealed as an intermediary in her reconciliation efforts). He was a lawyer who was widely liked but also respected for his humanitarian efforts to reform the barbaric English penal code. Byron had paid him a retainer so that he could call on his services if needed but, when Lady Byron asked him for advice, Romilly forgot his previous commitment (he was so successful, he received many retainers), and obliged her.[17] It was a betrayal Byron found impossible to forgive. When, shortly after topping the poll in the election of members of

Parliament for Westminster, and following the sudden death of his wife, Romilly cut his throat, Byron was in no mood to let bygones be bygones:

> This Man little thought when he was lacerating my heart according to law – while he was poisoning my life at it's sources – aiding and abetting in the blighting – branding – and Exile that was to be the result of his Counsels in their *indirect effects* – that in less than thirty six Moons – in the pride of his triumph as the highest Candidate for the representation of the Sister-City of the mightiest of Capitals – in the fullness of his professional Career – in the Greenness of a healthy old age – in the radiance of Fame – and the Complacency of self-earned Riches – that a domestic Affliction would lay him in the Earth – with the meanest of Malefactors – in a Cross road with a Stake in his body – if the Verdict of Insanity did not redeem his ashes from the sentence of the Laws he had lived by inter- preting or misinterpreting, and died in violating.[18]

That Byron often contemplated suicide himself does not save Romilly from his long accumulated fury, and he goes on to recall that, 'It was not in vain that I invoked Nemesis in the Midnight of Rome from the awfullest of her Ruins.' His response to Romilly's death, with its concluding boast of the effectiveness of his curses (he had visited Rome in 1817), comes in a letter to Lady Byron which he signs off with the ominous 'Fare you well'. It could hardly fail to remind her that she had been cursed also and condemned to be her own 'proper Hell'. There is some evidence that this is what she in fact became, although certainly not because of any magical properties in her husband's thought processes. Lady Byron did not commit suicide and she lived far longer than her husband, not dying until 1860; but she spent much of her life obsessed with proving to the world that she had acted with total moral rectitude during and after the separa- tion crisis. Attacking him as much as she could through Augusta, she made sure that as many people as possible heard her side of the story. Yet his direct contact with the public through his popular writings gave him a head start which always put her at a frustrating disadvantage and is likely to have prevented her from (in the modern jargon) 'moving on'. There was a sense therefore in which her relationship with him did prove a curse, one which she could never escape and which poisoned her existence.

14

Old Friends

From the time he settled in at the villa Diodati, Byron had been expecting John Cam Hobhouse, with whom he had always intended to move on to Italy. There had been numerous delays on Hobhouse's side but he eventually appeared on 26 August, and not alone, but with another close friend of Byron's, Scrope Berdmore Davies. The newcomers were just in time to meet Shelley, who was to leave for England three days later, on the morning of the 29th. The four men spent the intervening evenings together, with Claire and Mary staying behind in the Maison Chapuis. Claire's final visit to Diodati appears to have been on the 25th, when Lewis had left and Hobhouse and Davies had not yet arrived; but while she, Mary and Shelley were packing on the 28th, Byron called to say goodbye. This was probably a collective farewell, since in the letter she wrote to him on her way back home Claire said that she would have been happier to 'have seen & kissed you once before I left'.[1]

Slightly older than Byron, Hobhouse and Scrope Davies had first met him at Cambridge and transformed his time there with their warm friendship. The political views of the three men were similar and they were all members of a Whig club which Hobhouse had founded (he had also established an 'Amiable Society' but that had to be disbanded because its members were always quarrelling). If politics united them, they were bound together even more by long evenings of drinking and whoring, and it helped that Davies shared Byron's interest in sport, being a proficient boxer and crack shot. The tone within this group of wild young men about town was one which Byron clearly found congenial, although it is now hard to recover. A hint of it perhaps lies in the story he told when in 1819 Murray complained that in the first cantos of *Don Juan* there were 'approximations to indelicacy'. The phrase reminded him, he said, of a quarrel at Cambridge between Scrope Davies and George Lamb whose mother, Lady Melbourne, had been notorious in her youth for the number of her lovers. Sir, Lamb had protested to Byron, he 'hinted at my illegitimacy', to which Davies had retorted, 'Yes, I called him a damned adulterous bastard'.[2] As this riposte might suggest, the relationship between the three friends was not always smooth sailing. Another incident Byron remembered took place at Brighton in 1808 where an 'infinitely intoxicated' Davies, after having exchanged angry words, attempted to throttle Hobhouse, who retaliated by stabbing his assailant in the arm. Covered in blood and bubbling with fury, Davies then wanted to either shoot Hobhouse or himself, the latter alternative being one that Byron said he was willing to support as long as his own pistols were not used since, in the case of suicide, they would be forfeited to the Crown. But with the dawning light, wiser counsels prevailed and a doctor was called to dress Davies's wound, so that 'the quarrel was healed as well as the wound – & we were all friends as for years before and after'.[3] The truth of these last words had been demonstrated when Hobhouse and Davies stood by their friend after his wife had left, and there were movements in society to ostracise him. They visited Byron regularly and were the ones who had accompanied him down to Dover when he left England in April, waving goodbye as his ship left the quay.

There was nothing namby-pamby about Byron's friends but at the same time there were unusual among their contemporaries of the same class and habits in placing a very high premium on intelligence, and what they admired above all was wit. This is not so obvious in Hobhouse, whose writings are humourless and who developed into something of a prig; but when he visited Coppet, Madame de Staël described him as '*fort spirituel*', and Byron thought Hobhouse could have been as witty as Davies had he possessed more self-assurance.[4] But it was the witticisms of Davies which he was later to remember so fondly. What they helped to reinforce was an inclination to view serious matters in a comic light which Byron had manifested long before he went to Cambridge. This is a tendency apparent in his letters, with their frequent references to comic situations in eighteenth-century comedies or to Falstaff, and is what helps to make them so entertaining. An anecdote he was particularly fond of concerns the Methodist preacher who saw a 'profane grin' on the face of a member of his congregation and thundered, 'No hopes for them as laughs'.[5] Byron was one of those members of the world's congregation who could not stop himself from grinning at what he considered the comedy of life. He liked Shelley a great deal and found his earnest interest in intellectual questions stimulating, but to

be once again exchanging witticisms with his old friends must have been like
sinking back into a warm bath.

For many, Byron's tendency to see weighty matters in a comic light was a
weakness and a sign of his 'flippancy'. This was certainly the opinion of Lady
Byron, who warned Augusta against her brother's 'levity & nonsense which he
likes for the worst reason, because it prevents him from reflecting seriously'.[6]
What Shelley thought of it is not apparent, but while he was in Switzerland he
wrote not only 'The Hymn to Intellectual Beauty' and 'Mont Blanc' but also two
sonnets, one of which is entitled 'To Laughter'. This begins 'Thy friends were
never mine thou heartless fiend', and, after enumerating some of the weaknesses
of laughter, Shelley then continues,

> Thou canst not bear the moon's great eye, thou fearest
> A fair child clothed in smiles – aught that is high
> Or good or beautiful. – Thy voice is dearest
> To those who mock at truth and Innocency,
> I, now alone, weep without shame to see
> How many broken hearts lie bare to thee.[7]

This poem was never published and we have no idea of the circumstances in
which it was written, but it is possible that it represents a private response to
Byron's fondness for ridicule and mockery. He was a man who loved to laugh –
better that than cry, he would say – and some of his ways of provoking laughter
certainly involved teasing or making fun of others. One of the reasons he felt so
comfortable in Augusta's company was that they could always make each other
laugh. Describing to her his Italian mistress, Teresa Guiccioli, he said that she
had 'a good deal of *us* too – I mean that turn for ridicule like Aunt Sophy and you
and I & all the B.s'.[8] Ridicule was clearly in his family background and, whatever
initial tendencies he had in that direction, they were strengthened at Cambridge
in the company of men like Hobhouse and Davies. With them, as with Byron
himself, it did not pay to be too thin-skinned. This was a discovery Polidori had
made as he tried to impress others with his literary abilities, or assert his rights
to intellectual and social equality.

In all the ribbing, joshing or ridicule in which young men characteristically
indulge there is an inevitable element of cruelty; yet whether Byron's own
laughter was predominantly or even ever 'the heartless fiend' to which Shelley
refers in his sonnet is doubtful. Certainly his fondness for it was due less to
any lack of feeling than to depression and a hopelessness about the futility of

all human endeavour. An admirer of Dr Johnson's *Vanity of Human Wishes*, he believed that 'the infinite variety of lives conduct but to death, and the infinity of wishes lead but to disappointment' (an attitude of which Shelley was severely critical).[9] With Byron therefore it was not so much a question of 'no hope for them as laughs' as 'them as laughs do so because they have no hope'. And yet to trace all his humour to that source would be false. No-one can read his letters, *Beppo*, the *Vision of Judgement* or, above all, *Don Juan* and feel that all of what is comic in them can be ascribed to some kind of compensation mechanism. Byron found much of human life absurd but he often took what can be described as an intrinsic delight in its absurdity, and there is frequently in his comedy the geniality of a man conscious enough of his own inadequacies not to be too obsessed with those of others. When he exchanged witticisms with Hobhouse and Davies, and especially the latter, he must have manifested a high degree of animal exuberance and intellectual vivacity which, depressed though he often was, found its natural outlet with these friends, but which can be felt also in his work. Byron laughed because he would rather do that than cry, but he also laughed because he enjoyed laughing.[10]

On the same day that the Shelley party left, the three friends, together with Polidori, set out for Chamonix. They stayed at St Martin as the Shelley party had done but from there, instead of hiring mules, they took two or three light carriages (*char-à-bancs*) to take them to their destination. On their way into Chamonix they stopped at the Bosson glacier since it came, as it still does, almost down to the road. With a bevy of guides, one of whom cut steps in the ice with a pickaxe, they clambered up one side of the glacier to a point at which they could walk across a broad stretch of it and then down the other side, an excursion which was 'not a little perilous, especially to Byron' according to Hobhouse.[11] On the evening of their arrival in Chamonix, they were taken to see the sources of the Arveiron, just as the Shelley party had been. The following day it might have been expected that they should climb up the Montenvers in order to view more of the *mer de glace*, but with the weather worsening they decided to head for home almost immediately so that, stopping once again at St Martin, they were back in Diodati by 1 September. All Byron had time to do on the morning of their departure was buy a few trinkets made from specimens of local rock formations which he could send back to England for the children of Augusta, and for his own Ada. The summer of 1816 had once more belied its name and the trip lived most in Byron's memory because of the crowds which, in spite of the weather, he encountered on its way. Mary had complained of '*beaucoup de monde'* and so did he, recalling that one Englishwoman asked, as she faced Mont Blanc, '"did you ever see anything more *rural?*" It was as if she were in Highgate, or Hampstead, or Brompton, or Hayes,' he expostulated. '"*Rural!*" quotha! – Rocks, pines, torrents, Glaciers, Clouds, and Summits of eternal snow far above them – "*Rural!*"'.[12] He must then have felt rather like Coleridge who, happy to have lighted after long and careful deliberation on 'majestic', for the effect on him of the waterfalls on the river Clyde, was gratified when a fellow traveller used the same word; but less pleased when the gentleman in question went on, 'Yes Sir, it is very majestic, it is sublime, & it is beautiful and it is grand & picturesque', while his female companion added, 'Aye, it is the prettiest thing I ever saw'.[13] But then both Byron and Coleridge were professionals at finding the appropriate words for their feelings, and even they cannot always be said to have succeeded.

The circumstances of the Mount Blanc trip made it disappointing but in the course of it there was an incident of some interest and significance. When Shelley had made his excursion in July, he appears to have been irritated by an entry in the visitors' book at one of the hotels in Chamonix. This was written by someone who signed himself a 'methodist' and concluded:

> when he commands us, we cannot command him, when he judges us, we cannot judge him, but when he 'Loves' us, o! assuredly, we can 'love' him. Such scenes as these, then, inspire most forcibly the love of God.[14]

The final claim here was the theme of Coleridge's 'Hymn before Sunrise', and was indeed what everybody was expected to feel in the presence of landscape so impressive. How could such splendours not strengthen one's belief in God and had not Coleridge, in his prefatory note to his poem, said, 'Who *would* be, who *could* be an Atheist in this valley of wonders?' But Shelley was very interested in astronomy and knowledge of the vastness of the universe had made him feel how limited and parochial was the context in which Christianity fashioned its Romantic adaptations of the argument from design. As 'Mont Blanc' suggests, he found the conventional response to mountains small-minded and he there-fore wrote in the visitors' book his own name followed by a declaration in Greek that he was a lover of mankind, a democrat and an atheist. When, following in Shelley's footsteps, Byron saw this entry, he discussed with his friends what it was best to do and then decided to scratch it out. He must have felt that Shelley was too young to understand fully what a red rag to the bull of English public opinion the word 'atheist' would be, and how quickly news of its offensive presence would be spread by the many male travellers in the Mont Blanc area who could read Greek. Never one to back away when it came to challenging the public himself, he now decided to do so on Shelley's behalf. This was a strange action – and one that turned out to be futile since Shelley had written similar messages in at least three other visitors' books, all of them ending in a defiant declaration of his atheism. The result was that news of the scandal did quickly get back to London and was used by various writers in attacks on both him and Byron.

Davies and Hobhouse had been to Ferney on their own before the Chamonix excursion but, after it, they contented themselves with trips into Geneva. On one of these, they visited a tennis club which had been established by a committee in which Marc-Auguste Pictet was heavily involved. It was there that Davies had what Hobhouse describes as a 'hard match' against the marker.[15] This would have been the old, indoor 'real tennis' rather than its modern version, and the marker would presumably be what in our day is called the professional. If Davies challenged him, it would be a further sign of his interest in sport, as well as of his athletic ability; but since there might well have been money involved, it would also have been an indication of how he earned his living. The two close friends of Byron from Cambridge had originally been three but the third of them, Charles Matthews, had drowned in the Cam in 1811. None of these three held a title. Byron was proud of being a lord and very quick to react if he felt his aristocratic status was being neglected, but degrees of rank played no part in the formation of his friendships. This was illustrated in Davies, the second son of a country parson who had just enough influence to secure for Scrope a scholarship at Eton. After enduring barbaric conditions there (he and Shelley would have been able to exchange interesting reflections on the material shortcomings of their former school), he made what was at that time a semi-automatic move to King's College in Cambridge and, clever as he no doubt was, soon became a Fellow. This assured him of an annual income of between £100 and £150 a year, which was far too small for his needs, especially as even in his last days at Eton he had already chosen the life of a dandy. The dandies of the Regency period were the epitome of what would now be called 'cool', managing to assert temporarily, in those parts of high society where they were accepted, the superiority of style, elegance and wit over rank and inherited wealth. But it was an expensive pose to keep up, not only in the clothing department, and on their way to Switzerland, Davies and Hobhouse had called on its most celebrated victim, George 'Beau' Brummell, who was then languishing in Calais after his debts in England had finally caught up with him. To support his own way of life, Davies took to what was in effect professional gambling. He bet regularly on his prowess as a tennis player but, much more intensively, he haunted the racecourses, taking bets for others and making multiple wagers of his own on the same horse. Above all, he spent a great deal of time in the London clubs throwing dice for high stakes in a game justifiably known as hazard. That this Fellow of King's had a good head for figures and could work out probabilities made him an efficient gambler.

Dandy as he also was, Davies more than held his own in a world of country-house parties, extravagantly expensive dining out, carriages and servants; but he knew that he walked a knife edge. Byron remembered how, on a bad losing streak in a gambling den, Davies was once entreated by friends, 'one degree less intoxicated than himself', to come home and how, when he refused, they felt they had no option but to leave him to 'the demons of the dice-box'. Calling on him the next day at two, they found him sound asleep, 'not particularly encumbered with bed-cloathes', but with a chamber pot by his bed brimful of banknotes.[16] He does not say how much was in the chamber pot but Hobhouse could recall one evening when Davies won £3700 at a single sitting.[17] Byron himself gave up gambling relatively early in his life but was always intrigued by its appeal, noting that 'women – wine – fame – the table – even Ambition – *sate* now & then – but every turn of the card – & cast of the dice – keeps the Gambler alive', before then adding, characteristically, 'besides one can Game ten times longer than one do anything else'.[18] He was intrigued also by the dandies and proud that, thanks no doubt in part to Davies, they had accepted him among their company. He reflected that on the whole he felt more at home with them than with writers, the exceptions being Walter Scott and Tom Moore, who were men of the world, and Shelley, whom Byron felt was a visionary and who therefore fell into a quite separate category.

No-one ever knew the exact state of Davies's finances, although Hobhouse claimed that you could tell when his friend Scrope – it rhymed with 'soup' – was running short because he began talking about marriage. This was always an encouraging sign, Byron would joke, because then he might at last beget 'some Scrooples'.[19] Before his trip to the Levant, Byron had persuaded Davies to guarantee a loan of nearly £5000 and he always tended to assume that his friend was worth quite a lot: somewhere between thirty and fifty thousand pounds. In 1816 he was in fact down to £5000 and needed to get back home quickly to recoup. His duties as a Fellow of King's were not onerous and he tended to stay in Cambridge only in the Autumn term when Parliament was no longer sitting and London social life had become dispersed. But if he wanted to return from Diodati to make various arrangements at King's, he would also have had in his diary certain dates in Newmarket where he was expected to appear and where he hoped to use his skill to build up his funds again. This at least was Hobhouse's explanation of why Davies felt he had to leave on 5 September, only ten days after he had arrived. Because he was going home, Byron could entrust him with the presents he had bought in Chamonix for Augusta's children and Ada, as well as with various manuscripts. He also asked him to take with him his servant Rushton, who must by this stage have been missing his family back in Nottingham. Since he was breaking up his household in preparation for his move into Italy, he might in addition have thought now of sending back his valet Fletcher, who had a wife in England. But he and Fletcher had been together for a long time and, despite periodic arguments and a good deal of roughhouse fun by Byron at his valet's expense, they had come to depend on each other. Leporello to his employer's Don Giovanni, Fletcher would follow Byron to Italy, and then to Greece, and be at his bedside when he died.

15

Polidori Does Not Suit

With the departure of the Shelley party and of Davies, Byron and Hobhouse were left on their own. But not for long. Between Davies's leaving on 5 September and their own setting out to see more mountains on the 17th, they saw or entertained a number of visitors. It was in that fortnight, for example, that Lady Jersey and her husband were in the area. One of the formidable aristocratic ladies who decided who should or (perhaps more importantly) should not be invited to the fashionable social gatherings periodically held in Almack's Assembly Rooms in London, Lady Jersey was a major arbiter of Regency fashion and it had therefore been important that she had not dropped Byron when the tide of public opinion was running against him. Now she gave the lie to Brougham's assertion that all the English in the Geneva area shunned him. Someone who did the same, and who also visited Diodati at this time, was Richard Sharp. He was thirty years older than Byron, had met Boswell and Johnson and known Fox before becoming a friend of Lord Holland, and most of the other prominent Whigs. He was particularly close to Samuel Rogers, the poet and banker more responsible than anyone else for introducing Byron to the fashionable world after the success of *Childe Harold*. Like Rogers, Sharp came from a Dissenting background and had represented the Dissenting interest in Parliament. An impressive speech he gave attacking Britain's pre-emptive strike on neutral Denmark in 1807, when Copenhagen was bombarded and there were many civilian casualties, led to his being known as 'Copenhagen' Sharp, although later his reputation as a diner-out who could talk in an informed manner on a wide variety of topics meant that 'Conversation' was substituted for 'Copenhagen'. Byron had at one point thought of going to the continent in the company of 'Conversation' Sharp but the plan had fallen through. Now that he was in

Switzerland, Sharp could visit not only Byron but also Madame de Staël, so that, having entertained him at Diodati, the two young men would see him again at Coppet, as they would also Lord and Lady Jersey.

These visitors were reminders of a world Byron had left behind, but on Saturday 14 September there were dinner guests who pointed forward to the future. Nicolas and Francis Karvellas were young Greeks, one of them already a doctor and the other studying law in Padua, and they had probably been recommended to Byron by Madame de Staël. Like so many of their contemporaries, these two brothers were preoccupied with the possibility of Greece throwing off Turkish rule and regaining her independence. As Byron rattled away with them in Italian, seeds were no doubt sown which would germinate later, especially after 1821 when the Greek war of independence had finally broken out. Although he shared the philhellenism characteristic of many classically educated Englishmen of his generation, any struggle for national liberation made a direct and uncomplicated appeal to Byron's radical sympathies. While he was in England he had been persuaded to join a Hampden club by Lady Oxford, the woman whose lover he became after he had abandoned Caroline Lamb. There were Hampden clubs all over the country and they were dedicated to bringing together the more liberal Whigs with radical reformers who were usually much less well born. But Byron was made uneasy by any push towards the ground occupied by figures such as Henry 'Orator' Hunt or William Cobbett. In his idealised view aristocrats like himself, educated in leadership, would guide the people to a more equitable way of life and he would sometimes remember with disquiet what had happened in France in 1793 when there had been a very rapid shift of power to those with no previous experience of exercising it. Contemplating the possibility of a revolution in England inspired by the more demagogic representatives of left-wing opinion, he would say, 'If we must have a tyrant – let him at least be a gentleman who has been bred to the business, and let us fall by the axe and not by the butcher's cleaver.' These were feelings which meant that his support for radical causes could sometimes be less than whole-hearted. Encouraging those anxious to throw off a foreign oppressor was a much more straightforward matter. The Italians he met at Coppet sharpened an interest in Italian independence which, when he was living in Italy, culminated in his joining the Carbonari, the revolutionary secret societies dedicated to the overthrow of foreign rule. His reception of the Karvellas brothers was part of a process which would later lead him to put his life and fortune at the disposal of the Greek insurgents. As he indicated when he gave the name 'Bolivar' to the boat he had built in Italy, here were the kind of political issues with which he was comfortable, and in relation to which he had no doubt where he stood.

Now that his days at Diodati were nearing their close, it was time for Byron to think about the make-up of his household and in particular what he should do about Polidori. It told against the young doctor that Hobhouse had arrived since, back in England, he had strongly disapproved of Byron's choice. Because Hobhouse was strangely jealous of anyone with the opportunity of getting closer to Byron than he felt he was, this disapproval might not have meant much but, in this case, Polidori had given several reasons for thinking it justified. Yet separating himself from anyone he had got to know quite well was often difficult for Byron and an indication of a profoundly conservative aspect of his temperament. There were all kinds of levels at which this trait manifested itself. His financial affairs, for example, would have been in far less disarray if he could have brought himself to sack his lawyer and engage someone who was less appallingly dilatory and self-interested. But he had known John Hanson since he was a boy and appears never to have thought seriously about breaking off such a long relationship. When he moved into rooms in Albany in 1814, the most chic of London addresses for a bachelor, friends were surprised to see that he brought with him an old crone of a charlady because she had been in his employ before and he was used to her; and then there was of course Fletcher, who was a permanent fixture despite several irritating misdemeanours. The security of employment was far greater in working for Byron than was usual in his day, and it illustrated an attachment to the familiar which is deeply characteristic of the man and which may throw at least some light on why he was so devoted to Augusta.

Although this last suggestion may seem surprising it can be pursued a little with reference to a writer who, in publishing terms, is his fairly exact contemporary but who is otherwise usually thought of as his antithesis. In Jane Austen's *Mansfield Park*, the heroine is taken from a poor household in Portsmouth to be brought up with her first cousins in all the splendours of a great household. When she reaches marriageable age, she doggedly refuses the advances of a scintillating young man from outside the family circle, not so much because she disapproves of Henry Crawford but because she is helplessly in love with her older cousin Edmund. Since she has spent so much of her early life with Edmund, his eventual recognition of her value allows a certain kind of reader to indulge in the fantasy, not so much of marrying one's first cousin (a practice remarkably common among aristocratic families of Byron's generation), but of going one better and marrying one's brother. The temperamental conservatism this suggests is also glimpsed in Jane Austen's other novels, and what is surprising about Byron sharing it is that, in so many other respects, he is the very opposite of unadventurous or timid.

Getting rid of Polidori was hard for Byron but he would have had to admit to himself that his doctor was a heap of trouble. At one point in his excursions to Geneva, for example, Polidori had discovered a brothel. This was no easy task in the city of Calvin, which was one reason why it was so favoured by English tourists; but his visit there had ended in what would not be the last of his brushes with the local police. On another occasion he became involved in a street fight after the vehicle he and a friend were driving brushed against a cart whose owner responded by cracking his whip in their direction. But the most serious incident was perhaps the one involving the magnesia. This was Byron's medicine of choice but there appears to have been some difficulty in securing sufficient amounts of the right quality. Polidori bought some from a local chemist which he suspected of being impure and he therefore invited the seller back to Diodati so that he could watch it being tested. There was then an altercation which ended when Polidori, in his own telegraphic report, 'collared him, sent him out, broke spectacles'.[2] A writ was issued and Polidori then had to engage a lawyer and appear before five judges. In the event he escaped with a bill of costs and twelve florins for the broken spectacles, but the trouble which had been caused cannot have pleased Byron. It was not of course that he was without aggression himself. 'I like a row, & always did from a boy', he once told Walter Scott;[3] and it is true that, sent off to Harrow with a club foot and at least the remnants of a Scottish accent, he had very early learned how to look after himself. When he was living in Italy he cheerfully described to friends how once, in a very crowded theatre and with a lady on his arm, he had to punch a man in the stomach in order to make some room; or how, riding in the country and jeered at by someone in a coach he had passed, he went back to give the individual involved a violent slap in the face and invite him to step out (which he wisely declined to do). Byron had a 'rapid response' approach to insult which could get him into trouble, but it was one thing to have to worry about the possible effects of his own behaviour and another to be bothered with those of his more indiscriminately hot-headed doctor. As he said to Murray, explaining why he felt obliged to let Polidori go, 'I have enough to do to manage my own scrapes'.[4]

The volatility of Polidori could be problematic in several different ways – according to Moore, he was so upset after one dispute at Diodati that only a spontaneous gesture of reconciliation from Byron prevented him from committing suicide. But another and quite different problem was that he was not much use. During his last weeks in England, Byron had been in a very poor physical state. There had always been times before when he was a heavy drinker – when he used to dine with Davies, for example, the pair of them would regularly polish off six bottles of claret in addition to all that came before and after; but in the final stages of his marriage, he drank much more heavily than usual and consumed large quantities of brandy. The effect on a digestive system already made fragile by eccentric dieting must have been catastrophic. As she headed home, Claire Clairmont warned him against taking too much wine, but in no other references to Byron while he was in Switzerland is there any allusion to his drinking too much. Even before he arrived there, while he was in Koblentz, Polidori had written: 'Lord Byron's health is much improved, his stomach returning rapidly to its natural state. Exercise and peace of mind, making great advances towards the amendment of his *corps delabré*, leave little of medicine to patch up.'[5] It seems as if the more regular and sober mode of existence he adopted in Geneva (and which Geneva encouraged), and the limitation of his social life to the Shelley party and Coppet, allowed his system to continue to recover from the excesses of the previous months and he was therefore no longer ill. This meant that a private doctor was surplus to requirements. It is true that Polidori seems to have been entrusted to keep the accounts but there are suggestions in his diary that his performance as a bookkeeper was not regarded as satisfactory. It is true also that he was meant to be Byron's companion, but that role had been quickly usurped by Shelley, and then by Hobhouse. 'Lord Byron determined upon our parting,' Polidori wrote in his diary, ' – not upon any quarrel, but on account of our not suiting.'[6] There seems to have been no acrimony in the separation and the doctor did not complain about the £70 he was given to send him on his way. Yet regret may have been mingled with the relief which Byron felt when, on 16 September, Polidori set off to visit his relations in Italy, and there is no reason to doubt the doctor's own report that Madame Brelaz, the Portuguese lady he had fallen in love with, wept to see him go. Madame de Staël had no cause to weep but she demonstrated that kind-heartedness for which Byron would always later praise her by giving Polidori three letters of introduction to influential friends or acquaintances of hers in Italy.

On the morning of the 17th Byron got up uncharacteristically early, as he would on each subsequent day of his trip, and was ready to set off by seven o'clock. Having been a little disappointed by the Mont Blanc expedition, he and Hobhouse were now heading for the mountains which lie south of Berne in what is known as the Bernese Oberland. Leaving Fletcher behind to hold the fort, Byron was accompanied by Berger while Hobhouse had with him a similar combination of servant and guide whom he had hired in England on 15 June at £60 a year. He was called Joseph Poisson, came from Fribourg in Switzerland, and spoke all the necessary languages. The transport of the party was the same kind of light carriage or char-à-banc which they had used to get from St Martin to Chamonix. This was normally hired along with a driver and was useful in rough terrain, although notoriously uncomfortable. Yet it was less the prospect of discomfort than the need for exercise which prompted Hobhouse to undertake at least the first part of the day's trip to Lausanne on foot. He and Byron had travelled together before and must have worked out protocols for dealing with the fact that, although Byron liked nothing better than exercise, his deformed foot never allowed him to walk as far, and at the same speed, as other people. Setting out two or three hours before the char-à-banc was a procedure Hobhouse followed on nearly every subsequent day of the trip. When there was a temporary pause in their travelling, or at the end of the day when it was over, he would indulge in one of his favourite pastimes and go fishing, and he and Byron did not take every meal together. There was an independence in their activities here which helped to ensure that the two travellers remained pleased with each other's company throughout the whole excursion.

Since Hobhouse would have been picked up by the char-à-banc at either Nyon or Morges, two of the stages on their journey, he and Byron arrived together in Lausanne around five in the afternoon and from there they went down to the hotel in Ouchy where Byron had previously stayed with Shelley. Byron then ate alone while Hobhouse went back to Lausanne in order to dine with a wealthy Englishman called Okeden whom he had seen five days before at Coppet and to whom he had promised a copy of his book on the hundred days. A fellow diner from Lausanne who was also at the dinner relayed a number of anecdotes about Gibbon and insisted that there was still a 'very chosen society' in the town, although he admitted that 'the English character' had fallen 'since the peace'. What he presumably referred to by 'the English character' were those English who had chosen to live in Lausanne after 1815. Byron was of course also invited to this gathering but, maintaining the relatively anti-social stance he had adopted since his arrival in Switzerland, he chose to stay behind.

The next day Hobhouse rose early and set off on foot at six o'clock. After three hours he was picked up by Byron in the carriage so that by ten they were both in the 'beautiful market place' of Vevey,[7] the large open space which slopes gently down to the lake and which would still be beautiful now, were it not for the car-park in its centre. Vevey was a town Byron had of course already seen and been impressed by, but on his visit there with Shelley in June neither of them appears to have bothered with St Martin's church, which stands well above the market place, slightly to the east, and which contains memorials to two Englishmen of the seventeenth century, Edmund Ludlow and Andrew Broughton. They were both members of the court which sentenced Charles I to death, Broughton being the court's clerk and therefore the one who had to read out the eventual judgement. After the Restoration, they were members of a small group of regicides who fled the country and found refuge in the canton de Vaud. If Vevey was small and obscure in 1816, it must have been even more so a hundred and fifty years before, but it was safer than Lausanne, where one of their fellow regicides was assassinated by agents from England. Ludlow lived there for over thirty years before his death, and Broughton almost as long. Contemplating their memorials in St Martin's, Hobhouse improvised a few verses:

> It is not cowardice to fly
> From tyranny's triumphant face
> It is not banishment to die
> An exile only from disgrace.[8]

These are sentiments Byron would have echoed. Anti-monarchical in general, his contempt for the British ruling family had been strengthened when the Prince of Wales, who had formerly been friendly to the Whigs, failed to bring them into government after he became Prince Regent. Byron had little time for the House of Hanover and does not appear to have felt that the disappearance of these comparative recent arrivals in England would compromise his own status as a member of an aristocratic family which claimed to be able to trace back its origins to the Norman Conquest.

After Hobhouse and Byron had eaten breakfast in Vevey, there was a confusion which meant that their carriages and servants set off without them and Hobhouse had to run quite a way along the road to bring them to a halt. They then made their way to Clarens and the same house in which Byron and Shelley had stayed previously. In Clarens itself, Hobhouse was suitably impressed: 'Rousseau did well to fix on this spot for his Julie';[9] and he was impressed also when Byron took him on to Chillon and they saw again Bonnivard's dungeon and the execution rail. But the guide this time was drunk and he was also deaf, so that (Byron reports) 'thinking everyone else so – [he] roared out the legends of the Castle so fearfully that H got out of humour'.[10] Back in Clarens for a light dinner, the two travellers then walked up to the nearby château de Châtelard which (like Chillon) is more what the English think of as a castle and stands on a very steep little hill just behind the town. It was here that Byron and Shelley had previously picked roses, but now the flowers were gone 'with their summer'[11] and the château had been rented out to a certain Lady Mary Ross and her family. Looking out over the lake from the terrace of this impressive structure and seeing, as they made their way down from it, the spot where the 'bosquet de Julie' had been destroyed by the monks, Hobhouse noted that 'no romance has ever received such a complete local habitation' as Rousseau's had.[12] He and Byron had been able to visit the château, despite the temporary absence of its tenant, and they had been shown a painting in the drawing room which was supposed to represent Julie. It is clear that they were also taken to a turret room in one of the château's towers, since a tourist who made the same visit only a week later – although this time while Lady Mary Ross was present – recorded that both Byron and Hobhouse had followed what must have been the custom and written down their names there. Because a turret room in a castle would be a strange place to keep a visitors' book, one has to assume that the names were written or carved on the ancient walls and that therefore the name of Byron, still visible on one of the pillars of Bonnivard's dungeon in Chillon, may well be authentic after all.[13]

16

The Jungfrau

Vevey, Clarens and Chillon were familiar to Byron from his previous boat trip with Shelley, but on Thursday 19 September he and Hobhouse set out for what was new territory for them both. They were using a well-known guide book for travellers in Switzerland by Johann Gottfried Ebel, a French translation of which Hobhouse had acquired before he left England. The route they followed roughly corresponds to what is tour number 33 in Ebel and they both gave day-to-day accounts of it, Hobhouse in his diary and Byron in a long letter he wrote to Augusta in diary form. Sending Joseph and the char-à-banc on the easier road which passes through Bulle to the lake of Thun, they themselves (accompanied by Berger and a local guide) tackled the mountainous country behind Montreux on horseback, climbing steeply through the villages of Chernex and Les Avants until they reached what is known as the col de Jarman. Byron was surprised there by just how high in the mountains there was pasture for cattle. He was enchanted by the constant noise of cow bells with which he was then surrounded, and by the sounds of the shepherds (as he describes them) calling to each other on the crags above, or playing their pipes. It was an idyllic scene, which realised perfectly all he had ever heard or seen of what he called 'a pastoral existence', and which also chimed in conveniently with the contemporary image of Switzerland as not only a country full of high mountains where visitors could find their better selves or communicate with higher powers, but also one made up of small peasant communities that were hardy, austere, republican, and uncorrupted by modern life.[1]

The col they had reached lies just below the 'Dent de Jarman' and the two travellers began climbing this massive rocky projection so that they could enjoy the splendid view back to the lake and all the surrounding countryside

(Hobhouse made it to the top but Byron had to stop twenty yards below). Scrambling down again to recover their horses, they pressed on to the village of Montboven where they met the main road from Bulle and stayed the night. Blessed with fine weather, they continued on their way through Chateau d'Oex and Zweisimmen until, on 21 September, they arrived in Thun. From their inn there they were able to walk along the right bank of the river Aare to visit the château de Schadau. The present building dates from the middle of the nineteenth century but its predecessor must have been similarly impressive, since this visit had been warmly recommended to them by that seasoned traveller, 'Conversation' Sharp. Particularly striking is the site of the château, just at the point where the Aare enters the lake. Nothing could be more picturesque, a term which applies equally to the lake of Thun as a whole, as Byron and Hobhouse must have discovered when, the next day, they were rowed all the way down it to what is now a part of Interlaken (the horses and carriage were taken by their servants round the water so that they would be there when they disembarked). The journey took three hours and Byron was surprised to discover that those who did the rowing were female. Already from the boat they had been able to see facing them the mountain chain which is dominated by the Jungfrau, but once landed they headed for the Lauterbrunnen valley so that they could inspect this landscape at close quarters. The inn at Lauterbrunnen was full but they were happy to lodge at the house of the local pastor, especially as it was directly opposite the huge Staubbach waterfall. Nine hundred feet high, this dominates the village and Byron said of the great curve of the waterfall, as it thundered down in front of his lodging, that it was like 'the *tail* of a white horse streaming in the wind – such as it might be conceived would be that of the *"pale* horse" on which *Death* is mounted in the Apocalypse'.[2] The idea of a horse's tail might have come to him from the way the force of the water at the top of the cliff projects out into a slight upward curve before falling down. What then perhaps made him associate this equine feature with paintings he had seen of the white horse of the Apocalypse was the manner in which, as it falls, the water vaporises and can therefore begin to look ethereal. From the Staubbach, he and Hobhouse rode further down the valley to view the spot where three separate waterfalls, fed from the Eiger and the Jungfrau, could be observed. As they watched but also listened to this irresistible mass of water crashing down, a storm broke out with thunder, lightning and hail – 'all in perfection – and beautiful' Byron reported to Augusta. This was the epitome of what in the late eighteenth century was called the sublime ('All which expands the spirit, and yet appals', as he had put it in *Childe Harold* III[3]), and he was overwhelmed by what he saw, calling it 'wonderful – & indescribable'.[4]

Byron was so impressed by the scenery in and around Lauterbrunnen that he decided to set the rest of *Manfred* in this mountainous region. As a result, many of the phrases which he uses when describing his trip to Augusta, including the one that compares the waterfall to the tail of a white horse, pass directly into his poem. He had begun with echoes of Goethe's *Faust* but, as *Manfred* developed, its protagonist became an increasingly recognisable Byronic hero, endowed with magical powers perhaps but also haunted by the memory of inexpiable crimes committed in the past, conscious of being old before his time and, above all, utterly weary of both the world and himself. Disgust with self and the world is in Manfred so extreme that he wants to commit suicide and in the second scene of the first act, which is set on 'the Mountain of the Jungfrau',[5] he is standing on a cliff about to throw himself off. It is a chamois hunter who drags him back from the edge, Shelley having garnered during his trip to Chamonix a good deal of information about hunting the chamois which he may have passed on to Byron. Later in the action, insofar as this somewhat static 'dramatic poem' could be said to have such a thing, a venal Abbot offers to undertake Manfred's spiritual regeneration if he will become truly penitent and give all his lands to the monastery. In reply, Manfred calls up the demon Ashtaroth and instructs him to take the Abbot to spend the night on the top of the Schreckhorn (a mountain in the Jungfrau range whose name particularly struck Byron). 'Let him gaze and know / He ne'er again will be so near to Heaven' he says,[6] whereupon Ashtaroth spirits the Abbot off with a song about worldly monks and pregnant nuns. There is an anti-Catholicism here similar to that in Byron's note about the monks who destroyed Julie's bower, but he later revised *Manfred* and made the Abbot a much more reasonable and decent figure, although one no less ineffectual in preventing the hero's death at the end of the poem.

Ashtaroth is a spirit who is called up by Manfred but there are many others who appear spontaneously. The third scene of the second act, for example, which also takes place on 'the summit of the Jungfrau Mountain', is a festival in which various supernatural agencies congratulate themselves – much like the witches in *Macbeth* – on the misery they have caused; and in the following scene they congregate together in the 'Hall of Arimanes', the Zoroastrian spirit of evil. What characterises Manfred when he appears among them is his refusal to be intimidated: told to kneel in front of Arimanes he says he will do so only if they all also kneel to the 'overruling Infinite' above.[7] In his dealings with the

spirit world, he displays a defiant pride much like that of Prometheus or Milton's
Satan, and indeed much like that of Byron himself who, very hard on his own
failings, contested the right of any but his closest associates to be hard on them
also, and was not a man (as his behaviour during the separation crisis showed)
to allow any guilt he might feel for past actions to undermine his strength to
resist challenges from outside. At the end of *Manfred*, when a spirit appears in
order to take the hero away (as the spirit of the Commandatore appears at the
end of *Don Giovanni*), he repels it, determined to retain control over his own
dying. Insofar therefore as the poem is a psychodrama, it tracks the defiance of
the hero in his struggle to dominate the phantoms, many of which he himself
has conjured up.

Manfred is presented by Byron as a completely isolated individual, alienated
from society. The only person he has felt close to in the past is the Lady Astarte,
whom he feels he had gravely injured and who is now dead: 'my embrace was
fatal', he confesses.[8] Many readers identified Astarte with Augusta and in 1817 one
English reviewer of the poem, asking why we should feel sorry for Manfred in his
isolation, said that it was only because he was guilty of 'one of the most revolting
of crimes. He has committed incest'. The reviewer then added, sensationally
enough, 'Lord Byron has coloured *Manfred* into his own personal features'.[9] Few
others were so blunt in public, whatever they might have felt in private; yet there
is considerable evidence that Byron did have Augusta chiefly in mind when he
created Astarte. In the second scene of Act 2, for example, where Manfred is
recalling a past without the usual human ties, he says there was nevertheless one,

> like me in lineaments – her eyes,
> Her hair, her features, all, to the very tone
> Even of her voice, they said were like to mine;
> But soften'd all, and temper'd into beauty ...[10]

It is of this person that he then asserts, 'I loved her, and destroy'd her'. In the
third scene of Act 3, the servant Manuel says that the Lady Astarte was the sole
companion of Manfred's wanderings and adds that she was 'the only thing he
seem'd to love – / As he, indeed, by blood was bound to'.[11] There are other hints
like these but, if Byron was indeed thinking of Augusta when he conceived
Astarte, then there is a special poignancy in the episode in 2.iv when Manfred
insists on the spirits calling up Astarte and then, while admitting that it was 'the
deadliest sin to love as we have loved',[12] asks her either to forgive or condemn
him. But the ghost of Astarte gives no direct reply. Manfred is not of course

identical with Byron, yet it is hard not to think here of the way the latter was bombarding his sister with fervent expressions of warm feeling at this time and getting very little in return. 'Love me as you are beloved by me',[13] he was to end the journal-letter describing his trip, and a fortnight before he had written:

> What a fool I was to marry – and *you* not very wise – my dear – we might have lived so single and so happy – as old maids and bachelors; I shall never find any one like you – nor you (vain as it may seem) like me. We are just formed to pass our lives together, and therefore – we – at least – I – am by a crowd of circumstances removed from the only being who could ever have loved me, or whom I can unmixedly feel attached to.[14]

These words occur in letters which by this time Augusta was passing on to Lady Byron, who welcomed them as further confirmation of what had initially been only suspicions. Perhaps also they excited in her a degree of jealous resentment which made the tormenting of the woman to whom they were addressed appear all the more necessary.

By no means all the details of mountain landscape which appear in Byron's *Manfred* can be associated with the hours he spent in the Lauterbrunnen valley, impressive though he found it. On the day after their night there, Hobhouse set out for the Alpine village of Grindelwald on foot, with Byron following an hour or so later on horseback, but with an extra horse for his friend. They were rejecting Ebel's alternative of an easy road via the valley and opting instead for a route through the mountains which would take them six, seven and even, on one occasion, eight thousand feet high. By mid-morning they had reached the Kleine Scheidegg, a mountain pass where they had clear views of the north face of the Eiger and the Jungfrau. By half past eleven they tethered their horses and allowed them to drink in a mountain pool while they themselves spent fifty minutes clambering to the top of a nearby summit (believed now to be the Lauberhorn[15]). From there the views were even more magnificent: the slope they had climbed up was relatively gradual but opposite there was a 'vast precipice' with, Byron says, a 'boiling sea of cloud, dashing against the crags on which we stood'.[16] ('The mists boil up around the glaciers; clouds / Rise curling fast beneath me' says Manfred as he contemplates suicide in 1.ii.[17]). While they were on the Lauberhorn, both Byron and Hobhouse wrote their names on 'a bit of paper which we hid under a small stone near a blue flower'.[18] This was a strange gesture given the fragility of the medium, but one that seems to indicate an inclination to record their presence strong enough to suggest that the carving of

Byron's name on Bonnivard's pillar in Chillon may not be the forgery it is usually taken to be. On their way down from the mountain, an exuberant Byron pelted Hobhouse with snowballs. The rest of the journey to Grindelwald took three hours, with the noise of avalanches ringing in their ears and the sight all around of what Byron describes as '*whole woods of withered pines – all withered –* trunks stripped and barkless'. They reminded him, he says, 'of me & my family'.[19]

After a night in Grindelwald, the two travellers set off on 24 September towards Meiringen on a rough track still closed today to ordinary motorised traffic (although they do not say so, their char-à-banc had presumably again been sent on by the longer and easier route). On the way they were able to view the glacier at Rosenlaui which Hobhouse thought more impressive than Bosson, the one glacier in Chamonix which the weather had allowed them to walk on (Byron disagreed), and the Reichenbach falls, which at that time of course were without the literary associations they were later to acquire. After Meiringen, they were soon back on the flat and making for Brienz, the town which gives its name to the lake that would be a continuation of the lake of Thun were it not for the isthmus on which Interlaken stands. As they approached Brienz, it began to rain, so that they arrived wet through but not discouraged because, according to Byron's calculations, they had only had four hours of rain in eight days. Somewhere on their way out of the mountains, if it was not on their way into them, they had a brief encounter with a former acquaintance. When he was dismissed by Byron, Polidori had decided that he would save money by walking into Italy. Lonely, severely depressed and footsore, he met up with two Englishmen in a char-à-banc and on 21 September agreed to travel with them. It was in the next couple of days that his party crossed Byron's. 'We saluted' is all Polidori says, but neither Hobhouse nor Byron makes any mention of this chance meeting.[20]

By the time they were at Brienz, Byron and Hobhouse were on their return journey, although at Thun, instead of retracing their steps further, they made their way home via Berne, Fribourg and then Iverdon. Somewhere between Berne and Fribourg Byron bought a dog, a very ugly one with no tail according his own description, and '*très méchant*' according to the seller's.[21] He justified the purchase by saying that he needed a dog to 'watch the carriage' (presumably because it was carrying his luggage), but it is a fact that, like many other people who find human beings disappointing, he was inordinately fond of animals. In the epitaph he had written for a favourite dog which died at Newstead from rabies in 1808, he had contrasted the tributes paid to a dead human being ('Who knows thee well must quit thee with disgust, / Degraded mass of animated dust!') with the silence which usually greets an animal's disappearance; and he ended his 'Inscription on the Monument of a Newfoundland Dog' with, 'To mark a friend's remains these stones arise, / I never knew but one, and here he lies'.[22] Hobhouse, who must have asked himself what kind of friend of Byron this made him, quipped that the last phrase ought to read, 'here *I* lies',[23] but then he had little sympathy with the more plangent, melancholic or depressive aspects of Byron's character. Writing to Augusta on 8 September, Byron had said 'the Separation – has broken my heart – I feel as if an Elephant had trodden on it'; and ten days later, responding to what seem to have been some complimentary phrases from Augusta about his wife, he asked her to remember what Lady Byron had done to him and added, 'I do not think a human being could endure more mental torture than that woman has directly & indirectly inflicted on me'. Yet referring to his low spirits, he had asked Augusta to say nothing about them to Hobhouse, since 'I wish to wear as quiet an appearance with him as possible'.[24] In his *London Journal*, Boswell describes how one of his friends wondered how he could complain of being miserable when he seemed always to have such a 'flow of spirits', and he then reflected, 'Melancholy cannot be clearly proved to others, so it is better to be silent about it'.[25] As far as his relations with Hobhouse were concerned, Byron must have come to a similar conclusion. It was because he knew that there were whole sides of his nature with which his friend had no patience that he did not show him his 'Stanzas to Augusta'. That this was a reasonable decision became evident when Hobhouse saw the poem in print and wrote a parodic commentary on it which began:

> Dear Byron this humbug give over;
> Never talk of decay or decline,
> No mortal alive can discover
> The cause of so causeless a whine…[26]

Clearly, as far as misery was concerned, Hobhouse was of the 'cheer up', 'snap out of it' or 'things are never as bad as they seem' school.

On 28 September the travellers left Iverdun at nine in the morning but then waited for a few hours in the village of Cossonay so that Berger could see some of his relatives. Unlike Joseph Poisson, Berger was, it turns out, a native of the pays de Vaud, and he told Hobhouse that the Vaudois would have been willing to fight if in 1814, at the Congress of Vienna, they had been returned to where they were before the French Revolution and subjected once again to the government

of Berne. (The way in which the Vaudois had been freed from Bernese control
by the invasion of Switzerland by French troops in 1798 could be regarded as an
exemplification of Shelley's claim that, although Napoleon had outraged democracy, he was also its representative.) By early evening they were all in Aubonne,
at an inn from the terrace of which, Byron and Hobhouse agreed, there was the
best of all possible views of Lake Geneva. They were lucky to have rooms there
since a German princess, who had almost prevented them from finding decent
accommodation in Iverdun, had moved with her suite to Aubonne at the same
time as they did. The result was that an English family called the Clintons, whom
they had come across several time on their trip, and who arrived later than them
at the Aubonne inn, were turned away. All this suggests that they were by no
means the only ones following Ebel's tours and, indeed, on that summit between
Lauterbrunnen and Grindelwald where they wrote their names on paper, they
were just congratulating themselves on how many fewer tourists there were in
those mountains than in the Chamonix area when their solitude was interrupted
by the approach of three women on horseback. Yet in general the presence of
quite a few fellow travellers does not seem to have bothered them much. The
great difference from the Chamonix trip, and a major reason why Byron would
later say that he had found the Alps in Switzerland more impressive than those
in Savoy, was that, on the whole, the weather had held up. After so much rain and
cold the weather gods had finally relented and given them almost a fortnight of
more or less fine days.

All in all, therefore, the trip to the Bernese Oberland had been highly
successful, as Byron acknowledged at the end of his diary-letter to Augusta:

> In the weather for this tour (of 13 days) I have been very fortunate – fortunate in
> a companion (Mr. H[obhous]e) fortunate in our prospects – and exempt from
> even the little petty accidents & delays which often render journeys in a less wild
> country – disappointing. – I was disposed to be pleased – I am a lover of Nature
> – and an Admirer of Beauty – I can bear fatigue – and welcome privation – and
> have seen some of the noblest views in the world.

These are the words of a happy and satisfied traveller; yet Byron immediately
continued,

> But in all this – the recollections of bitterness – & more especially of recent & more
> home desolation – which must accompany me through life – have preyed upon
> me here – and neither the music of the Shepherd – the crashing of the Avalanche
> – nor the torrent – the mountain – the Glacier – the Forest – nor the Cloud – have

for one moment – lightened the weight upon my heart – nor enabled me to lose my own wretched identity in the majesty & the power and the Glory – around – above – & beneath me.[27]

By the time Byron wrote this letter, his stay in Switzerland was well nigh over – back at Diodati on 28 September, there was just time for a farewell dinner at Coppet with Madame de Staël before he and Hobhouse left for Italy on 5 October. What his words indicate is the failure of what might be called a reconstitution of the self. He had arrived in Geneva disgusted with the London society which had rejected him and without any defined role or purpose in life. A social circle reduced to a few intimates, and the consolations to be found in the natural world, constituted his recipe for re-establishing his equilibrium. In his 'Epistle to Augusta' he had talked of 'Alpine landscapes' which 'create / A fund for contemplation', and said that to be lonely amongst them was not to be desolate. Nature had after all been, he had reminded Augusta, 'my early friend – and now shall be / My Sister – till I look on thee again.'[28] It is quite true that, unlike Gibbon or Madame de Staël, Byron had always enjoyed and appreciated the natural world in its wilder aspects, and one of his earliest poems was a celebration of a Scottish mountain ('Lachin Y Gair'), which he had known as a boy.[29] But through Shelley he had been introduced to that closer relationship with landscape so often evoked in the poetry of Wordsworth. This was the one in which, in the well known words of 'Tintern Abbey', even the memory of much-loved scenes induces

> that serene and blessed mood,
> In which the affections gently lead us on, –
> Until the breath of this corporeal frame
> And even the motion of our human blood
> Almost suspended, we are laid asleep
> In body, and become a living soul.[30]

There was a degree of consoling intimacy which Byron was seeking in his visit to the Swiss Alps and which he clearly did not find. In his notes to canto 3 of *Childe Harold*, he talks of the atmosphere surrounding Clarens, and other sites associated with Rousseau's *Julie*, and says that the spirit of love, that 'great principle of the universe', was so powerfully evident there that 'knowing ourselves a part we lose our individuality, and mingle in the beauty of the whole'.[31] Yet if he did momentarily lose his individuality on the trip round the lake, he very soon recovered it. In 1806, after a visit to Chamonix and the *mer de glace*,

Chateaubriand had launched a vigorous attack on his contemporaries' interest in mountains. Citing the passage from *Julie* which is quoted in the first chapter of this book, the one in which St Preux claims that the higher one climbs, the more one seems to leave behind base and earthly sentiments, Chateaubriand commented that unfortunately man's soul was independent of geography and 'a heart full of grief is no less heavy in the high places than in the valleys'.[32] Byron similarly found that, even in the Bernese Oberland, there was no possibility of escaping from what he calls, in his letter to Augusta, his 'wretched identity'.

Something of this state of affairs is reflected in *Manfred*. This was a work which became both popular and influential, especially in Europe. Its central figure clearly caught the European imagination, with his alienation from the social world and his intense *Weltschmerz*. Tortured by remorse though he may be, he has at the same time a feeling, which seems to have resonated with many readers, that the world in which he finds himself is wholly inadequate to his own powers and aspirations. Much of the drama is made up of the protagonist's speeches but their context was also important for the impact it made. Byron wisely insisted that *Manfred* was not suitable for stage performance, and it is true that most of what he writes calls rather to be declaimed than spoken, and that there is very little dramatic interaction, the chamois hunter, the Abbot (in both his manifestations), and Manfred's servants all being characters with very little definition. And yet the numerous spirits which continually appear might well be called dramatic, or at least theatrical, reminiscent of the pantomimic effects in the Gothic melodramas which Byron must have seen when he was associated with the theatre in Drury Lane. And the same might be said of the drama's setting. This had certainly been provided by his trip to the Jungfrau and yet it is theatrical in the sense that precipitous cliffs or cow bells have so little influence on the psychology of the central figure that the action might just as well have taken place on Salisbury Plain. In spite of its abstraction, Shelley's 'Mont Blanc' does demonstrate interaction with a mountainous landscape whereas, in *Manfred*, it is never anything more than a backdrop and offers no alleviation for the miseries of its hero. His letter to Augusta clearly shows that it provided none for Byron either. Much as he had enjoyed his trip with Hobhouse, its effect was to make him realise how little Nature could help him to recover from his misfortunes and that he was stuck with working through his misery on his own. At one point in *Manfred* the hero says, 'I have pray'd / For madness as a blessing – 'tis denied me'.[33] Similarly denied that drastic remedy for his acute unhappiness, Byron had to wait for a new *human* environment which would eventually allow it to moderate, if not entirely fade away. The four months he had spent in Switzerland were very important for his poetic development, and also for his friendships, but they had not allowed him to forget the pain and humiliation of the separation from his wife, or to decide what he now ought to do with his life.

Afterwords

1

Lewis, de Staël and 'Poor Polidori'

After Byron's stay in Switzerland, several members in the supporting cast of the story of his life there did not fare too well. Matthew Lewis, for example, spent a year on the continent after leaving Diodati, visiting Rome, Florence and Naples (where he had a married sister), and in July 1817 again calling in on Byron, who by then was established in Venice. But Lewis was back in England in October of that year worrying about his slaves and in November he sailed again for Jamaica. His main aim on this trip was to institute further humanitarian reforms on a second plantation which he had previously only partly owned but to which he had now acquired the rights to do with as he pleased. It was on the road back from this second plantation that he stayed in an inn in which a couple of residents had recently died of yellow fever. Lewis took the ship back home in May 1818 but the fever declared itself while he was on board and he died in mid-ocean at the age of forty-two. While he was in Italy he had engaged a valet called Falcieri, a sturdily built Venetian with an imposing black beard who, according to Shelley's later report, had 'stabbed two or three people' but was nonetheless 'the most goodnatured … fellow'.[1] After Lewis's death, Falcieri – or Tita as he was known – made his way back to Italy, where he was taken on by Byron and became one of his most trusted servants. It was Tita who, along with Fletcher, was with Byron when he died in Greece.

By the time of Lewis's death, his old antagonist, Madame de Staël, had been gone almost a year. The summer of 1816 proved to be her last season at Coppet and in October she moved to Paris, disturbed to find the city still crawling with foreign troops. She began to exert herself in her usual way, seeing all the people that mattered and trying to persuade them that since the Allies' quarrel was not with France but Bonaparte, it would make sense to liberate the capital as soon as possible. So active was she that her old friend the Duke of Wellington found himself forced to warn her to be more discreet. Discretion was, however, quickly forced on her by failing health. She found it hard to sleep and, hyperactive as she was, complained that insomnia made life too long since one day could never hold enough interest for a full twenty-four hours. It was on the staircase leading to the door of the Minister of the Interior that she had her first major collapse. Taken home, she quickly became bed-ridden and gangrenous splotches began to appear on her skin. Madame de Staël died on 14 July 1817 at the age of fifty-one, attended by old friends like Chateaubriand and Madame Récamier, and surrounded by her family. Her young husband Rocca was also there, but he was tubercular and would survive his wife by only a few months.

Byron was distressed to learn that de Staël had died. On 12 August 1817 he wrote to Murray: 'I have been very sorry to hear of the death of Me. de Staël – not only because she had been very kind to me at Coppet – but because now I can never requite her. – In a general point of view she will leave a great gap in society & literature.'² His subsequent references to de Staël convey the same appreciation, often expressed in warmer terms. But that warmth did not prevent Byron from having some mild fun at her expense. Her secret marriage was known to him by the time he saw her at Coppet but he may only have discovered later that in 1812, when she was forty-six, she had given birth to Rocca's child. Byron alludes to this event in some comic doggerel which he included in a letter to Murray written only nine days after his expression of regret at de Staël's death. The premises in Albermarle Street where Murray carried on his business were a meeting place for a number of prominent writers, journalists and politicians. They came there to exchange news and views, or to give advice on various manuscripts he had received (Byron referred to them as the 'synod', or Murray's 'parlour boarders'). In the doggerel he sent to his publisher on 21 August, he suggests that these people might just then be 'in discussion / On poor De Staël's late dissolution', and goes on to imagine what the topics of their discussion would be:

> 'Tis said she certainly was married
> To Rocca – & had twice miscarried,
> No – not miscarried – I opine –
> But brought to bed at forty-nine, …

The factual error in the last line here can be blamed on the need to find a rhyme for 'opine', but as Byron continues it is clear that he is in any case mimicking the idle and inaccurate gossip of the time (a 'hum' is Regency slang for a false rumour):

> Some say she died a Papist – Some
> Are of opinion *that's* a Hum –
> I don't know that – the fellow Schlegel
> Was very likely to inveigle
> A dying person in compunction
> To try the extremity of Unction.[3]

These lines make it evident enough that the recently dead were always likely to be as fair game for Byron as the living, but his regard for Madame de Staël was genuine and he never forgot the kindness she had shown him.

The references to de Staël in the verses Byron wrote for his publisher are incidental. Their main topic was Polidori, who had recently sent one of his poetic dramas to Murray in the hope that he would publish it. Not wanting to do so, Murray had asked Byron how best to manage the rejection, which is why the verses begin,

> Dear Doctor – I have read your play
> Which is a good one in it's way
> Purges the eyes & moves the bowels
> And drenches handkerchiefs like towels …[4]

The fact that Polidori had sent his play to Murray was a sign that he was still hovering between medicine and literature. He had arrived in Milan in September 1816, weary and depressed, but the abbé de Brême, whom he had known in Coppet, took him up and introduced him to the best society. Polidori thus found himself again associating on easy terms with Hobhouse and Byron, once these two had arrived in Milan, and he began to enjoy himself until he became involved in yet another 'scrape'. Finding himself behind an Austrian officer with a large hat in La Scala, he asked for the hat to be removed. There was an altercation and in no time at all he found himself arrested. Byron and Hobhouse were also at the opera that night and, hearing of the arrest, hurried down from de Brême's box to see what they could do. By establishing his own identity, Byron was able to procure Polidori's immediate release, but that did not prevent the young doctor from being told later that he would have to leave what was at this period Austrian-controlled territory within twenty-four hours.

After Milan, Polidori went to stay with an uncle for a while but he then moved on to Pisa where he studied under Andrea Vaccà Berlinghieri, an old school friend of his father's but also a distinguished surgeon with an international reputation (he was the doctor Byron would rely on for medical advice when he moved to Pisa). Polidori kept a journal of Vaccà's methods which he hoped to have published in England, but his main aim seems to have been to use the letters of introduction he had been given by Madame de Staël in order to find a position similar to the one he had held with Byron. One of these letters was to Lady Westmoreland, the mother of Lady Jersey, but although nothing very tangible came of that he was, while still in Pisa, called to the sickbeds of Lord Guilford, the senior member of the influential North family; of Francis Horner, journalist and parliamentarian; and of a child of the writer Thomas Hope (whom he had met on his trip to Chamonix). It nourished one of Byron's running jokes about Polidori that all these three patients died ('The Doctor Polidori ... has no more patients – because his patients are no more'[5]), but by the Norths, at least, he was not blamed and they engaged him to accompany the corpse of their relative back to England. Byron was intrigued to learn that what he calls the carcass of the deceased travelled separately from the internal organs. 'Conceive a man going one way, and his intestines another and his immortal soul a third!', he commented, 'Was there ever such a distribution?'[6]

While he was still in Italy, Polidori had joined a scheme to practise medicine among the settlers in Brazil and asked Byron whether he could smooth the way with the Portuguese authorities. Having so recently dispensed with his former doctor's services, Byron had a difficult letter to write to Murray, but he attributed Polidori's faults to 'a pardonable vanity & youth' and he went on,

> I know no great harm of him – & some good – he is clever – & accomplished – knows his profession by all accounts well – and is honourable in his dealings – & not at all malevolent – I think with luck he will turn out a useful member of society (from which he will lop the diseased members) & the college of Physicians. – If you can be of any use of him – or know anyone who can – pray be so – as he has his fortune to make.[7]

Byron sent his request to Murray because he was a person who, through his 'synod', had high-level contacts in London's political and diplomatic world. Anyone who has ever had to write a reference for someone in whom their confidence was not complete will appreciate the skill and even generosity of what he wrote. But his efforts were in vain because, back in England by the summer of 1817, Polidori decided against Brazil and chose instead to go to Norwich, where he had spent some time after graduating, to try to establish a practice there. His success was only moderate, perhaps because, as his sending his play to Murray in August 1817 suggests, he was not wholly committed to doctoring. By the following year he was back in London and in April 1819 his literary career began with *The Vampyre*. Whether or not he had any part in the attribution of that story to his former employer, its appearance under Byron's name damaged Polidori's literary reputation even before he began to have one. *Ernestus Berchtold* failed and he had no more success when the poetic drama he had offered to Murray was finally published by someone else, or with his collected poems and an ambitious religious work entitled *The Fall of Angels*. A failed doctor and an unsuccessful writer, Polidori's tendency to depression may have been exacerbated by a serious head injury he sustained in a driving accident in Norwich although, after his death, the chief talk was of the heavy gambling debts he had incurred. Whatever the precipitating circumstances, when, around midday on 24 August 1821, a maid went to open the shutters of the room in his father's house which Polidori then occupied, she found him in a desperate state and, although medical assistance was called, he died very shortly afterwards.

The coroner's verdict was that Polidori had died of natural causes, although it was widely assumed afterwards that he had committed suicide by swallowing prussic acid, a highly toxic liquid made chiefly from bitter almonds. When Byron heard the news of his death he said to Shelley's cousin, Thomas Medwin, that 'poor Polidori' was 'always talking of prussic acid, oil of amber, blowing into veins, suffocating by charcoal, and compounding poisons'.[8] The vial of poison he himself kept close by for emergencies had no doubt been procured by Polidori and was almost certainly prussic acid also. In 1822 Shelley asked a friend to find him a small quantity of 'Prussic acid, or essential oil of bitter almonds' because, although he had no intention of committing suicide at present, it would comfort him to own 'this golden key to the chamber of perpetual rest'.[9] Prussic acid is a very fast-acting poison but in minute doses it can be useful as a sedative and it may be therefore, since Polidori did not die especially quickly, that he had not meant to kill himself (or even that prussic acid was not involved at all). A few weeks before his twenty-sixth birthday he was nonetheless dead, and then buried in old St Pancras churchyard, where Mary Wollstonecraft's tombstone could be found and where her daughter had first declared her love for Shelley.

2

The Shelley Party and Allegra

After the Shelley party had arrived back in England, the two men continued to write to each other and Claire also tried to correspond with Byron; but her several heart-rending letters, begging him to keep the promise she claimed he had made to communicate with her, received no reply. She was taken by Mary and Shelley to Bath to await the birth of her child, and established in a boarding house there, away from any of her previous contacts in London (that she was pregnant was successfully hidden from her parents). Her baby was born on 12 January 1817 and initially called Alba, in allusion to Byron's nickname. At his request this was later changed to Allegra. Claire clearly hoped that Allegra would alter Byron's attitude to her, but that never happened. She was thus entirely dependent for moral as well as financial support on Shelley, who quickly had many other matters to preoccupy him. In December 1816, for example, his deserted wife, Harriet, drowned herself in the Serpentine. He spent many subsequent months trying to recover from Harriet's family the two children he had had with her and, in order to make him seem more respectable to the legal authorities who would decide the issue, married Mary. This second sacrifice of his ideological objections to marriage cut no ice with the Court of Chancery, where it was pointed out that Shelley had shown very little previous interest in his two children by his first wife; that he had abandoned her; and that he held, in any case, such extreme political and religious views that he was unfit to be a parent. Lord Eldon, the government's Tory Lord Chancellor in charge of the proceedings, must have been only too happy to endorse this last view and Shelley's request that his two children by Harriet should come to live with him and Mary was denied. The fact that Samuel Romilly acted on behalf of Harriet's family in this affair cannot have endeared him further to Byron, who was drawn closer to Shelley by it (had they not both been deprived of their children?), and who would worry later that by putting his name to his more unorthodox writings, he might compromise any hope he still had of recovering his own daughter.

The agreement had been that it would be best for Allegra's future prospects that she should be handed over to Byron and brought up as the daughter of a lord. Her becoming old enough for that to be feasible coincided with a combination of difficulties which made Shelley want to leave England for Italy. This he did in March 1818 when, along with Mary, Claire and Allegra, he settled in the Milan area. His hope was that Byron would visit them all there and at the same time pick up his daughter. But once he was firmly established in a place, as he was in Venice, Byron was very hard to move and he had, in any case, developed a horror of any more contact with Claire. In April, therefore, Shelley sent Allegra off to Venice with Elise, the Swiss nursemaid he had taken back to England with him, where she had not only looked after William but also the baby girl to whom Mary had given birth in September 1817. It was as Allegra was being despatched that Shelley made his most determined, surviving effort to plead Claire's case, pointing out how difficult it was for a mother to give up her child and how cruel it would be not to allow her to keep in touch. Byron seems to have agreed that Allegra's mother had an obvious right to continue to visit her, but he would find it harder and harder to reconcile his acceptance of this principle with his wanting never to see Claire again.

In August 1818 Shelley went to visit Byron in Venice. Hiding from him that he had travelled there with Claire, he said that he had left her, Mary and his children in Padua. A difficult situation was resolved when Byron offered the whole Shelley party a villa at Este which he had rented but was not using, and where Allegra could be sent to visit them. Meanwhile the two friends met often in Venice and renewed a friendship which *Julian and Maddolo* suggests was just as warm as it had been in Geneva. Although Shelley criticises Byron's misanthropy and hopelessness in this poem (through the thinly veiled portrait of Count Maddolo), he continued to praise him as 'a person of the most consummate genius', and he took care to inform the general public that in social life no one could be 'more gentle, patient, and unassuming' as well as 'cheerful, frank, and witty'.[1] Glad as he had been to see Byron however, and stimulating though he found his company, Shelley reverted to a critical mode once he was away from Venice (just as he had done in 1816 after the trip round the lake). Peacock had written to say that he thought the fourth canto of *Childe Harold's Pilgrimage*, which had recently appeared, was 'really too bad' and that one ought to take a stand against 'the encroachments of black bile'.[2] Two weeks into December 1818 Shelley wrote to say that he agreed and that if the spirit in which the canto was written was insane, it was 'the most wicked & mischievous insanity that ever was given forth'. Moreover, the true source of Byron's expressions of contempt and desperation was anything but sublime. It was rather a result of his association with Italian women, than whom no human beings could be more contemptible. Even Italian countesses, he complained, 'smell so of garlick that an ordinary Englishman cannot approach them'. But it was not chiefly with countesses that Byron consorted but rather with loose women from the lower classes, parents who were ready to sell their daughters, and men who 'do not scruple to avow practices which are not only not named but I believe seldom even conceived in England'. 'You many think,' he lamented, reverting to Allegra's original name in a gesture of defiance against Byron, 'how unwillingly *I* have left my little favourite Alba in a situation where she might fall again under his authority. But I have employed arguments entreaties every thing in vain, & when these fail you know I have no longer any right'.[3]

It was quite true that the life Byron was living in Venice at this time provided a highly unsuitable environment for the rearing of an infant girl. Conscious of this himself, he had handed her over temporarily to a respectable married friend called Richard Hoppner (the English consul in Venice), and hence the reference to the danger of Allegra falling once again under Byron's authority in Shelley's letter to Peacock. The general situation improved somewhat when in December 1819 Byron, now happy with just one mistress, followed Teresa Guiccioli to Ravenna, her home town; but Claire was still enraged that Allegra was not constantly in her father's care, as she always claimed it had been agreed she should be. In April 1820, not having seen her daughter for more than eighteen months, and knowing that the little girl had not been able to stay with the Hoppners all that time, she warned Byron that she would be coming to fetch Allegra so that she could bring her back to the Pisa area for the summer. In Venice and Ravenna, she claimed, the child's health had suffered and she would make arrangements to look after her properly, during the summer months, in a healthy environment. Stung by the implicit accusation of neglect and acting through the intermediary of Hoppner, Byron responded by insisting, 'I can only say to Claire – that I so totally disapprove of the mode of Children's treatment in their family – that I should look upon the Child as going into a hospital [i.e. should she be sent back to her and the Shelleys]. Is that not so? Have they *reared* one?' This last remark is an unkind reference to the fact that all three of the children Mary had had by Shelley – William and his sister as well as a baby girl born before she met Byron – were by this time dead. His aim, he said, was in a year or two either to send Allegra to school in England or put her in an Italian convent, but on no account, he went on, in the strongest criticism he ever made of Shelley's principles, would he allow her to go off with Claire 'to perish of Starvation, and green fruit – or be taught to believe there is no Deity.' As for Claire herself, 'whenever there is convenience of vicinity and access – her mother can always have her with her – otherwise no. – It was so stipulated from the beginning'.[4]

In March 1821, almost certainly following Teresa Guiccioli's advice, Byron placed Allegra in a convent school a dozen miles from Ravenna. It was a move to which Claire was violently opposed: was it not because they were convent-educated, she protested, that Italian women were 'licentious & ignorant', 'bad wives & most unnatural mothers?'[5] She must have assumed that Shelley's principles would lead him to oppose the move also, but in April he told Byron that 'Mary, no less than myself, is perfectly convinced of your conduct towards Allegra having been most irreproachable, and we entirely agree in the necessity, under existing circumstances, of the placing her in a convent near to yourself'.[6] By this date he had not seen Byron for more than two and a half years, but in August 1821 he went to Ravenna to renew the friendship and to find information which would reassure Claire about the well-being of her daughter. His admira-tion for Byron's powers as a poet had not lessened and he was exhilarated once again by his conversation. The only bar to his enjoying his friend's company as much as ever, therefore, was a charge which had been made against him by Richard Hoppner and which Byron, with his characteristic openness (or indis-cretion), laid before him. This referred to events which still remain obscure and which revolve round the fact that in February 1819, when Shelley was in Naples, he registered the birth of a certain Elena Adelaide Shelley, and that in June of the following year this baby's death was recorded. Elise had assured Hoppner that the baby in question was Claire's, but scholars have subsequently conjectured that it was perhaps Elise's own; that of a mysterious English admirer who had followed Shelley round Italy; or a child the Shelleys had chosen to adopt. It was not so much the claim that he had had sexual relations with Claire, or even that she had been pregnant by him, which scandalised Shelley, but rather the sugges-tion that he had given her medicines to procure an abortion and joined her in treating Mary with contempt. He urged his wife to write a letter which denied these charges and which could be passed on via Byron to the Hoppners. This is what Mary did, pointing out in the strongest terms the many reasons why Elise, whom the Shelleys had felt obliged to dismiss, might have for telling lies; but it is doubtful whether Byron did pass the letter on (doing so would reveal that he had ignored Hoppner's request to keep the matter quiet). When he had first heard the charges almost a year before, he had been inclined to believe them, although he questioned Elise's reliability as a witness. Whether or not Mary's letter cleared up all his doubts, he clearly did not allow the matter to affect his relations with Shelley – he suspected that his friend had slept with Claire before he himself had met her and he knew that there was nothing in Shelley's belief about free love to prevent him from doing the same afterwards; but what Hoppner told him may well have strengthened his determination to keep Allegra with him, and not give her back to Claire.

By the time Shelley saw Byron, Teresa Guiccioli had managed to acquire a legal separation from her husband, while her father and brother had been expelled from Ravenna on account of their political activities. It was therefore a question of where they all (Byron included) should go to live next. The Gambas, as Teresa's family was called, were thinking of Geneva and Byron therefore asked Shelley to write to her and explain all the disadvantages for him of living in an area full of English visitors. Shelley wrote this letter with some enthusiasm because he hoped that he and Byron might soon be able to live close to each other in Italy, and because he had a plan to bring Leigh Hunt over from England so that, with the help of Byron's money, they could launch together a new liberal journal. The Shelleys were by then established in Pisa and it was there that the Gambas moved in August, with Byron following them in November 1821. By this time, to Mary's great relief, Claire had been living apart from the Shelleys in Florence for over a year.

Byron and Shelley were now together once again, but their companionship was far less exclusive than it had been in Geneva. Attracted to Pisa by one or both of them was a group with mild literary aspirations which included Thomas Medwin, Edward Williams, a former army officer, and Edward Trelawny, who had been a sailor and modelled his public persona on Byron's poem *The Corsair*. These young man were congenial companions for Byron when he rode out beyond the town to practise pistol-shooting, or when he organised dinners; but Shelley found the tone established among them oppressive and, while still admiring Byron's works, became increasingly disenchanted with their author. Matters seem to have come to a head in February 1822 when he told Claire that it was vitally important to them, and 'to Allegra even', that 'I should put a period to my intimacy with LB, and that without *éclat*. No sentiments of honour or justice restrain him (as I strongly suspect) from the basest insinuations'.[7] Shelley does not make clear quite what these insinuations were which he only suspected Byron of making, but they almost certainly involved his relations with Claire. On 10 April, however, he told Hunt that perhaps he had been too 'misanthropical and suspicious' on the subject of Byron. What was nevertheless certain was that 'Lord Byron has made me bitterly feel the inferiority which the world has presumed to place between us and which subsists nowhere in reality but in our own talents, which are not our own but Nature's – or in our rank, but which is not our own but Fortune's'.[8] He was sorry if this 'jealousy of my Lord Byron' had interfered with the question of the money Byron had undertaken to provide in order to bring Hunt, his wife and their six children over to Italy. There is no sign that Byron was aware of the jealousy or of how disgruntled Shelley was feeling, but then around this time he was coping with the fact that the Gambas had once again been exiled, and with information from the convent school where he had left Allegra that on 20 April she had died of a fever. Shelley agreed to break this news to Claire, who for months had been concocting wild schemes to steal her daughter back from Byron.

Shelley did not tell Claire of Allegra's death until after 30 April when he and Mary, along with Edward Williams and his partner Jane, had moved from Pisa to a house on the coast near La Spezia and Claire was staying with them. He was relieved that her reaction was less violent than he had feared. If the move was a way of putting some distance between himself and Byron, it was also a sign of his continuing fascination with sailing. He had had a boat built which was much smaller that Byron's *Bolivar* but very fast through the water. Shelley had no experience of sailing on the sea, and his friend Williams had very little, but on 1 July 1822 the two of them succeeded in sailing this craft from the bay of Lerici to Leghorn where they met up with Byron and the only recently arrived Hunt family. It was a week later, when sailing back, that their boat was caught in a storm and they were both drowned, along with a young cabin boy they had hired as crew. The fate of Williams suggests that Shelley's inability to swim made no difference. Their bodies were washed up on different parts of the shore and buried in the sand by the locals. Later Byron and Trelawny led a party to recover and cremate them, largely in response to Mary's wish that Shelley's ashes should be taken to Rome and buried in the Protestant cemetery where the body of her son William already lay.

Following his first wife's suicide, Shelley had revised the will he had made after his narrow escape from drowning on the lake of Geneva; but its provisions regarding Mary and Claire remained essentially the same and Byron was still an executor. There was, however, precious little to execute while Shelley's father was still living. Anxious about Mary's future and her surviving child (a baby boy born in November 1819), Byron established contacts with Sir Timothy Shelley. But the old man, who would live to be so much older, was in an unforgiving mood and only prepared to make financial provision for Mary's child if the baby boy were given up to him. She was angered by Byron's view that, in the circumstances in which she found herself, she ought perhaps to accept this condition; and furthered annoyed when it seemed to her that he was less forthcoming that he ought to have been in providing the money which would allow her to return home. There were misunderstandings between the two which Leigh Hunt, who was himself in an uncomfortable position of financial dependence, stoked up. But that Mary and Byron parted on bad terms did not mean that he felt any less severely the loss of her husband. He had always spoken well of him (if not of his principles) and at the beginning of August 1822 insisted to Murray, whom he knew was disapproving, 'You are all brutally mistaken about Shelley who was without exception – the *best* and least selfish man I ever knew. – I never knew one who was not a beast in comparison.'[9]

3

The Road to Greece

With the death of Shelley in July 1822, four of those who had been with Byron on the Lake of Geneva six years before were gone, and he would not live much longer himself. The failure of de Staël to reconcile him with his wife had been a turning point in his life and from then on he did all he could to put his marriage behind him. What aided him in the methods he first chose to achieve this objective was that the Venice in which he settled in November 1816 was a very different town from Geneva. There was in the first place a plentiful supply of prostitutes and then a good number of middle-aged or frankly old men who accepted, with more or less good grace, that their much younger wives should have one designated admirer (a *cavalier servente*). The attitude to sex was more relaxed in Venice and, as its Carnival illustrated, there was there a belief in enjoyment which was the very antithesis of Calvinism. Byron found the atmosphere congenial and threw himself into a long period of dissipation. In February 1817 he would tell his sister that if Lady Byron 'would rejoin me tomorrow – I would not accept the proposition',[1] and although he never ceased to love Augusta, he began to realise that she was now lost to him.

Byron's method for putting the past behind him was only brought to an end when, in April 1819, he fell in love with the 21-year-old Teresa Guiccioli, the third wife of a rich count almost three times her age. The situation of a *cavalier servente* he found humiliating but that he followed Teresa to Ravenna shows that he accepted it. The first phase of the relationship was tumultuous, with a good deal of excited love-making in situations where he and his mistress were in imminent danger of discovery, and much jealousy on Byron's part of Teresa's husband and other men she knew. He would emphatically insist at one point that he would not survive losing her; but eventually, and especially after Teresa's

influential family persuaded the Papal authorities to endorse a separation from
her husband, the two of them settled into a quasi-domesticity. Byron and Teresa
did not often live in the same building, and very rarely in the same rooms, but
when it was possible they saw each other every day and in many other respects
lived liked man and wife. Fondness and loyalty replaced the passion of their
first encounters and Byron's interest in other women, and in other sexual experiences, largely evaporated.

Developments in Byron's emotional life rarely altered the steady pace at
which he produced new work. He finished *Manfred* after his arrival in Italy and
there then followed a whole series of more austere dramas, perhaps the most
successful of which, and certainly the most controversial, was *Cain*. This was the
story of a man who slept with his sister because no-one else was available, but
the controversy it aroused had less to do with sexual than with religious matters.
Like all of Byron's plays, *Cain* is a somewhat static piece, much more so than *The
Cenci*, the poetic drama which Shelley wrote in 1819 and which is better adapted
for the stage. Stage production was what Byron was anxious to avoid for what are
in his case really dramatic poems and, although he admired the talent displayed
in *The Cenci*, he thought it too reliant on the Elizabethan or Jacobean theatre.
His own models, he insisted, were now classical, and it was in the same spirit in
which he made this claim that he increasingly argued the case for Pope, a writer
he had always admired but whom he now came to appreciate even more warmly.
All the important poets of his generation, he began to feel, were on 'a wrong
revolutionary poetical system', including Wordsworth. Yet since he himself had
done as much as anyone else to foster an 'exaggerated & false taste' in the public,
he would later admit how fitting it was that his efforts to be more classical in
his dramas should be coolly received.[2] 'Back to the standards of the eighteenth
century' became in many ways his mantra, and it was partly because Keats, who
exemplified a further development of the new 'Romantic movement' so trium-
phantly, had attacked Pope (as Wordsworth had before him), that he took such
a strong dislike to his poetry.

Byron's evolving thought on how poetry should be written did not stop him
composing the fourth and final canto of *Childe Harold's Pilgrimage* while he
was in Venice. Although never as popular as his earlier works, all his writing in
this mode was very successful, to the despair of Shelley, who was beginning to
produce some of his greatest poems and finding either that he could not get them
published or, when he could, that they were almost completely ignored. Byron's
poetic voice was one the public was always keen to hear but in the final years

of his writing career it underwent a radical change. The trigger was the arrival in Venice in September 1817 of a copy of *Whistlecraft*, a poem in which John Hookham Frere successfully adapted the Italian *ottava rima* for comic purposes. After his enjoyment of the volume of Casti given him in Brussels, Byron had developed an interest in Italian poets from earlier periods, such as Boccaccio and Pulci, who also used this form, and, with Frere's example before him, he now eagerly seized on it for *Beppo*, a light-hearted illustration of Venetian moral standards told in a constantly engaging, digressive and comic manner. He used it again for *The Vision of Judgement*, a parody or, more accurately, a travesty of Robert Southey's commemorative verses on the death of George III in 1820, and also one of the funniest and most entertaining political poems in English. But it served him best for *Don Juan*, the long comic poem whose first two cantos he had published the year before. At the beginning of canto 4 he tried to sum up the progress which had brought him to the composition of this work:

> As boy, I thought myself a clever fellow,
>   And wished that others held the same opinion;
> They took it up when my days grew more mellow,
>   And other minds acknowledged my dominion;
> Now my sere Fancy "falls into the yellow
>   Leaf", and Imagination droops her pinion,
> And the sad truth which hovers o'er my desk
>   Turns what was once romantic to burlesque.[3]

Although this stanza is very much in the general manner of *Don Juan*, it seriously undersells the poem. In the first place, the comic framework of *Don Juan* allows Byron to display some of his best 'Romantic' writing without the danger of sentimentality and, in the second, far from his imagination having fallen into what Macbeth calls the 'sere and yellow leaf', it remains as lively as ever in *Don Juan*. Much more dramatic than his poetic dramas, the poem exhibits Byron's story-telling abilities at their best and is infused with the same verve and humour found in his letters. When he first sent it to England, however, Hobhouse and other friends strongly advised against its being published. They were alarmed by what could be recognised as – all things considered – some genial mockery of Lady Byron in the first canto; and perhaps also by the fact that, although the poem's hero is a naïve, well meaning youth and not the charismatic seducer of legend, he nonetheless continually finds himself in compromising sexual situations. Teresa Guiccioli also disapproved of the poem (which she read in French prose), upset by its depiction of passion as always and necessarily transitory. But it is entirely to his credit that, as he got to know it, Shelley was overwhelmed and confirmed in his self-damaging belief that his friend was able to reach heights to which he could never aspire. Soon after leaving Geneva he had written to Byron and suggested that with his great gifts he owed the world a major work, some 'greater enterprise of thought', perhaps on the French Revolution.[4] *Don Juan* would eventually run to more than sixteen cantos but, though of epic length, it is always only ever *mock* heroic in manner. Recognising immediately its distinctive quality and its originality, Shelley nonetheless declared it the finest long poem in English since *Paradise Lost*.

Byron took a moderate interest in his literary career but 'scribbling', as he habitually called it, was not enough to satisfy his need to find some significant aim in life. He was fortunate in that members of Teresa's family were deeply immersed in nationalist politics and it was with their encouragement that he joined a local Ravenna branch of the Carbonari. When a revolt in Naples in 1820 succeeded in wresting democratic concessions from the Sardinian authorities, it seemed as if there could be similar activity in the North of Italy, but the members of the so-called Holy Alliance became alarmed and an Austrian army was sent to restore the status quo. At this point Byron was firmly convinced there would be fighting, but the Carbonari were faced with overwhelming numbers and, to Byron's dismay, any thought of coordinated resistance soon faded away. After this disappointment he looked vaguely towards the newly liberated countries in South America, but the decisive moment came with the outbreak of the Greek war of independence in 1821. In support of the Greek cause a committee was formed in London of which Hobhouse was a member and it was one of its representatives who urged Byron to go to Greece to report on the situation on the ground, give what help he could, and estimate what further aid might be required. Having already visited the country, he was under no illusions about the difference between modern Greeks and those depicted in his classical reading, and he had no particular animus against the occupying Turks. Championing Christianity against the Moslem faith was also never on his agenda. But he had a deep, instinctive conviction that people ought to be free and in the future freedom of the Greeks he at last found a cause for which he felt it was worth getting up in the morning (as he often found he had to when he arrived in Greece and discovered so many official papers to read and so much business to transact). In sailing from Leghorn in July 1823 he was abandoning Teresa Guiccioli. Yet if he was indeed beginning to feel that his relationship with her was stifling, he fully expected to come back to Italy; there was no other woman involved; and he had with him Teresa's brother, Pietro, an even more enthusiastic supporter of the Greek cause than he was and by that stage a close friend.

When he arrived in Greece Byron found, as he rather thought he might, not a united band of brothers ready to lay down their lives for each other but a chaos of competing factions, often more hostile to their fellow countrymen than to the Turks. Anxious to demonstrate that his decision to come was not a result of naïve idealism, he accepted the realities of the situation and devoted all his energy and financial resources to furthering the cause in any way he could. While he had been in Italy, his attitude to money had radically changed. From being thoughtlessly extravagant, he had become careful of what he spent and even miserly. But once in Greece he spent money freely wherever he felt it was needed, bringing in supplies and maintaining an armed group of over five hundred soldiers. He went first to one of the Ionian islands because, captured by the British during the Napoleonic wars, they had been formed into a British Protectorate. From there he was able to observe the war and decide where his presence might be most useful. At the end of 1823 he sailed for Missolonghi, a Greek bridgehead on the Ottoman side of the Dardanelles, and narrowly avoided capture on the way. There he was commissioned by one of the Greek leaders to plan an assault on Lepanto, the town which gives its name to the sea battle in which Cervantes famously took part. But this came to nothing and in April 1824 Byron caught the fever from which he would quickly die.

Since Polidori had been let go, he had managed without a private doctor but he took with him to Greece a young Italian who may have been a better choice from a personal point of view (there are no records of Dr Bruno getting into scrapes), but who in medical terms was hardly an improvement since he was a fervent advocate of bleeding. Byron hated the practice and claimed that many more people were killed by the lancet than by the lance; yet he became so weak that he found it impossible to resist the entreaties of not only Bruno but three other, English doctors who were present in the vicinity. In an essay on medicine in the Romantic period, Roy Porter has said that it was only towards the end of the nineteenth century that doctors began to cure more patients than they killed.[5] Bruno may not have killed Byron but he and his English associates so weakened his system by copious bleeding that they took away any hope it may have had of resisting his disease. On 19 April 1824 Byron died, roughly three months after his thirty-sixth birthday.

4

Last Rites

There are conflicting accounts of Byron's last words and final wishes but one of the English doctors in attendance reported him as saying: 'One request let me make to you. Let not my body be hacked, or be sent to England. Here let my bones moulder. Lay me in the first corner without pomp or nonsense.'[1] In declaring this preference he may have been thinking of Polidori's unfortunate patient, Lord Guilford, who was shipped back to England from Italy in bits. This is exactly what happened to Byron, except that the Greeks insisted on keeping his lungs. They were anxious to have some memento of a man whose fame throughout Europe had not only added lustre to their cause but would also eventually help to ensure that it was successful. When the rest of Byron's body arrived home, Murray was urged by Hobhouse to enquire about the possibility of burial in Westminster Abbey. Nothing could have been less appropriate, as the Abbey authorities were only too ready to confirm. It was not until the 1960s that objections were overcome and a stone commemorating Byron was laid in 'that curious mason's yard of sculptural litter' known as Poets' Corner.[2]

As an executor of Byron's will, and his loyal friend, Hobhouse took care of the funeral arrangements. For a few days the body was displayed in a room in the centre of London so that those who wished could apply to pay their respects. For both Hobhouse and Augusta, meeting Byron again in this manner was a less distressing process than they anticipated because the corpse they saw was unrecognisable as his. The teeth of which he was so proud had been discoloured by the embalming fluid and there were marks of a hacksaw – or similar instrument – on his forehead. His features had been further distorted by the removal of his brain and eyes. One visitor who may well have found the sight shocking nevertheless was Mary Shelley because, as she had periodically made clear,

Byron was always physically attractive to her. It was decided that he should be buried with his ancestors in the church at Hucknall, one of the manors on the Newstead estate (now no longer of course in the Byron family). A funeral procession of carriages therefore set out northwards from central London on 12 July and the hostile feelings which Mary Shelley had latterly entertained about Byron softened as she saw it go by. 'Connected with him in a thousand ways,' she wrote to Trelawny, 'admiring his talents & with all his faults feeling affection for him, it went to my heart when the other day the herse that contained his lifeless form, a form of beauty which in life I often delighted to behold, passed my window going up Highgate Hill on his last journey.'[3] A few years later, when Moore was preparing his biography of Byron, she declared – much to the disgust of Claire – that she was happy to help with information, not least about the time she had spent with him in Geneva.

Of the members of the Genevan group still alive in 1824, and who might therefore have viewed Byron's body or attended his funeral, there were two principal absentees. Scrope Davies would certainly have done one or both but in 1820 his gambling luck had run out and, like his friend Beau Brummell, he had been forced to escape his debts by retreating to the continent. Because his political principles did not allow him to go to Paris, he holed up initially in Bruges and Brussels, keeping body and soul together thanks to the annual payment of his King's Fellowship. His sad after-life of the involuntary exile lasted a long time and he did not die until 1852. People who met him noted that, although he could still be amusing, his Regency mannerisms and wit wore distinctly thin. He talked freely about Byron and had a plan at one point of making his own contribution to the huge volume of biographical literature on his friend; but nothing ever came of it.

The other, more notable absentee was Claire Clairmont. From the time of his elopement with Mary, Shelley had supported Claire, but after his death she was thrown on her own resources. For single women in her situation there were very few options and she became a governess, sometimes in places as far away as Moscow. Her musical abilities and her facility with languages made her well qualified for that career, but not perhaps her temperament. There was an inevitable feeling of having fallen short, the origins of which she had expressed when she complained of being brought up in the Godwin household: 'in our family, if you cannot write an epic poem or novel that by its originality knocks all other novels on the head, you are a despicable creature, and not worth acknowledging.'[4] Her bitterness towards Byron had grown and settled into firm hatred after the death of Allegra. Already in November 1820 she had imagined a series of caricatures of him which would have made Gillray proud. One of these was to have Byron drinking spirits at a table opposite one of his mistresses from whose mouth emanate fumes to be described in a bubble as 'garlick'. An English footman just entering the room is knocked back by the smell. Meanwhile Byron is issuing instructions on how to be 'a great pathetic poet':

> Ist. Prepare a small colony, then dispatch the Mother, by worrying & cruelty, to her grave; afterwards to neglect & ill-treat the children – to have as many & as dirty mistresses as can be found; from their embraces to catch horrible diseases, thus a tolerable quantity of discontent and remorse being prepared, to give it vent on paper, & to remember particularly to rail against learned women. This is my infallible receipt by which I have made so much money.[5]

Much later Claire told Trelawny that Byron had been 'the merest compound of vanity, folly, and every miserable weakness that ever met together in one human being'.[6] Although she attracted strong interest from other men (Peacock and Trelawny included), she did not seem willing to commit herself. Her relationship with Byron had been the defining episode of her life and her commitment there had hardly done her much good. It did not help her general sense of failure that her stepsister Mary enjoyed considerable success with *Frankenstein* and was able afterwards to pursue a modest literary career.

The lives of both women were greatly eased when in 1844 Shelley's father finally died. There were some suggestions then that Claire's £12,000 was twice as much as Shelley had intended because Allegra was now dead, but she stuck to the letter of the law and became very comfortably off. The financial security which Sir Timothy's death also brought Mary lasted only a few years since she died in 1851, but Claire lived for almost thirty after that, eventually settling in Florence and, despite her previous hostility to convents, converting to Roman Catholicism. Henry James was surprised to discover how recently she had been a resident there when he visited Italy in the 1880s and he used his knowledge of her case to write a novella in which an unscrupulous biographer tries to persuade or trick a secretive old lady into showing him personal documents relating to the relationship she has had with a famous Romantic poet many years before. This biographer is the narrator of *The Aspern Papers* and the surprise he expresses at the beginning of the story that the old lady in question is not dead must have been very close to James's own when he found out how recently Claire Clairmont had been living in Florence: 'The strange thing had been for me to discover … that she was still alive: it was as if I had been told that Mrs Siddons was, or Queen Caroline, or the famous Lady Hamilton, for it seemed to me that she belonged to an extinct generation.'[7] In the 1870s Claire must have felt that her generation was indeed extinct. Of the three near-contemporaries to whom James's narrator implicitly compares her, it is the last who is most relevant since she too was well known, not for any of her own achievements, but because of the famous man she happened to have slept with.[8]

In its own way the fame of Byron when he died was almost as great as Nelson's had been and, although he did not die in battle, it was augmented by his having lost his life in the service of what liberals all over Europe regarded as a noble cause. That his burial was such a relatively low-key affair was therefore perhaps surprising. While the funeral cortege was still in central London, it consisted of over forty carriages, but most of these were empty. People felt they needed to show their respect but, at the same time, they did not want to be associated too closely with a highly controversial figure. Notorious at the time of his separation, Byron had added to his reputation for immorality with poems such as *Don Juan* and strengthened the false impression that he was an infidel with plays such as *Cain*. Since he had left England, in the middle of the Regency, the tone of public life had in any case begun to change. It was as if when a drunken Sheridan had told a member of the watch that his name was Wilberforce, he had already seen the writing on the wall. A religious revival had taken strong hold in all classes of society and there was much less tolerance in its upper reaches of irregular behaviour. With more seriousness came an increase of the *cant* against which Byron waged a continual war from his outposts abroad.

The change in the public mood may well have influenced the attitude Hobhouse adopted to an autobiographical memoir Byron had written while he was in Italy. Because this included an account of the breakdown of his marriage, he had invited his wife to look a copy over and point out anything she thought inaccurate, but she declined. Knowing his friend Moore was in financial difficulties, Byron gave the memoir to him with the proviso that it should only appear after its author's death. What he suggested was that, in the meantime, Moore could raise money by selling the future publishing rights to Murray (which he did, and for 2000 guineas). Jealous as always of anyone whom he felt might be closer to Byron than he was, Hobhouse interpreted this transaction, not as an act of generosity but as a method of paying for favourable publicity after one's death. Without having read the memoir himself, he became convinced that it could only do Byron's posthumous reputation harm and ought therefore to be destroyed, a view supported by both Lady Byron and Augusta, who had not read it either. In one of the greatest of all acts of literary vandalism, and before Byron's body arrived back in England, the memoir was therefore burned in a fireplace in Murray's rooms in Albermarle Street, despite the protests of Moore, who then felt obliged to give Murray his money back. The pity of this is that Byron's letters are now rightly regarded as a major part of his work, and there must always therefore be a regret that he did not write more prose.

Byron would have been distressed to learn that his memoir had been destroyed. He was a firm believer in telling the truth as he saw it, no matter what, and he always felt that his side of the separation quarrel had never been properly expressed. More than that however, he had an almost religious or superstitious respect for anything the dead left behind, clearly feeling that it was largely through their relics that they could be remembered. Sceptical of any other kind of after-life, he believed that the principal way in which the dead survived was in the minds of others. Working hard in his poetry to preserve the memory of those he admired, he no doubt hoped to be remembered himself (which is perhaps why he kept all his correspondence). As young men both he and Shelley were intensely ambitious, and wanted to make names for themselves; and yet, paradoxically enough, they both quickly came to realise how hollow and insubstantial fame could be. Shelley expresses this familiar theme in 'Ozymandias', one of the best of his shorter poems. A traveller in the desert has come across the broken statue of the great Egyptian pharaoh of the title:

> And on the pedestal, these words appear:
> 'My name is Ozymandias, king of kings,
> Look on my Works, ye Mighty, and despair!'
> Nothing beside remains. Round the decay
> Of that colossal wreck, boundless and bare
> The lone and level sands stretch far away.[9]

This is a highly successful evocation of the eventual futility of human achievements and aspirations, especially when they involve social or military power. Referring also to one of the pharaohs, Byron expresses a similar if broader feeling in verses from *Don Juan* which, while they in no way suggest all that marks him off him from Shelley, do indicate the alternative path his poetic career eventually took, and a major difference in the temperaments of the two men whose important friendship was first forged on the shores of Lake Geneva:

What are the hopes of man? Old Egypt's King
    Cheops erected the first pyramid
And largest, thinking it was just the thing
    To keep his memory whole, and mummy hid;
But somebody or other rummaging
    Burglariously broke his coffin's lid:
Let not a monument give you or me hopes,
    Since not a pinch of dust remains of Cheops.[10]

Although this is the kind of gloomy thought which, by the time of *Don Juan*, Byron had reconciled himself to expressing humorously, that does not make its pessimism any less authentic. His general outlook would not have been brightened by the knowledge that his own version of his life as a married man would be turned by his friends, not to dust but to ashes, and that not a pinch of those would remain either.

Notes

In the main, these notes only refer to direct quotations. For further information about my sources, readers should consult the bibliography. Two abbreviations are used: *L. & J.* for Leslie Marchand's edition of Byron's letters and journals; *P. W.* for Jerome McGann's edition of Byron's poetical works.

Place of publication is London unless otherwise indicated.

Preface

1. Phyllis Grosskurth, *Byron: The Flawed Angel* (Hodder and Stoughton, 1997), pp. 39, 41, 48, 112, 152.
2. Benita Eisler, *Byron: Child of Passion, Fool of Fame* (Hamish Hamilton, 1999), pp. 384–85, 500.
3. Fiona MacCarthy, *Byron: Life and Legend* (John Murray, 2002), pp. 34, 73, 116, 147.
4. MacCarthy, *Byron*, pp. xiii, 233.
5. Edna O'Brien's *Byron in Love* (Weidenfeld and Nicolson, 2009) and Daisy Hay's *Young Romantics: The Shelleys, Byron and Other Tangled Lives* (Bloomsbury, 2010) appeared when this book was largely completed. The first is hardly relevant in that O'Brien misses out the summer of 1816, according it only two short error-strewn paragraphs when she is discussing the death of Shelley. Hay's book is a far more interesting, skilfully constructed account of a large number of early nineteenth-century writers centred on Leigh Hunt. Byron remains a peripheral figure, however, and there is little on his writings (although more than in O'Brien).

Chapter 1

1. Stendhal, *Voyages en Italie*, ed. Victor del Litto (Paris: Pléiade, 1973), p. 153.
2. See Ghislain de Diesbach, *Madame de Staël* (Paris: Librairie Académique Perrin, 1983), p. 133.

3 Eisler, *Byron*, p. 26.

4 See Byron's appendix to his play *The Two Foscari*, *P. W.*, vol. 6, p. 223, although also stanza 81 in canto 3 of *Childe Harold's Pilgrimage* where he adopts the conventional view of the practical effects of Rousseau's writings (*P. W.*, vol. 2, pp. 106–107).

5 Mavis Coulson, *Southwards to Geneva: 200 Years of English Travellers* (Gloucester: Allan Sutton, 1988), p. 22.

6 Edward Gibbon, *Memoirs of My Life and Writings*, ed. A. O. J. Cockshut and Stephen Constantine (Keele University Press, 1994), pp. 109–10, 203.

7 Jean-Jacques Rousseau, *Œuvres Complètes*, vol. 2 (*Julie ou la Nouvelle Héloïse*), ed. Henri Coulet et al. (Paris: Pléiade, 1964), p. 78.

8 S. T. Coleridge, *The Complete Poems*, ed. William Keach (Penguin Books, 1997), pp. 324–25.

9 For details of Coleridge's indebtedness, see Adrien Bonjour, *Coleridge's 'Hymn Before Sunrise'* (Lausanne: Imprimerie La Concorde, 1942) and Norman Fruman, *Coleridge: The Damaged Archangel* (New York: George Braziller, 1971), pp. 26–30.

10 William Wordsworth, *The Prelude*, ed. Ernest de Selincourt (Oxford: Oxford University Press, 1959), p. 194, line 353.

11 The observer was John Galt. See Ernest J. Lovell (ed.), *His Very Self and Voice: Collected Conversations of Lord Byron* (New York: Macmillan, 1954), p. 57.

Chapter 2

1 See R. Glynn Grylls, *Claire Clairmont: Mother of Byron's Allegra* (John Murray, 1939) and Robert Gittings and Jo Manton, *Claire Clairmont and the Shelleys* (Oxford: Oxford University Press, 1992).

2 See Mary Shelley and P. B. Shelley, *History of a Six Weeks' Tour: 1817* (Oxford: Woodstock, 1989), p. 58.

3 Michael Glover, 'The Lavalette Affair, 1815: Rescuing a Victim of French Vengeance', *History Today*, vol. 27, issue 9 (September 1977), pp. 600–606.

4 Jane Dunn, *Moon in Eclipse: A Life of Mary Shelley* (Weidenfeld and Nicolson, 1978), p. 60.

5 *The Clairmont Correspondence: Letters of Claire Clairmont, Charles Clairmont and Fanny Imlay Godwin*, ed. Marion Kingston Stocking (Baltimore: Johns Hopkins University Press, 1995), vol. 1, p. 24.

6 Stocking (ed.), *The Clairmont Correspondence*, p. 29.

7 See Richard Holmes, *Shelley: The Pursuit* (Harper Collins, 1994), p. 320.

8 Dunn, *Moon in Eclipse*, p. 59.

9 Stocking (ed.), *The Clairmont Correspondence*, vol. 1, p. 38.

10 'Stanzas for Music', *P. W.*, vol. 3, p. 379. McGann is confident that this poem, which dates from March 1816, refers to Claire, but others have associated it with Edelston, in which case 'None of Beauty's daughters' would of course have a different meaning.

11 The case for believing that Shelley's poems about Claire's singing indicate that he had been sexually involved with her before the meeting with Byron was first made

by K. N. Cameron in *Shelley: The Golden Years* (Cambridge, MA: Harvard University Press, 1974), pp. 296–97. It is taken up by James Beiri, *Percy Bysshe Shelley: A Biography* (Baltimore: Johns Hopkins University Press, 2008), pp. 387–88.

12 Stocking (ed.), *The Clairmont Correspondence*, vol. 1, pp. 39, 40.

13 Stocking (ed.), *The Clairmont Correspondence*, vol. 1, p. 42.

14 *Letters of Mary Wollstonecraft Shelley*, ed. Betty J. Bennett (Baltimore: Johns Hopkins University Press, 1980–), vol. 1, p. 11.

15 Stocking (ed.), *The Clairmont Correspondence*, vol. 1, p. 43.

Chapter 3

1 *L. & J.*, vol. 3. p. 210.

2 Malcolm Elwin, *Lord Byron's Wife* (Macdonald, 1962), p. 456.

3 Her name was Elizabeth Pigot. See *L. & J.*, vol. 1, p. 123.

4 *L. & J.*, vol. 10, p. 203.

5 See Leslie A. Marchand, *Byron: A Biography*, 3 vols. (John Murray, 1957), vol. 1, pp. 170, 346–47.

6 *L. & J.*, vol. 5, p. 75.

7 *L. & J.*, vol. 5, p. 73.

8 Gordon left an account of his meeting with Byron in the second volume of his *Personal Memoirs, or, Reminscences of men and manners at home and abroad during the last half century* (Colburn and Bentley, 1830).

9 *L. & J.*, vol. 5, p. 76.

10 *P. W.*, vol. 2, pp. 77–78.

11 H. J. C. Grierson (ed.), *Letters of Sir Walter Scott: 1815–1817* (Constable, 1933), pp. 296–97.

12 *P. W.*, vol. 2, p. 79.

13 *P. W.*, vol. 3, p. 380.

14 *P. W.*, vol. 3, pp. 382–83.

15 *P. W.*, vol. 2, p. 76.

16 *P. W.*, vol. 2, pp. 84–85.

17 *P. W.*, vol. 2, pp. 82–83.

18 *L. & J.*, vol. 5, p. 80.

19 *L. & J.*, vol. 5, p. 77.

20 *P. W.*, vol. 2, pp. 93, 99 (stanzas 46 and 60).

21 *L & J.*, vol. 5, p. 77.

22 *The Diary of Dr. John William Polidori: 1816*, edited and elucidated by William Michael Rossetti (Elkin Mathews, 1911), pp. 11, 33.

23 *L. & J.*, vol. 5, pp. 76–77.

24 *L. & J.*, vol. 5, pp. 73, 76.

25 Gibbon, *Memoirs*, p. 143.

Chapter 4

1 Stocking (ed.), *The Clairmont Correspondence*, pp. 46, 36, 47.
2 *L. & J.*, vol. 5, p. 92.
3 As reported to Thomas Moore and recorded in his *Life and Letters of Lord Byron*, first published by John Murray in 1830. See p. 53 in the one-volume edition published by Chatto and Windus in 1875.
4 Moore, *Life and Letters of Lord Byron*, p. 524. (It is Moore who also tells the Rogers anecdote. Other friends of Byron said that after dining with Rogers, he went off to eat a beefsteak, but that seems to have been a canard.)
5 *L. & J.*, vol. 11, p. 22.
6 For more on Byron's aversion see Ernest J. Lovell (ed.), *Medwin's Conversations of Lord Byron* (Princeton: Princeton University Press, 1966), p. 41 and several references in Peter Cochran (ed.), *Lord Byron's Life in Italy* by Teresa Guiccioli, translated by Michael Rees (Newark, DE: University of Delaware Press, 2005).
7 *L. & J.*, vol. 3. p. 217.
8 See Lovell (ed.), *His Very Self and Voice*, p. 265.
9 Arthur H. Beaven, *James and Horace Smith* (1899), p. 137.
10 Bennett (ed.), *Letters of Mary Wollstonecraft Shelley*, vol. 1, p. 18.
11 Claire-Eliane Engel, *Byron et Shelley en Suisse et en Savoie* (Chambéry: Librairie Dardel, 1930), pp. 4–5.
12 The account of this episode occurs in the 'Extract from a letter from Geneva' which preceded Polidori's *The Vampyre*, first published in 1819.
13 Rossetti (ed.), *Diary of Dr. John Polidori*, pp. 70, 105.
14 Rossetti (ed.), *Diary of Dr. John Polidori*, p. 105.
15 *L. & J.*, vol. 5, p. 165.
16 Mary Shelley reported her impressions of Byron in Geneva to Thomas Moore, who included them in the third volume of his *Letters and Journals of Lord Byron*.
17 I prefer 'life-long depressive' to the 'manic-depressive' or 'bi-polar' which has been common since K. R. Jamison's *Touched with Fire: Manic-Depressive Illness and the Artistic Temperament* (New York: Free Press, 1993). Byron was certainly volatile and moody but there is little evidence of sustained periods of gloom followed by equally sustained periods of euphoria and activity. His problem was that, as he complains himself, he woke up feeling gloomy *every* morning (*L. & J.*, vol. 8, p. 15).
18 *P. W.*, vol. 2, p. 118.
19 *On Poetry and Poets* (Faber and Faber, 1957), p. 201.

Chapter 5

1 Coulson, *Southwards to Geneva*, p. 25.
2 See William S. Clark, 'Milton and the Villa Diodati', *The Review of English Studies*, vol. 11, no. 41 (January 1935).
3 Rossetti (ed.), *The Diary of Dr. John Polidori*, p. 108.

4　For an incomparable description of Byron's financial affairs, see Doris Langley Moore, *Lord Byron: Accounts Rendered* (John Murray, 1974).

5　Stocking (ed.), *The Clairmont Correspondence*, pp. 77, 83.

6　Marchand, *Byron*, vol. 2, p. 547.

7　*L. & J.*, vol. 5, p. 107.

8　*P. W.*, vol. 1, p. 236.

9　Shelley, *Poetical Works*, ed. Thomas Hutchinson and G. M. Matthews (Oxford: Oxford University Press, 1970), p. 526.

10　Lovell (ed.), *Medwin's Conversations of Lord Byron*, p. 194.

11　*P. W.*, vol. 4, p. 447.

12　Jerome McGann seems to have no such difficulties. For a challenging account of a poem he regards as 'splendid' and 'sadly neglected', see his *Byron and Romanticism* (Cambridge: Cambridge University Press, 2002), pp. 179–81.

13　*P. W.*, vol. 2, p. 103.

14　*The Journal of Thomas Moore*, ed. Wilfred S. Dowden (University of Delaware Press, 1983), vol. 1, p. 355.

15　William Wordsworth, *Poetical Works*, eds. Thomas Hutchinson and Ernest de Selincourt (Oxford: Oxford University Press, 1970), p. 164.

16　*P. W.*, vol. 2, pp. 103–104.

17　*L. & J.*, vol. 4, p. 324.

18　*L. & J.*, vol. 5, p. 159.

19　*P. W.*, vol. 2, p. 108.

20　Wordsworth's line reads 'The only sound / The dripping of the oar suspended' (see his *Poetical Works*, p. 7).

21　*P. W.*, vol. 2, pp. 108–10.

Chapter 6

1　Moore, *Life and Letters of Lord Byron*, p. 519.

2　For details of the effect the Italian's prediction had, see Jeffrey Vail, '"The bright sun was extinguish'd": The Bologna Prophecy and Byron's "Darkness"', *The Wordsworth Circle*, vol. 28, no. 3 (summer 1997), pp. 183–92.

3　See Henry and Elizabeth Stommel, *Volcanic Weather: The Story of 1816, the Year Without a Summer* (Newport, Rhode Island: Seven Seas Press, 1983).

4　Shelley, *Poetical Works*, pp. 771–72.

5　*P. W.*, vol. 2, p. 111. Byron himself assigns a date to this storm.

6　Holmes, *Shelley: The Pursuit*, pp. 258–62.

7　This line was omitted when Coleridge published the (still unfinished) poem in 1817. See Coleridge, *Complete Poems*, pp. 194, 509.

8　John William Polidori, *The Vampyre* and *Ernestus Berchtold*, ed. D. L. Macdonald and Kathleen Scherf (Calgary: Broadview Editions, 2008), p. 107.

9　*L. & J.*, vol. 9, p. 23.

10　See *Lord Byron: The Complete Miscellaneous Prose*, ed. Andrew Nicholson (Oxford: Oxford University Press, 1991), pp. 58–63.

11 The issue is dealt with at length in D. L. Macdonald's excellent *Poor Polidori: A Critical Biography of the Author of 'The Vampyre'* (Toronto: University of Toronto Press, 1991).

12 *The Vampyre* and *Ernestus Berchtold*, p. 39.

13 Moore, *Life and Letters of Lord Byron*, pp. 523–24.

14 *L. & J.*, vol. 6, p. 126.

15 Mary Shelley, *Frankenstein*, ed. J. Paul Hunter (New York: Norton Critical Editions, 1996), p. 133.

Chapter 7

1 Rossetti (ed.), *The Diary of Dr. John Polidori*, p. 106.

2 Shelley went on reading *Julie* after his return from his lake trip and, in the letter he sent to Peacock on 27 July, did refer to its 'prejudices', although he then went on immediately to say that it was 'an overflowing of sublimest genius & more than mortal sensibility'; see K. N. Cameron et al. (eds.), *Shelley and his Circle*, vol. 7 (Cambridge, MA: Harvard University Press, 1986), p. 33. The following day, in writing to Hogg, he said that *Julie* was 'in some respects absurd & prejudiced' and yet was 'the production of a mighty genius, & acquires an interest I had not conceived it to possess when giving and receiving influence from the scenes by which it was inspired. Rousseau is indeed to my mind the greatest man the world has produced since Milton'; see Cameron et al. (eds.), *Shelley and his Circle*, vol. 4, p. 719.

3 The liberal in question was Henry Brougham. See Cameron et al. (eds.), *Shelley and his Circle*, vol. 7, p. 14.

4 *L. & J.*, vol. 5, p. 81.

5 See Frederick L. Jones (ed.), *The Letters of Percy Bysshe Shelley* (Oxford: Clarendon Press, 1964), vol. 1, p. 482.

6 See Charles E. Robinson (ed.), *Frankenstein or the Modern Prometheus: The Original Two-Volumed Novel of 1816–1817 from the Bodleian Library Manuscripts* (Oxford: Bodleian Library, 2008), p. 89.

7 *Julie, ou la Nouvelle Héloïse*, p. 65 (first part, letter 26).

8 Shelley, *Letters*, vol. 1. pp. 482–83.

9 *P. W.*, vol. 2, p. 107.

10 *L. & J.*, vol. 1, p. 78.

11 See *L. & J.*, vol. 6, p. 126, where Byron gives an account of the episode to Murray.

12 Reproduced in Edouard Chapuisat, *L'auberge de Sécheron* (Geneva: Editions du Journal de Genève, 1934).

13 Cameron et al. (eds.), *Shelley and his Circle*, vol. 7, p. 32.

14 *L. & J.*, vol. 1, p. 237.

15 *P. W.*, vol. 5, p. 121.

16 *L. & J.*, vol. 5, p. 124.

17 The text of the will is printed, with a very helpful commentary, in volume 4 of Cameron et al. (eds.), *Shelley and his Circle* (pp. 702–15).

18 *L. & J.*, vol. 5, p. 162.
19 In a letter to the *Times Literary Supplement* of 11 August 1995, Curtis Bennett insisted that Shelley was indeed the father of Claire's baby, which, Bennett argued, was born in the autumn of 1816 rather than the January of the following year. According to him, Byron was deliberately misinformed of the birth date so that he would believe the baby his. But this case requires so much elaborate and detailed lying on the part of Shelley, Claire and Mary that it seems far-fetched.

Chapter 8

1 Most of what Shelley says about his lake trip can be found in the long letter he wrote to Peacock on 17th July. He relied in writing this letter on notes made while he was travelling with Byron (see *The Journals of Mary Shelley: 1814–44*, ed. Paula Feldman and Diana Scott-Kilvert (Oxford: Oxford University Press, 1987), vol. 1, pp. 480–88); and he published an edited version of it in his and Mary's *History of a Six Weeks' Tour*, pp. 119–22. In 1975 the manuscript of this letter appeared, with a number of details not in the prevous versions, and a transcript of it has been published in vol. 7 of Cameron et al. (eds.), *Shelley and his Circle*. The phrase referring to Villeneuve is there (p. 32).
2 Shelley, *Letters*, vol. 1, p. 485.
3 *P. W.*, vol. 1, p. 223.
4 *L. & J.*, vol. 5, p. 229.
5 See *P. W.*, vol. 4, pp. 4–16.
6 In her *Byron et Shelley en Suisse et en Savoie*, Engel states categorically that Byron did not write his name on the pillar (p. 39). Her main argument is that no-one who was with him at this time mentions his having done so; but she does say that other people were talking of having seen the name by 1822 at the latest (pp. 100–101).
7 Cameron et al. (eds.), *Shelley and his Circle*, vol. 7, pp. 33–34.
8 *P. W.*, vol. 2, pp. 312–13.
9 See Nicholson (ed.), *Complete Miscellaneous Prose*, p. 37.
10 Shelley, *Letters*, vol. 1, p. 480.
11 Jean-Jacques Rousseau, *Les Confessions et autres textes autobiographiques* (Paris: Pléiade, 1959), pp. 152–53.
12 *P. W.*, vol. 2, p. 312.
13 Cameron et al. (eds.), *Shelley and his Circle*, vol. 7, p. 34.
14 *L. & J.*, vol. 5, p. 82.
15 *Memoirs*, p. 205.
16 *L. & J.*, vol. 8, pp. 21–22.
17 Reported by Hazlitt in 'On My First Acquaintance with Poets'. See his *Complete Works*, ed. P. P. Howe (1933), vol. 17, p. 117.
18 Shelley, *Letters*, vol. 1, pp. 487–88.
19 Shelly, *Letters*, vol. 1, p. 486.
20 *Memoirs*, p. 115.

21 Cameron et al. (eds.), *Shelley and his Circle*, vol. 7, p. 28.
22 *P. W.*, vol. 2, p. 116.

Chapter 9

1 Stocking (ed.), *The Clairmont Correspondence*, p. 52.
2 Marchand, *Byron*, vol. 2, p. 628; Ralph Milbanke (Earl of Lovelace), *Astarte: A Fragment of Truth Concerning Lord Byron* (Christophers, 1921), p. 60.
3 Most of my information about Madame de Staël comes from the remarkable biography by Ghislain de Diesbach (Paris: Librarie Académique Perrin, 1983).
4 *L. & J.*, vol. 3, p. 12.
5 Diesbach, *Madame de Staël*, p. 159.
6 *L. & J.*, vol. 9, p. 45.
7 *L. & J.*, vol. 3, p. 160.
8 *P. W.*, vol. 3, p. 436.
9 *L. & J.*, vol. 3, p. 235.
10 *L. & J.*, vol. 3, p. 241.
11 Henry Brougham – see Cameron et al. (eds.), *Shelley and his Circle*, vol. 7, p. 14.
12 Byron's version of the encounter with Elizabeth Hervey is in Medwin (see Lovell (ed.), *Medwin's Conversations of Lord Byron*, p. 12); for details of the woman herself see Cameron et al. (eds.), *Shelley and his Circle*, vol. 7, p. 55. A copy of her letter describing her encounter with Byron can be found in the Lovelace papers but there is an extract from it in Lovell (ed.), *His Very Self and Voice*, p. 191.
13 This is what Bonstetten describes him as doing when he visited Coppet with Hobhouse; see Lovell (ed.), *His Very Self and Voice*, p. 190.
14 See Nancy Goslee, 'Pure Stream from a Troubled Source: Byron, Schlegel and Prometheus', *The Byron Journal*, vol. 10 (1982).
15 Rossetti (ed.), *The Diary of Dr. John Polidori*, p. 146.
16 Stendhal, *Voyages en Italie*, p. 155.
17 *Gazette de Lausanne*, 15 November 1816.

Chapter 10

1 *Souvenirs, 1785–1876 du feu duc de Broglie* (Paris: Calmann Lévy, 1886), p. 361.
2 *L. & J.*, vol. 3, pp. 231–32.
3 Benjamin Constant, *Oeuvres*, ed. Alfred Roulin (Paris: Pleaide, 1957), p. 77.
4 Constant, *Oevures*, p. 81.
5 *L. & J.*, vol. 5, pp. 86–87.
6 Lady Caroline Lamb, *Glenarvon*, ed. Deborah Lutz (Kansas City: Valancourt Books, 2007), p. 159.
7 *L. & J.*, vol. 5, p. 131.
8 *Glenarvon*, pp. 200, 236.

9 Byron tells this anecdote in *L. & J.*, vol. 9, p. 15; there are good accounts of Sheridan's career in Linda Kelly, *Sheridan: A Life* (Sinclair Stevenson, 1997) and Fintan O'Toole, *ATraitor's Kiss: The Life of Richard Brinsley Sheridan* (Granta Books, 1997).

10 *P. W.*, vol. 4, pp. 20–21.

Chapter 11

1 Madame de Staël, *De l'Allemagne* (Paris: Garnier-Flammarion, 1968), p. 65.

2 Shelley, *Letters*, vol. 1, p. 493.

3 See Emily E. Sunstein, 'Louise Duvillard of Geneva, the Shelleys' Nursemaid', *Keats-Shelley Journal*, vol. 29 (1980), pp. 27–30.

4 *Journals of Mary Shelley*, vol. 1, p. 113.

5 See Stocking (ed.), *The Clairmont Correspondence*, p. 53, note 2.

6 *Journals of Mary Shelley*, vol. 1, p. 115.

7 Shelley, *Letters*, vol. 1, p. 495.

8 See *P. W.*, vol. 2, p. 100 (stanza 62).

9 Shelley, *Letters*, vol. 1, pp. 494–95.

10 *L. & J.*, vol. 5, p. 86.

11 Shelley, *Letters*, vol. 1, p. 499.

12 *Journals of Mary Shelley*, vol. 1, p. 118.

13 Shelley, *Letters*, vol. 1, p. 500.

14 Shelley, *Poetical Works*, pp. 529–31.

15 *Frankenstein*, p. 64.

16 Shelley, *Poetical Works*, pp. 532–35.

17 See Marchand, *Byron*, vol. 1, p. 78.

18 *P. W.*, vol. 4, p. 28.

19 *L. & J.*, vol. 5, p. 165.

20 *P. W.*, vol. 4, pp. 28–29.

21 *P. W.*, vol. 4, p. 30. The fragment begins, 'Could I remount the river of my years'.

22 Lovell (ed.), *His Very Self and Voice*, p. 299.

23 See R. J. Dingley, '"I had a Dream … Byron's "Darkness"', *The Byron Journal*, no. 9 (1981), p. 25.

24 *P. W.*, vol. 4, pp. 40–43.

Chapter 12

1 *Journals of Mary Shelley*, vol. 1, p. 123.

2 Stocking (ed.), *The Clairmont Correspondence*, p. 43.

3 Stocking (ed.), *The Clairmont Correspondence*, pp. 69–70.

4 Moore, *Life and Letters of Lord Byron*, p. 527.

5 Stocking (ed.), *The Clairmont Correspondence*, p. 51.

6 Stocking (ed.), *The Clairmont Correspondence*, p. 52.

7 Stocking (ed.), *The Clairmont Correspondence*, p. 52.

8 *P. W.*, vol. 2, p. 95.

9 *P. W.*, vol. 4, p. 33.

10 *P. W.*, vol. 4, pp. 35–40.

11 Shelley, *Letters*, vol. 1, p. 506.

12 The letters are reprinted in the 1921 edition of *Astarte*, pp. 197–262.

13 Coleridge's attack is quoted in Peter Cochran (ed.), *The Gothic Byron* (Cambridge Scholars Publishing, 2009), p. 34.

14 *P. W.*, vol. 1, p. 237. There is a good account of Lewis's life in L. F. Peck, *A Life of Matthew G. Lewis* (Cambridge, MA: Harvard University Press, 1961).

15 *Journals of Mary Shelley*, vol. 1, p. 126.

16 *P. W.*, vol. 5, pp. 712–13.

Chapter 13

1 *L. & J.*, vol. 9, p. 18.

2 *L. & J.*, vol. 3, p. 241.

3 *L. & J.*, vol. 5, p. 206.

4 See his *Journal of a Residence among the Negroes of the West Indies*, published by Murray in 1834.

5 See *P. W.*, vol. 4, p. 463.

6 See *P. W.*, vol. 4, pp. 53–59.

7 *P. W.*, vol. 2, p. 78.

8 *Journals of Mary Shelley*, vol. 1, p. 130.

9 *L. & J.*, vol. 5, p. 88.

10 The review is reprinted in Andrew Rutherford (ed.), *Byron: The Critical Heritage* (Routledge and Kegan Paul, 1970), pp. 27–32. I would not have 'worn the motley mantle of a poet / if some one had not told me to forego it', says Byron in canto 15 of *Don Juan* (stanza 24).

11 *P. W.*, vol. 1, pp. 245, 409.

12 See Doris Langley Moore, *The Late Lord Byron* (John Murray, 1961), pp. 126–27.

13 This letter, which is the archives of the De Broglie family, is transcribed by Robert Escarpit in his 'Madame de Staël et le ménage Byron', *Langues Modernes*, July–August 1951, pp. 238–42. Escarpit also reproduces the letter Lady Romilly sent to de Staël, reporting her failure to make any headway with Lady Byron.

14 *P. W.*, vol. 4, pp. 43–45.

15 *P. W.*, vol. 4, p.61.

16 See *P. W.*, vol. 4, p. 466.

17 Romilly appears to have withdrawn from the case once he realised there had been a conflict of interest. See Hobhouse's diary for 15 March 1816.

18 *L. & J.*, vol. 6, p. 80.

Chapter 14

1 Stocking (ed.), *The Clairmont Correspondence*, p. 69.
2 *L. & J.*, vol. 6, p. 138.
3 *L. & J.*, vol. 9, p. 39.
4 Madame de Staël's judgement was reported by Hobhouse himself in his diary; Byron's is in *L. & J.*, vol. 9, p. 21.
5 Byron repeats this anecdote several times, but see *L. & J.*, vol. 5, p. 144.
6 See Peter Gunn, *My Dearest Augusta* (Bodley Head, 1968), p. 192.
7 This sonnet was in a notebook which Scrope Davies took back to England with him. It was only discovered when the trunk Davies had deposited with his bank in 1820 was opened in the 1970s. The text I quote is from Judith Chernaik and Timothy Burnett, 'The Byron and Shelley Notebooks in the Scrope Davies Find', *The Review of English Studies*, New Series, vol. 29, no. 113 (1978), pp. 40–41.
8 *L. & J.*, vol. 8, p. 235.
9 *L. & J.*, vol. 8, pp. 19–20.
10 For a broader discussion of this issue see my own 'Byron's Sense of Humour', *Romanticism*, vol. 17, no. 1 (2011).
11 See Hobhouse's diary entry for 30 August 1816.
12 *L. & J.*, vol. 5, p. 97.
13 S. T. Coleridge, *Lectures 1808-19 on Literature*, ed. R. A. Foakes (Princeton: Princeton University Press, 1987), vol. 1, p. 193.
14 Quoted by Gavin de Beer in his 'An "Atheist" in the Alps', *Keats-Shelley Memorial Bulletin*, vol. 9 (1958), p. 10.
15 See the entry in Hobhouse's diary for 4 September 1816 and also Rossetti (ed.), *The Diary of Dr. John Polidori*, p. 152.
16 *L. & J.*, vol. 9, pp. 38–39.
17 Reported in T. A. J. Burnett's admirable *The Rise and Fall of a Regency Dandy: The Life and Times of Scrope Berdmore Davies* (Oxford: Oxford University Press, 1983), p. 71.
18 *L. & J.*, vol. 9, p. 23.
19 Burnett, *The Rise and Fall of a Regency Dandy*, p. 37.

Chapter 15

1 *L. & J.*, vol. 7, p. 44.
2 Rossetti (ed.), *The Diary of Dr. John Polidori*, p. 136.
3 *L. & J.*, vol. 9, p. 86.
4 *L. & J.*, vol. 5, p. 163.
5 Quoted in Franklin Bishop, *Polidori! A Life of Dr. John Polidori* (Gargoyle Press, 1991), p. 31.
6 Rossetti (ed.), *The Diary of Dr. John Polidori*, p. 152.
7 Details of Hobhouse's time with Byron in Geneva are in his manuscript diary in the British Library, but there is a printed version of that part of the diary which relates to the Bernese Oberland excursion in John Clubbe and Ernest Giddey, *Byron et la*

Suisse (Geneva: Droz, 1982), to which Clubbe provides an excellent introduction. The reference to Vevey is on p. 38 of this book.

8 Clubbe and Giddey, *Byron et la Suisse*, p. 30.
9 Clubbe and Giddey, *Byron et la Suisse*, p. 30.
10 *L. & J.*, vol. 5, p. 98.
11 *L. & J.*, vol. 5, p. 97.
12 Clubbe and Giddey, *Byron et la Suisse*, p. 40.
13 The tourist who saw the names was John Waldie and his diary is in the Charles E. Young Research Library Department of Special Collections in the University of California, Los Angeles (see http://escholarship.org/uc/item/1xj193gd). I am grateful to one of the present owners of the château de Châtelard, the Baron Pierre-Hubert Fornerod, for informing me that the room in which Byron and Hobhouse wrote their names (now alas whitewashed) does exist.

Chapter 16

1 *L. & J.*, vol. 5, p. 99; for the two aspects of the image of Switzerland in the early nineteenth century, see Claude Reichler's introduction to his and Roland Ruffieux's *Le voyage en Suisse: anthologie des voyageurs français et européens de la Renaissance au vingtième siècle* (Paris: Laffont, 1988), as well as this same writer's *La découverte des Alpes et la question du paysage* (Geneva: Georg, 2002).
2 *L. & J.*, vol. 5, p. 101.
3 *P. W.*, vol. 2, p. 100.
4 *L. & J.*, vol. 5, p. 101.
5 *P. W.*, vol. 4, p. 62.
6 *P. W.*, vol. 4, p. 468.
7 *P. W.*, vol. 4, p. 82.
8 *P. W.*, vol. 4, p. 70.
9 *Day and New Times*, 23 June 1817; see Marchand, *Byron*, vol. 2, p. 699.
10 *P. W.*, vol. 4, p. 74.
11 *P. W.*, vol. 4, p. 96.
12 *P. W.*, vol. 4, p. 85.
13 *L. & J.*, vol. 5, p. 105.
14 *L. & J.*, vol. 5, p. 96.
15 The itinerary I describe is the one established by Clubbe in his introduction to his transcript of Hobhouse's diary in *Byron et la Suisse* (see pp. 23–26). It is Clubbe who gives the height of the Lauberhorn as 8111 feet.
16 *L. & J.*, vol. 5, p. 102.
17 *P. W.*, vol. 4, p. 65.
18 Clubbe and Giddey, *Byron et la Suisse*, p. 50.
19 *L. & J.*, vol. 5, p. 102.
20 Rossetti (ed.), *The Diary of Dr. John Polidori*, p. 158.
21 *L. & J.*, vol. 5, p. 103.

22 *P. W.*, vol. 1, p. 225.

23 See Marchand, *Byron*, vol. 1, p. 161.

24 *L. & J.*, vol. 5, pp. 91, 95, 94.

25 Frederick A. Pottle (ed.), *Boswell's London Journal: 1762–1763* (Heinemann, 1950), pp. 261–62.

26 See Marchand, *Byron*, vol. 2, p. 646.

27 *L. & J.*, vol. 5, pp. 104–105.

28 *P. W.*, vol. 4, pp. 37–38.

29 See *P. W.*, vol. 1, pp. 103–104.

30 Wordsworth, *Poetical Works*, p. 164.

31 *P. W.*, vol. 2, p. 312 (see p. 64 above).

32 Chateaubriand's *Le Mont Blanc: Paysages de Montagne* has been edited by Philippe Antoine in *Œuvres Complètes*, ed. Béatrice Didier (Paris: Champion, 2008), vol. vi–vii, pp. 809–37.

33 *P. W.*, vol. 4, p. 74.

Afterword 1

1 Shelley, *Letters*, vol. 2, p. 324.

2 *L. & J.*, vol. 5, p. 256.

3 *L. & J.*, vol. 5, p. 260.

4 *L. & J.*, vol. 5, p. 258.

5 *L. & J.*, vol. 5, p. 210.

6 *L. & J.*, vol. 5, p. 210.

7 *L. & J.*, vol. 5, pp. 163–64.

8 Lovell (ed.), *Medwin's Conversations of Lord Byron*, p. 104.

9 Shelley, *Letters*, vol. 2, p. 433.

Afterword 2

1 Shelley, *Poetical Works*, p. 189.

2 Nicholas A. Joukovsky (ed.), *The Letters of Thomas Love Peacock* (Oxford: Oxford University Press, 2001), vol. 1, p. 123.

3 Shelley, *Letters*, vol. 2, p. 58.

4 *L. & J.*, vol. 7, p. 80.

5 Stocking (ed.), *The Clairmont Correspondence*, p. 163.

6 Shelley, *Letters*, vol. 2, p. 283.

7 Shelley, *Letters*, vol. 2, pp. 391–92.

8 Shelley, *Letters*, vol. 2, p. 405. Envy of Byron's success became a crucial element in Shelley's feeling for him, as I try to explain in 'Who is King of the Cats? Byron, Shelley and the Friendship of Poets', *Cambridge Quarterly*, vol. 39, no. 1 (2010), pp. 61–71, where matters which here have been somewhat drastically summarised are dealt with in a little more detail.

9 *L. & J.*, vol. 9, pp. 189–90.

Afterword 3

1 *L. & J.*, vol. 5, p. 175.
2 See *L. & J.*, vol. 5, p. 265 and vol. 9, p. 161.
3 *P. W.*, vol. 5, pp. 203–204.
4 Shelley, *Letters*, vol. 1, pp. 507–508.
5 See Roy Porter's chapter on medicine in Iain McCalman (ed.), *An Oxford Companion to the Romantic Age* (Oxford: Oxford Uuniversity Press, 2001), pp. 170–78.

Afterword 4

1 Lovell (ed.), *His Very Self and Voice*, p. 591.
2 Not alas my phrase but that of Doris Langley Moore in *Lord Byron: Accounts Rendered*, p. 507.
3 Bennett (ed.), *Letters of Mary Wollstonecraft Shelley*, pp. 436–37.
4 See Grylls, *Claire Clairmont*, p. 193.
5 Marion Kingston Stocking (ed.), *The Journals of Claire Clairmont* (Cambridge, MA: Harvard University Press, 1968), pp. 183–84.
6 Grylls, *Claire Clairmont*, p. 219.
7 Henry James, *'The Aspern Papers' and 'The Turn of the Screw'* (Penguin English Classics, 1984), p. 47.
8 In *Young Romantics: The Shelleys, Byron and Other Tangled Lives* (Bloomsbury, 2010), Daisy Hay has uncovered an interesting new document in which, towards the end of her life, Claire Clairmont denounced both Shelley and Byron as apostles of free love (pp. 307–309). This is of course a mistake on Claire's part: Byron never had that excuse for his bouts of promiscuity and never railed against marriage as an institution. Although the surprising hostility she expresses in this document against Shelley could be wholly explained by her conversion to Catholicism, it does make marginally more likely the already strong possibility that her involvement with him was at some point sexual.
9 Shelley, *Poetical Works*, p. 550.
10 *P. W.*, vol. 5, p. 79. This conclusion was written before I discovered that Peter Cochran had also brought together 'Ozymandias' and this stanza; see his *'Romanticism' and Byron* (Cambridge Scholars Publishing, 2009), pp. 362–64. His commentary is excellent.

Bibliography

Manuscript material: Byron is such a well known figure that most of the information a biographer needs is in printed form. Until very recently parts of the diary of John Cam Hobhouse which are relevant to this study could only be consulted in the British Library, but a transcript of the whole text is now available via the website of the remarkable Peter Cochran (http://petercochran.wordpress.com). Much useful and still unpublished material can be found in the Lovelace Papers in the Special Collections department of the Bodleian Library in Oxford; and the same is true of the Murray archive, now in the National Library of Scotland in Edinburgh.

Printed sources (place of publication is London unless otherwise indicated):

Beaven, Arthur H., *James and Horace Smith* (1899).

Beiri, James, *Percy Bysshe Shelley: A Biography* (Baltimore: Johns Hopkins University Press, 2008).

Bennett, Betty J. (ed.), *Letters of Mary Wollstonecraft Shelley* (Baltimore: Johns Hopkins University Press, 1980–).

Bishop, Franklin, *Polidori! A Life of Dr. John Polidori* (Gargoyle Press, 1991).

Bonjour, Adrien, *Coleridge's 'Hymn Before Sunrise'* (Lausanne: Imprimerie La Concorde, 1942).

Broglie, duc de, *Souvenirs, 1785–1876 du feu duc de Broglie* (Paris: Calmann Lévy, 1886).

Burnett, T. A. J., *The Rise and Fall of a Regency Dandy: The Life and Times of Scrope Berdmore Davies* (Oxford: Oxford University Press, 1983).

Butler, Marilyn, *Romantics, Rebels and Reactionaries: English Literature and its Background, 1760–1830* (Oxford: Oxford University Press, 1981).

Buxton, John, *Byron and Shelley: The History of a Friendship* (New York: Harcourt Brace, 1968).

Cameron, K. N., Reiman, Donald H., and others (eds.), *Shelley and his Circle* (Cambridge, MA: Harvard University Press, 1961–2002), 10 vols.

Cameron, K. N., *Shelley: The Golden Years* (Cambridge, MA: Harvard University Press, 1974).

Chapuisat, Edouard, *L'auberge de Sécheron* (Geneva: Editions du Journal de Genève, 1934).

Chateaubriand, François-René, *Œuvres Complètes*, ed. Béatrice Didier, vol. vi–vii: *Récits de voyages* (Paris: Champion, 2008).

Chernaik, Judith, and Burnett, Timothy, 'The Byron and Shelley Notebooks in the Scrope Davies Find', *The Review of English Studies*, New Series, vol. 29, no. 113 (1978).

Clark, William S., 'Milton and the Villa Diodati', *The Review of English Studies*, vol. 11, no. 41 (January 1935).

Clubbe, John, 'The Tempest-Toss'd Summer of 1816: Mary Shelley's *Frankenstein*', *The Byron Journal*, vol. 19 (1991).

Clubbe, John, and Giddey, Ernest, *Byron et la Suisse* (Geneva: Droz, 1982).

Cochran, Peter, *The Gothic Byron* (Cambridge Scholars Publishing, 2009).

Cochran, Peter, *'Romanticism' and Byron* (Cambridge Scholars Publishing, 2009).

Cochran, Peter (ed.), *Lord Byron's Life in Italy* by Teresa Guiccioli, translated by Michael Rees (Newark, DE: University of Delaware Press, 2005).

Coleridge, S. T., *The Complete Poems*, ed. William Keach (Penguin Books, 1997).

Coleridge, S. T., *Lectures 1808–19 on Literature*, ed. R. A. Foakes (Princeton: Princeton University Press, 1987).

Constant, Benjamin, *Oeuvres*, ed. Alfred Roulin (Paris: Pléiade, 1957).

Coulson, Mavis, *Southwards to Geneva: 200 Years of English Travellers* (Gloucester: Allan Sutton, 1988).

De Beer, Gavin, 'An "Atheist" in the Alps', *Keats-Shelley Memorial Bulletin*, vol. 9 (1958).

De Staël, Madame, *Corinne ou l'Italie*, ed. Simone Balayé (Paris: Champion, 2000).

De Staël, Madame, *De l'Allemagne* (Paris: Garnier-Flammarion, 1968).

Diesbach, Ghislain de, *Madame de Staël* (Paris: Librairie Académique Perrin, 1983).

Dingley, R. J., '"I had a Dream … Byron's "Darkness"', *The Byron Journal*, no. 9 (1981).

Douglass, Paul, *Lady Caroline Lamb* (Palgrave Macmillan, 2004).

Dunn, Jane, *Moon in Eclipse: A Life of Mary Shelley* (Weidenfeld and Nicolson, 1978).

Eisler, Benita, *Byron: Child of Passion, Fool of Fame* (Hamish Hamilton, 1999).

Eliot, T. S., *On Poetry and Poets* (Faber and Faber, 1957).

Ellis, David, 'Byron's Sense of Humour', *Romanticism*, vol. 17, no. 1 (2011).

Ellis, David, 'Who is King of the Cats? Byron, Shelley and the Friendship of Poets', *Cambridge Quarterly*, vol. 39, no. 1 (2010), pp. 61–71.

Elwin, Malcolm, *Lord Byron's Wife* (Macdonald, 1962).

Engel, Claire-Eliane, *Byron et Shelley en Suisse et en Savoie* (Chambéry: Librairie Dardel, 1930).

Escarpit, Robert, 'Madame de Staël et le ménage Byron', *Langues Modernes*, July–August 1951.

Fairweather, Marie, *Madame de Staël* (Robinson Publishing, 2006).

Fruman, Norman, *Coleridge: The Damaged Archangel* (New York: George Braziller, 1971).

Gibbon, Edward, *Memoirs of My Life and Writings*, ed. A. O. J. Cockshut and Stephen Constantine (Keele University Press, 1994).

Gittings, Robert, and Manton, Jo, *Claire Clairmont and the Shelleys* (Oxford: Oxford University Press, 1992).

Glover, Michael, 'The Lavalette Affair, 1815: Rescuing a Victim of French Vengeance', *History Today*, vol. 27, issue 9 (September 1977).

Gordon, Pryse Lockhart, *Personal Memoirs, or, Reminiscences of men and manners at home and abroad during the last half century* (Colburn and Bentley, 1830).

Goslee, Nancy, 'Pure Stream from a Troubled Source: Byron, Schlegel and *Prometheus*', *The Byron Journal*, vol. 10 (1982).

Graham, Peter W., *Byron's Bulldog: Letters of John Cam Hobhouse to Lord Byron* (Columbus, OH: Ohio State University Press, 1984).

Grierson, H. J. C. (ed.), *Letters of Sir Walter Scott: 1815–1817* (Constable, 1933).

Grosskurth, Phyllis, *Byron: The Flawed Angel* (Hodder and Stoughton, 1997).

Grylls, R. Glynn, *Claire Clairmont: Mother of Byron's Allegra* (John Murray, 1939).

Gunn, Peter, *My Dearest Augusta* (Bodley Head, 1968).

Hay, Daisy, *Young Romantics: The Shelleys, Byron and Other Tangled Lives* (Bloomsbury, 2010).

Hazlitt, William, 'On My First Acquaintance with Poets', in *Complete Works*, ed. P. P. Howe (1933), vol. 17.

Hobhouse, John Cam, *The Substance of Some Letters Written by an Englishman Resident in Paris During the lst. Reign of the Emperor Napoleon* (1816).

Holmes, Richard, *Shelley: The Pursuit* (Harper Collins, 1994).

James, Henry, *'The Aspern Papers' and 'The Turn of the Screw'* (Penguin English Classics, 1984).

Jamison, K. R., *Touched with Fire: Manic-Depressive Illness and the Artistic Temperament* (New York: Free Press, 1993).

Joukovsky, Nicholas A. (ed.), *The Letters of Thomas Love Peacock* (Oxford: Oxford University Press, 2001).

Kelly, Linda, *Sheridan: A Life* (Sinclair Stevenson, 1997).

Lamb, Lady Caroline, *Glenarvon*, ed. Deborah Lutz (Kansas City: Valancourt Books, 2007).

Lewis, Matthew, *Journal of a Residence among the Negroes of the West Indies* (John Murray, 1834).

Lewis, Matthew, *The Monk* (Oxford: Oxford University Press, 1998).

Lovell, Ernest J., 'Byron and Mary Shelley', *Keats-Shelley Journal*, no. 2 (January 1953).

Lovell, Ernest J. (ed.), *His Very Self and Voice: Collected Conversations of Lord Byron* (New York: Macmillan, 1954).

Lovell, Ernest J. (ed.), *Lady Blessington's Conversations of Lord Byron* (Princeton: Princeton University Press, 1969).

Lovell, Ernest J. (ed.), *Medwin's Conversations of Lord Byron* (Princeton: Princeton University Press, 1966).

MacCarthy, Fiona, *Byron: Life and Legend* (John Murray, 2002).

Macdonald, D. L., *Poor Polidori: A Critical Biography of the Author of 'The Vampyre'* (Toronto: University of Toronto Press, 1991).

Marchand, Leslie A., *Byron: A Biography*, 3 vols. (John Murray, 1957).

Marchand, Leslie A. (ed.), *Letters and Journals of Lord Byron*, vols. 1–11 (John Murray, 1981–).

McGann, Jerome J., *Byron and Romanticism* (Cambridge: Cambridge University Press, 2002).

McGann, Jerome J. (ed.), *Lord Byron: The Complete Poetical Works*, vols. 1–6 (Oxford: Oxford University Press, 1980–86).

Milbanke, Ralph (Earl of Lovelace), *Astarte: A Fragment of Truth Concerning Lord Byron* (Christophers, 1921).

Moore, Doris Langley, *Lord Byron: Accounts Rendered* (John Murray, 1974).

Moore, Doris Langley, *The Late Lord Byron* (John Murray, 1961).

Moore, Thomas, *Life and Letters of Lord Byron* (Chatto and Windus, 1875).

Naville, Paul, *Cologny* (Geneva: Edition du Journal de Genève et Roto Sadag, 1958).

Nicholson, Andrew (ed.), *Lord Byron: The Complete Miscellaneous Prose* (Oxford: Oxford University Press, 1991).

Nicolson, Marjorie, *Mountain Gloom and Mountain Glory: The Development of the Aesthetics of the Infinite* (New York: Norton, 1963).

O'Toole, Fintan, *A Traitor's Kiss: The Life of Richard Brinsley Sheridan* (Granta Books, 1997).

Peck, L. F., *A Life of Matthew G. Lewis* (Cambridge, MA: Harvard University Press, 1961).

Polidori, John William, *The Vampyre* and *Ernestus Berchtold*, ed. D. L. Macdonald and Kathleen Scherf (Calgary: Broadview Editions, 2008).

Porter, Roy, 'Medicine', in Iain McCalman (ed.), *An Oxford Companion to the Romantic Age* (Oxford: Oxford University Press, 2001).

Pottle, Frederick A. (ed.), *Boswell's London Journal: 1762–1763* (Heinemann, 1950).

Reichler, Claude, *La découverte des Alpes et la question du paysage* (Geneva: Georg, 2002).

Reichler, Claude, and Ruffieux, Roland, *Le voyage en Suisse: anthologie des voyageurs français et européens de la Renaissance au vingtième siècle* (Paris: Laffont, 1988).

Reiman, Donald H., *Percy Bysshe Shelley* (Boston: Twayne, 1990).

Robinson, Charles E., *Shelley and Byron: The Snake and the Eagle Wreathed in Flight* (Baltimore: Johns Hopkins University Press, 1976).

Robinson, Charles E. (ed.), *Frankenstein or the Modern Prometheus: The Original Two-Volumed Novel of 1816–1817 from the Bodleian Library Manuscripts* (Oxford: Bodleian Library, 2008).

Robinson, Charles E. (ed.), *Lord Byron and his Contemporaries* (Newark, DE: University of Deleware Press, 1982).

Rossetti, William Michael (ed.), *The Diary of Dr. John William Polidori: 1816* (Elkin Mathews, 1911).

Rousseau, Jean-Jacques, *Les Confessions et autres textes autobiographiques* (Paris: Pléiade, 1959).

Rousseau, Jean-Jacques, *Œuvres Complètes*, vol. 2 (Julie ou la Nouvelle Héloïse), ed. Henri Coulet et al (Paris: Pléiade, 1964).

Sangiorgi, Roberto Benaglia, 'Giambattista Casti's *Novelle Galanti* and Lord Byron's *Beppo*', *Italica*, vol. 28, no. 4 (December 1951).

Shelley, Mary, *Frankenstein*, ed. J. Paul Hunter (New York: Norton Critical Editions, 1996).

Shelley, Mary, *Journals: 1814–44*, ed. Paula Feldman and Diana Scott-Kilvert (Oxford: Oxford University Press, 1987), 2 vols.

Shelley, Mary and Shelley, Percy Bysshe, *History of a Six Weeks' Tour: 1817* (Oxford: Woodstock, 1989).

Shelley, Percy Bysshe, *Letters*, ed. Frederick L. Jones (Oxford: Clarendon Press, 1964), 2 vols.

Shelley, Percy Bysshe, *Poetical Works*, ed. Thomas Hutchinson and G. M. Matthews (Oxford: Oxford University Press, 1970).

Stendhal, *Voyages en Italie*, ed. Victor del Litto (Paris: Pléiade, 1973).

Stocking, Marion Kingston (ed.), *The Clairmont Correspondence: Letters of Claire Clairmont, Charles Clairmont and Fanny Imlay Godwin* (Baltimore: Johns Hopkins University Press, 1995).

Stocking, Marion Kingston (ed.), *The Journals of Claire Clairmont* (Cambridge, MA: Harvard University Press, 1968).

Stommel, Henry and Elizabeth, *Volcanic Weather: The Story of 1816, the Year Without a Summer* (Newport, Rhode Island: Seven Seas Press, 1983).

Sunstein, Emily E., 'Louise Duvillard of Geneva, the Shelleys' Nursemaid', *Keats-Shelley Journal*, vol. 29 (1980).

Tomalin, Claire, *The Life and Death of Mary Wollstonecraft* (Weidenfeld and Nicolson, 1974).

Vail, Jeffrey, '"The bright sun was extinguish'd": The Bologna Prophecy and Byron's "Darkness"', *The Wordsworth Circle*, vol. 28, no. 3 (summer 1997).

Wilkes, Joanna, *Lord Byron and Madame de Staël: Born for Opposition* (Ashgate, 1999).

Wood, Dennis, *Benjamin Constant: A Biography* (Routledge, 1993).

Wordsworth, William, *Poetical Works*, ed. Thomas Hutchinson and Ernest de Selincourt (Oxford: Oxford University Press, 1970).

Wordsworth, William, *The Prelude*, ed. Ernest de Selincourt (Oxford: Oxford University Press, 1959).

Index